IN MY SKIN

IN MY SKIN

a memoir

kate holden

ARCADE PUBLISHING
NEW YORK

FIRST NORTH AMERICAN EDITION 2006

This project has been assisted by the Australian Government through the Australia Council, its arts funding and advisory body.

Library of Congress Cataloging-in-Publication Data

Holden, Kate, 1972–
    In my skin : a memoir / Kate Holden. —1st North American ed.
        p. cm.
    ISBN-13: 978-1-55970-830-2 (alk. paper)
    ISBN-10: 1-55970-830-1 (alk. paper)
    1. Holden, Kate, 1972– 2. Drug addicts—Australia—Biography.
3. Prostitutes—Australia—Biography. 4. Heroin abuse—Australia—Case studies. I. Title.

    HV5805.H64A3 2005
    616.86'320092—dc22   2006018637
    [B]

Published in the United States by Arcade Publishing, Inc., New York
Distributed by Hachette Book Group USA

Visit our Web site at www.arcadepub.com

10 9 8 7 6 5 4 3 2 1

EB

PRINTED IN THE UNITED STATES OF AMERICA

This memoir is dedicated to my brave and beautiful family.
For everything.

Facilis descensus Averno…sed revocare…hoc opus, hic labor est.

To descend into hell is easy.
But to return—what work, what a labour it is!

VIRGIL

ACKNOWLEDGMENTS

This book would not have been possible without the support of my wonderful parents and my sister, my relatives, my patient and precious friends, and all those who lived this life with me. I thank you and treasure you all.

I would like to thank also the staff and students in the Professional Writing and Editing course at RMIT for their comments, encouragement and generosity. And everyone at Text Publishing, especially Michael Heyward, who helped make this book better.

To everyone who knew me then, and knows me now, who put up with my excitement and despair and who talked things through while I wrote this book, I extend my endless appreciation.

These are my own memories. To protect the privacy of others, names have been changed, characters conflated and some incidents condensed.

IN MY SKIN

WHAT DO I REMEMBER of being a prostitute?

I remember tenderness, boredom, the ice-creams we would eat at 3 a.m. in front of the television; the smell of cocks, shy men with silky skin, laughter; dark streets gleaming; boys in baseball caps slouching in the introduction lounge, heavy bellies pressing on me; conversations, sneaking cigarettes while fixing my make-up.

I remember the other girls being like sisters, and knowing that to tell them my real name was dangerous. I remember opening my heart to strange men and stroking their faces, smiling. I remember being pounded so hard my face was white with pain. I remember being a prostitute, and being proud of it, liking it.

But what I did is not normal. No? I was naked, I touched people's bodies, they touched mine, we were alone in a room. Like a masseur, like a dentist, like a beauty therapist. Yes, but I opened my body, they touched me there. Like a doctor. Yes, but inside.

Yes.

I sometimes wondered, with my legs spread over the face of some eager man, if I felt regret for the invasion of my most secret places. A man whom I've never met before is staring at my vagina. But what does this mean? It is just skin. Am I ashamed to have the crook of my knee examined? My ear? The inside of my mouth? Eyes leave no scar, I am not reduced by someone's gaze. My body is beautiful, and desired; I feel beautiful and desirable. Someone is looking at me. At the outside, at the membrane of flesh that veils me. I am still mine.

I do not like to judge others. I know now that everyone has their secrets. I write mine down. I carry them lightly inside me. They are almost invisible.

I walked dark and dirty footpaths in the middle of the night. I got into strangers' cars and got out swearing or smiling. I drove with men to grotty alleys and put stained tissues in my bag afterwards. I took their money and wiped my mouth and went to a small flat and pumped chemical relief into my vein, and returned to the rainy street. I slept on a dirty mattress in an empty room and shivered and woke every grey twilight wishing I could sleep forever. I lived on chocolate bars and bought a single cup of coffee for an afternoon, sheltering in warm cafés for comfort. I watched people in supermarkets and couldn't remember what it felt like to take ordinary things from the shelves. I stood in the dark on the footpath and gazed in on bright living rooms. I held down so much sorrow I couldn't feel anything anymore. The sadness and anger corroded all my feelings. The only thing I knew I wanted was heroin, and rest.

I made money I'd never imagined and I wore velvet dresses and shone in lamplight. I walked tall in crowds, knowing myself to be desired. I received luxurious gifts. I was a princess in my realm and men couldn't get enough of me. They waited hours for my company and I couldn't even remember their names. I had a house with a spa and hardwood floors; I lost track of fifty dollar notes, and found them adrift in pockets, inside books. I was everyone's favourite. I told people I was a prostitute, and smiled as I said it, and dared them to turn their gaze.

The smile that I give when I talk about it now is, I can feel, nostalgic, provocative. A brightness comes into my eyes. And, I'm told, a hard look too.

I WAS A SENSITIVE LITTLE girl, but perhaps not more than most. Sometimes the world was too big; other times, far too small. It took a long time to nudge out the right space in it.

My family was simple and close: two parents and a younger sister. We grew up in a nice suburb of Melbourne, in a large and comfortable old house, though the front lawn was a disgrace and the weatherboards flaked a little. We had two old lemon trees in the backyard. My sister and I used to 'paint' the boards with the hose, darkening the colour for just a moment. My parents were too busy with their books and work, and with raising us, to bother much about the dandelions in the lawn. Inside the big house we had all the warmth we needed. The place was cluttered, full of cracked treasures, odd objects in boxes, the smell of casserole.

My father was a scientist, bearded and genial, who gathered my sister and me into his arms and told us magical stories. Busy with a career in the community and education, my mother often seemed to me sterner, but at parties I sheltered behind her slim hip to watch the other children. Quick to hug and kiss me, she made sure I knew that I was always cherished.

It was the seventies. My mother taught me that men are not to be feared, that women are strong, that a person could become anything she wished, as long as she did it with passion and a good heart. My father showed me this also. I knew only kind men.

My parents bought me books: on cavemen, on gods, on unicorns, on deserts and beasts and adventures. Stories of forest paths and brave princesses. I grew up in a house insulated with books. They covered every wall; and as I was timid, they were my gentlest friends. From their pages I took dreams of a magical island, safely moated and quiet under a humming sun.

With some friends, my mother established a small alternative primary school. The fathers had beards, the women short hair and clean faces. There the dozen or so students were encouraged to develop their own interests without too many boundaries. Free to read all day if I chose, or to play with my friends, I grew up loving alternately the haven of solitude and the solace of a group. My soft little voice was often lost in the furore of the yard. When my friends played 'horses', I was a lone mare tossing my mane on the other side of the playground until they fetched me back. Sometimes it was easier to sit in a warm place and read.

When I was about nine, there was a day on which we were all to make cubby houses. Someone had donated cardboard boxes used for delivering fridges: sturdy, roomy boxes. There were parents of the children there, but my mother was in a meeting with the owners of the church building the school leased. I was feeling miserable.

The clatter of the room was too loud.

'Pair up, and you can decorate your cubby house,' we were encouraged. Everyone else coupled up and started getting thick paintbrushes and polystyrene off-cuts from the craft table, cutting doorways and windows, painting flowerboxes under the 'sills' and fluorescent trees against the 'walls'. The room was filled with the sound of happy children talking and planning. I looked at them, and didn't want to join. There seemed something foolish about the bother.

I found a box for myself. With a Stanley knife, I cut a low entrance. I jostled open the flap I'd made, and got in.

Inside, it was ochre-shadowed and warm. The cardboard muffled the noise of the other children; I curled up, chin to knees, crossed arms holding myself. My breath came back warm at my face. I grew drowsy with the silence and the peace.

I thought of gods in their grottoes, as I'd read in my mythology books. Safe caves, secret glades. Centaurs and nymphs, curled up in the roots of ancient trees. My face was damp with breath. It was so quiet in there. I thought I would never get out of this box where I could be me, alone, hardly anyone at all.

'Where's Kate? She—Kate? Are you in there?' Concerned voices outside, hollow thumps on the fragile wall. 'Are you coming out? Do you want some crayons? You haven't decorated!'

I sat there in my cocoon, besieged, becoming more and more resentful and furious. *Don't make me come out.* The voices went away; returned.

'Well, if you're just going to *sulk*—'

I clambered out, embarrassed and murderous, already realising that sometimes escape is not popular, that it needs to be more furtive.

*

My mother and I had arguments, shrieking at each other down the hall, slamming doors. What did she, what did everyone, want from me? My dark brows under the blonde fringe drew down in rage. In dumb fury I poured libations of bitter dregs from my father's wine bottle, murmuring something confused to ancient gods I almost believed in. On those days Athena, my goddess, loved not only wisdom but war.

Then it was time to leave the little alternative school. At a state high school I faltered. I withdrew behind my long hair, lowered my face. I could never quite understand what my new friends saw in me, gauche, try-hard, blushing with my gummy smile. But they took me in, and taught me to be welcomed, and though I looked in horror on their early experiments with drinking and smoking, I remained, hovering, on the rowdy fringe of teenage conspiracy. I was the one to bring glasses of water to tired, drunken friends, to call the taxi home. Being out was exciting but I loved going home.

There were my piano, my books, the sweet frail light that slipped down the hall in the afternoons, the familiar scorn of my little sister. My bedroom, where I could curl up and dream, and sometimes cry, and vanish. Inside me, that was where I found peace.

My schoolfriends were mostly girls, with sharp haircuts and a blade of sophistication in their talk. Sometimes I was forgotten, but other times we stayed over at someone's house, having baths together, giggling and talking secrets. I didn't say much, but I beamed shyly at them all, so glad to be included.

I was sixteen and no one had kissed me. Then seventeen, and finishing school. Matilda, Camille, Joey, they were all having sex by then. Short-sighted, I hated to wear glasses; perhaps a boy had smiled at me, but I didn't know. I touched myself sometimes, but it seemed silly. I didn't like the idea of men's bodies. I had a crush on a girl at school. The whole idea of sex was frightening. But I was miserable to be left out of the chance at it. It began to embarrass me; I waited.

To me, my body was revolting: I pawed at the flesh on my hips, at my unnecessary breasts, with frustration, and hid it all beneath too-large clothes, wallowing around, wishing I were invisible. I dreaded having someone see me naked, see me up close. I couldn't bear my body. And so I cherished my mind.

School was over, and as I waited to begin university I took a weekend job in a local bookshop. My new boss said kindly, 'You're shy, aren't you? It'll do you good. You'll have to talk to people.' I was almost too shy to admit it was true. But I learned to love my job, and to chat with customers, telling them what to read, laughing with them, finding confidence.

I'd expected university to be a haven, but amid the poised elite at Melbourne University I tottered to classes, where I kept my mouth shut and resented everyone for their confidence. Studying archaeology, classics and literature was a natural choice, it was my dream. I sat in the classics library in a dusty shaft of sunlight, fingering texts in ancient Greek, deciphering them. I was going to be an archaeologist who read Virginia Woolf in a tent. I had classes in fashionable cultural studies theory about sexuality and feminist irony. Now I wore a camouflage of black clothes and conceit. I avoided the gaze of other students. I wanted to be like them; I didn't like them. I loved the learning, but even that wasn't what I expected. Archaeology was dry and dusty. I wasn't quite as smart as I'd thought I was.

The friends from school were still around; they all moved into inner-city sharehouses together, while I stayed at home in the suburbs. My foothold on a social life was slipping in this muddle of loneliness and doubt.

I would hear my little sister and her boyfriend, giggling and smoking pot in her bedroom. I passed the closed door, and went to my room. I sat, forlorn in my black clothes, listening to The Cure, reading *Titus Groan* by candlelight, hating the cliché I was. Nineteen years old and feeling middle-aged.

Will was the first boy I kissed and the first boy who made love to me. I met him skulking at a party. As bashful as I was, as enthralled by fancy and fantasy, he gave me a precious year. Confessions. Poetry. Saturated kisses in dim afternoon rooms. I uncovered my body to him and somehow, now, it became beautiful. He gave me white roses because I loved them. I thought I'd found perfection, my twin, my mate. His pale body was beautiful, not frightening; it melted under my mouth, under the skimming of my palms. Through our long dyed-black fringes we smiled mischievously at each other. I told him everything. I was in love.

He was the first boy to break my heart. The girl he left me for had green hair, a nose ring and a crazed sort of charm. She was wild and bold. She was everything I was not; there was nothing I could do to fight for him. There was just me now, foolish and devastated. It was as if the world had broken.

On a day of parched, rough northerlies I sat at my window, scraped raw with hurt. I smoked my first cigarette and scratched my skin idly with a blunt knife. How nice I'd been, how stupid. Rage and humiliation blew their hot winds inwards. Slice, slice, just softly. I'd been so *open*. I learned the satisfaction of metal against skin and sealed myself up.

Soon after, aged twenty-one, I went to Europe for six months' backpacking. Roaming the strange streets, I learned self-sufficiency.

I tested my courage, my ability to survive; there were hard and lonely times when I wept on twilit roadsides, far from home. It toughened me. I sat at a window in a hostel in dusty boots and old clothes. Past the faded green shutters lay the grandiose city of Rome. The notebook in my hand was full of observations, quotations, pale pencil sketches of art I'd seen. I read Casanova's memoirs, and Byron, and Tacitus. Here no one knew me, no one observed. Alone, I was dreaming and at peace; like a maiden in a tower.

I sat in a piazza, drinking strong espresso, raising my face to the sunshine with a little smile of accomplishment at being there, at being an adult in the world. When I got back to Melbourne to go on with my studies, I had a new stride. It was the early nineties. Before I left, Nirvana had broken into the music scene, and now everything was a roar of energy.

'Can I have some?' I asked my friend, who was smoking a joint at a party. The marijuana dizzied me, lent me solace. The doze of it wasn't as frightening as I'd feared. It was warm.

'I'll have some,' I said to a friend pouring vodka at another party. And bought myself a bottle the next day. I feared losing control in front of others; I drank it alone.

'Sure, I'll move in with you,' I said to Matilda, my friend from school, who had a spare room in St Kilda. And finally it all began. At twenty-one I splashed into a new life, full of friends and music and bravado.

St Kilda was famous for its art deco flats and glossy cafés and bars, its well-loved old pubs; the foreshore, the craft market, the seaside kiosks; the ferals and the beautiful people; the strange characters and the bland crowds of tourists. At that time it was still cheap enough for students to live there, in tattered but elegant old flats in leafy streets, around the corner from the main street and the beach and the parks and each other. On weekends people came in from all over town, to drink, swim and loiter at shop windows in Acland Street; at night the place had certain streets where girls wore very little, even in winter, and there were cars going around and around. St Kilda was full of artists, bohemians, rich people, music, sex and drugs.

Suddenly I was in the middle of things. There were late nights staggering home from the pub, days of bumping into my friends in the street and going off for long afternoons of coffee and pool. Parties where I knew everyone. I was kissed up against walls, missed classes because I was in bed with a lanky, dreadlocked boy. We all had our noses pierced.

My happy group of friends breezed around the suburb. I smoked pot again. Something in me wanted to know, to conquer. I liked the dreaminess, the way it elucidated my thoughts. Then cigarettes as well. It seemed like progress, to be able to loosen my stern grip on myself. I liked to keep a cask of wine beside my bed. Before a rock gig, we all snorted speed, and I felt excitement flutter up through my belly. I learned to play bass guitar and found myself on a pub stage with a couple of friends, hammering out heavy sounds of glory. I thought, *I never imagined I'd be this brave.*

There was a body on my bed, a series of bodies, fervent young men clambering towards orgasm, my face making the right expressions, my mind blank. It wasn't bad sex but I valued the kisses, the lying together quietly afterwards. I wasn't in it for the pleasure. I didn't think my dull flesh could find it like this. Will and I had had pleasure, but he was gone. Now it was all about the glow of victory, about the scent on my skin afterwards, about manifesting something like desirability.

In sex, the edge of the world brimmed at the edge of me. I took the world into my own body, right inside my flesh. It gasped appreciation, and then I put it out again and my body remained immaculate. I learned this.

I wasn't sure why I had these affairs, except that I wanted to please and be seen to please. They were lovely boys, with their mouths tasting iron with nervousness but, still shamed by my body's appetites, I could not tell them what might make it sing. Those boys wouldn't stay, they weren't for keeps. In the morning when they left I waved goodbye bravely at the front door.

Afterwards I would read, relishing words, their magic transport to luminous worlds. I smoked a bong and flicked page after page, still dreaming.

For my honours year I wrote a thesis on Anaïs Nin, who recorded wild sprees of sex and love in her writings. The pathology of her behaviour excited me. Besotted by the similarities I saw in our natures—yearning, passionate, repressed, fragile—I dressed like her, in heavy thirties dresses and heeled shoes, red lipstick and a glossy bun. For a year I read Anaïs and wished for her elegance, her daring, her sexual fulfilment. I was in love with a charismatic young man called Max who admired Nin's lover Henry Miller. In his dim, sun-dappled room down the road from mine we talked and talked. Philosophy, art, writing. Occasionally he would take me to bed. And when a year later I wept inconsolably on his bedroom floor for our failure to be happy together, I told myself that Anaïs, too, had felt this pain and made of it something beautiful.

My life was surging and bright, like a wave in the sun. I stayed close to my family, whose house full of books and happy chaos and good humour had buoyed me all my life. I had an arts degree with

12

honours—the final grade wasn't what I'd hoped, but what could I expect when I'd spent most of my last year playing pool with Max and indulging in romantic melodramas? Now my bookshop employers offered me more part-time work. I wasn't going to get any further with my studies, but I was sure I would find a place in the world of literature somehow, and so selling novels was as good a way to start as any. The idea of a dour office job and professional career repelled me. I was twenty-three years of age, and my life was just beginning.

I moved out of Matilda's and into a large Victorian house closer to Acland Street. It had tall, pale ceilings, unused iron fireplaces and a rich garden full of flowers and marijuana plants. I lived there with Cathy and Dan, a slightly older couple who both played in rock bands and decorated the kitchen with bright painted ceramics. My room was dim and cool, its ceiling rose chipped. There was a kindly lemon tree outside my sashed window. I made the room as thirties as I could, with drapes and lamps; I hung my Anaïs dresses along one wall. The house always smelled of incense and pot.

I was still close to Max and his friends, though he and I were no longer lovers. In his house around the corner I said hello to a thin, intense young man with pensive eyes and a nervous habit of drawing in a sketchbook. We had met before, at parties and exhibition openings. I peered at what he was working on: a self-portrait, exaggerating his slouch, his skinniness, his glare of apprehension. And a picture of me, cute and thin also. Underneath, as I watched, James wrote, not looking at me, *I like you.*

Taking the pen from his hand, I angled the page towards me. *I think I like you too.*

*

13

Max passed behind James, and winked.

Love, love ran through me like sunshine.

In the summer evenings of St Kilda with James, down there by the sea, with our clever clothes and happy heads, holding hands, everything felt so young and fresh and possible.

Life was all lightness the summer I was twenty-three. The lightness of James's fingers across my breast in sleep, the lightness of my spirits as we roamed Acland Street in search of midnight chocolate and vodka. We sat on his front verandah in the twilight, dressed alike in short-sleeved gingham shirts, drinking sarsaparilla. James played on an old acoustic guitar. We lit each other's cigarettes.

James was my bliss. Though he was four years younger than I was he had the deep, thoughtful gaze of an old soul. He lived just around the corner with Jodie, the sister of one of Max's housemates; Jodie had a boyfriend, Sam; there were other hangers-on. And so I had found myself in a new circle of younger people.

There was underground art I'd never seen, and different music; something joyous and satisfying about their world, new things to talk about. They were so bright and cool, these people, with their wicked humour. I felt older and wiser, but not too much.

I stood on a stage under red lights, playing with my band, striking a pose for the benefit of James kneeling on the floor below, and laughed at him through the hot smoky air. On sunny days in parks I read him my favourite poetry by Yeats and Judith Wright and Stevie Smith, and he wrote me funny, melancholy ditties in return. We made love every day and beneath his hands and his slender body I found pleasure at last, was flushed through with it. I was late to work as James would sleepily reach out from the covers when I bent to kiss him goodbye and he'd pull me in; helplessly I'd sink back into his embrace. It didn't seem to matter. Love was the most important thing in the world.

And when, two months into our relationship, I found I was pregnant, even that seemed like some kind of adventure.

'I don't think we can—should—' I said.

'No. But—oh, Kate.'

It made me ill; that was the burden. We tried to imagine that there was a living thing inside me, but it was impossible. All I knew was that I felt dreadfully sick, and wanted it to stop. We didn't want a child: we each lived in a shared house with only a bedroom to ourself; James was twenty years old. It was all too early and rushed and accidental. When I went to the clinic for the termination, it was with relief. I refused the general anaesthetic, because I wanted to witness the moment, feel the pain. It hurt, but I felt maybe I deserved that.

Afterwards, things continued as they were. If James felt grief, he kept it from me. If I felt grief, I didn't know.

IT WAS THE NIGHT OF OUR three-month anniversary: a cool evening in April. All day James and I had been teasing each other, promising erotic delights, expensive liquor and luxurious pleasure to celebrate. I was brimming with anticipation, I clutched his hand tightly. And so it was a shock when, walking away from the pub after a drink with Sam and Jodie, James said he couldn't come back to my room after all.

'The others and me, we're doing something at my place.'

I stopped in the footpath. 'What? What are you doing?'

I was rotten with disappointment but I kept smiling. To show I understood.

'You don't want to do it. We're—' his face took on a kind of pride '—we're doing heroin.'

Heroin was all around us in St Kilda. We'd been to see a movie about junkies, there were fashion shoots of sullen anorexics in smeared make-up, and the suburb we lived in had a high population of tottering, lean-thighed people with harsh mouths and dirty jeans. But it was a scene I'd never known; it was something I passed in the street. I'd never seen the drug itself, except in films.

The idea of heroin, its swooning rush, strapped arms in hotel rooms, and the romantic tradition of laudanum, had always appealed to my adolescent dreams of exquisite oblivion but to me it was as foreign as motherhood, or speaking Chinese. A black hole, edged with a halo of glamour, radiating transgression. One of my school friends had dabbled in it a few years earlier; when I'd asked him about it, he'd said he didn't want ever to talk about it. I hadn't dreamed it would come any closer to me than that.

Now here it was, ruining the evening ahead, entering the house I spent time in, taking my boyfriend to a strange place I didn't know. I turned, left him, ran to Max's house numb with fright for tea and consolation. Then I spent the night alone.

The next day James came around, and hugged me. He looked at my face, and hugged me again. 'It was just something I wanted to try,' he said. 'I'm sorry.'

When we made love, I saw the tiny red mark on the inside of his arm. A little puncture, where something brutal and metal had pierced my beloved boy. I said nothing, but in the dim green light of the afternoon I surreptitiously kissed the tender flesh there.

The next time I went to his place there was a new shiver in the air. James, Sam, Jodie and another friend had the gleeful air of children with a secret. I sat there, all too aware of being the one not invited to share.

I looked at them as people who had crossed a river, who were going somewhere joyously while I stood alone on the other bank.

They'd done something I couldn't conceive of: they'd put a needle in their arms. They'd taken a hard drug. Marijuana and trips, they were one thing; this was like entering a world full of legends and awe. Sid Vicious, Billie Holiday, Kurt Cobain. Of course I felt the pull of that glamour, but I also remembered how all those people had died. What kind of courage was getting my friends past their fear?

That night, and again a week later, there came a point in the evening when looks were exchanged, and someone said, 'You might like to go home now, Kate.' As if I were a child to be protected. I could only set my face in a smile, and go away.

I knew this sensation: being judged too innocent, too immature, to remain part of the group, just when I'd found one. Playing horses by myself as a child. Being left behind when my high school friends went out. I was so appalled to find this feeling yet again. And I felt contempt too; I had dallied in the ragged life of the pot-smoking student, but I was still at heart a sensible prude, and I thought they were completely out of their minds to be doing heroin. They didn't seem to be taking it seriously. I looked at Jodie's beautiful young face, and I thought of James, sinking backwards on a bed in the ecstasy of a smack rush, with an almost erotic charge of horror.

I didn't know whether I despised or envied my friends. Fear, temptation, and panic all wrenched at me. All I wanted was to be happy again.

There was no single moment when someone looked at me and said, 'Just have one go.' No one made me try heroin. My friends told me to keep away. There was no enticement; just an inductive pressure, a sense that if I didn't, I would lose.

And so I thought perhaps I should try it. Just once, to know. To join them behind the closed door of someone's bedroom, to be able to say, *You really are insane, now I know what you're doing.* To leap over that river. To test myself.

James said no. 'I don't want you doing it,' he said. But then, later, making love to me, he had a little smile on his face and when I kissed him and asked what he was smiling at he said, into the side of my throat, 'I'm thinking bad things. Bad things about heroin,' and I, with the same smile, wanting to stay close to him, knowing what it meant, said, 'Me too.'

And the next night, after James had been done, and then Sam, and Jodie's sister Abbey, while the rest of us waited edgy and incandescent in the lounge, Jodie took me into her bedroom. James held my arm under the hard light of a lamp and Jodie kneeled in front of me, saying, 'I'll try not to hurt you too much, baby.' I smiled to hide my nervousness. Jodie's beautiful face was like a Flemish Madonna's in the blank light; I just stared at the immaculate skin in the crook of my arm, and thought, *In a minute I'll have taken heroin.* It was inconceivable, but here I was, and it seemed like what I wanted.

The metal approached my flesh; there was a sharp sting, the ridge of the needle under the skin, the sucking pressure of blood drawn out, and fluid pressed steadily in. James released my arm and I licked the tiny spot of blood. It tasted metallic with chemicals. He kissed me, in consolation or congratulation. My head felt dazzled, from my racing heart. But I didn't think I could feel much else. Sleepy, perhaps. A little spangled with sensation. Proud.

Then I decided that I needed another try before I could say I'd done heroin; I hadn't had the legendary rush of chemical bliss. It had taken a couple of tries with pot, too, before I'd really felt the effects. There seemed a varnish in me that had to be scratched before a chemical could enter. I didn't work up the nerve straight away. James and I went on with our kisses, drawing, smoking joints, hanging out. The next attempt was a week later; and this time I was aware of a happy thrill in my veins: a dizzy feeling; then dreaminess as I lay back on Jodie's bed. I was aware of a contented glow, warm in my marrow. I couldn't judge how much of that was the drug, and how much was the satisfaction at my own courage.

Heroin is like wading into the sea. The first fizz of water at your ankles is delicious, shocking. You're aware of every cold pulse of water against your skin. You wade further; your temperature accommodates; you walk more slowly. The water is still shallow, though the bottom slopes. You're delighted as you relax into the sway, the buckle of the waves. You grin with pleasure, and you think, Why didn't I come in sooner? How gorgeous, how thrilling! Then abruptly the sand drops beneath your next step, and you plunge into deeper water, and you can't feel the bottom anymore.

It took about two weeks before I began to realise we were in thrall. That every time the group of us got together the question was, *Shall we?* That we waited with shivering nerves and giddy smiles for Jake the dealer to arrive, in his shiny boots, with his well-tended hair and enigmatic drawl, with his little origami packets of treasure. That we were having a better time now than ever before; that if we didn't ring Jake for his wares we sat around listlessly drinking beer, the conversation more laden with effort.

Giggling at each other's pinned pupils. 'Butterflied,' we called it. 'You're so butterflied.'

We gloried in the secrecy, the ritual and the closed bedroom door. A deal was fifty dollars, split between four of us; the money wasn't an issue. The next day we didn't feel bad, but perhaps dozed a little longer in bed; it didn't matter since none of us had more than a part-time job, a few uni classes, the washing-up to do. The little red points on our skin healed within a day.

Heroin was a lure, a security, a delight. It calmed me, glossed me; the infusion of heat, the tickle of satisfaction. With junk in our veins, we were the most beautiful people in the world.

I liked how our eyes would all glitter as we waited for the dealer to arrive; how they'd soften after the fix. The sex was fantastic.

James and I always had lovely sex; but there'd been moments when we sat in pubs, in my room, just gazing at each other with nothing to say. Now, with the glee and balm of the drug in our systems, we couldn't stop talking, touching. When we made love it was for hours, in a cocoon of warmth, in drowsy low lamplight, his skin a miracle under my hands, his mouth rapturous on mine.

Max said, 'I don't like it. You don't know what you're doing with those kids. I've seen people who use smack, you're not like that. Do you even know what the fuck you're doing?'

'It's fine,' I said, my smile reaching him, my eyes already drifting away.

He didn't know how it was. There was something full of awe surrounding that drug, in our respect for it, the way our excited giggles would flatten into seriousness for the administration, and then rise again in the happiness afterwards.

My housemates, Cathy and Dan, knew something was up. We were watching a program about the heroin trade in Afghanistan. 'I've been doing some of that,' I said finally, off-hand. 'Heroin. It's kind of interesting.'

The television blared on; they stared at me. The room stiffened. It wasn't the reaction I was hoping for.

They stopped talking to me; when I walked into the lounge

room Cathy would leave, looking upset. They put a second television in their bedroom and I rarely saw them. Petulant and baffled, I decided to move out. My life could be so much better, fresher; something new was what I wanted. Now I was finished with university it was time to re-set. I would be clean and healthy, I would take myself in hand, firm myself up. I had a beautiful boy, wonderful friends. James and I decided to move in together.

We could find a deco flat, in the suburb of Elwood just nearby. I pictured myself reading in the afternoons, perhaps studying a little ancient Greek, and writing with a thick-nibbed pen. My hair smooth, my mind clear as water. There would be plane trees shading my window and pools of sunshine on the floor.

There were plenty of beautiful apartments, but all too expensive for a bookshop girl and a student. We ended up with a flat in a seventies building. Its exterior was the drab brown of a Communist foyer and inside were small, box-like rooms without decoration. The ceiling was like regurgitated porridge. 'We'll decorate,' we said. But my black-and-white nudes, my gauzy wall-hangings and my candlesticks looked a little odd against the bleak beige walls.

At our housewarming party there was no food or drink, since we had no money to buy any, and old friends mixed awkwardly with new. At the end of the evening, the non-drug users departed, leaving the rest of us to borrow money to score from the last to leave. I'd sworn to myself I'd never use if I didn't have the cash on me; but it was only twenty-five bucks. We liked two tastes each by now. James, Jodie, Sam, Abbey and I sat on the floor in a haze of contentment, and didn't care that the others had gone.

My parents came to see the new place. They'd visited me from time to time in St Kilda, though it was easier for me to go home to see them. In the past I'd usually stayed the night, but I hadn't done that for a while. Every now and then I'd catch up with them to see a film or have a meal. Now my parents looked around the new place.

'The ceiling's pretty low,' said my mother. 'It's a good thing you haven't much furniture, in this little room.'

'But look at the big plane tree outside the window!' I said, and directed her attention outside. Out of the corner of my eye I'd seen a forgotten swab wrapper lying on the carpet under the couch. I kicked it out of sight.

'It's nice, darling,' said my mother as we walked down the concrete stairwell and into the concrete carpark. 'I just hope you can afford it, you two.'

I started a new journal. On the front cover I stuck a picture of Anaïs, elegant and composed, at the brink of her career, and framed it with black velvet. In the back, I kept a list of the dates we used heroin, until there was no point because it was every day. I filled the pages with looping letters, chronicling a life that seemed to be moving beyond what I had ever expected.

It had been a couple of months since we started using. Already when we didn't score we felt the difference. A slight flush of sweat, loose bowels, thin fatigue. My skin dried out from the chemical. But the compensations seemed enough. The prickling excitement of fixing up, the gluttony; how sleek and luminous we were when the drug was inside us.

It was a good life for a while. I worked several days at the bookstore; I'd come home, up the leafy street still sunny with the last of autumn's warmth, with icy-poles for us to eat on the balcony. Jake lived in a flat across the road from us, so most nights one of us would go and visit him and come back to find the other waiting with teaspoons, syringes and a cup of water ready. We'd fix up, smoke a few cigarettes, talk, cook, watch television. It was a calm routine.

23

Jake was an exotic character who exactly fitted my expectations of a smack dealer. He wore black with rockster swagger and told outlandish stories from his life—his champion athlete days, kangaroo-shooting with his brothers, perilous car accidents he'd miraculously escaped. He was about the same age as me. His girlfriend Vicki was a morose blonde who said little and slumped on the couch. She was a street prostitute; Jake said she was tired from all the energy she used up working at night. They worked and dealt to cover their habit; they weren't flush with cash. There was a kind of cinema glamour to them, in their flat full of kitsch and cigarette smoke and discarded thigh-high stiletto boots. Vicki's eyes were smudged with make-up; they had a GI Joe doll on the mantelpiece, armed with an uncapped syringe. At first we begged needles off them, from a full box in a drawer; then they told us where to get clean fits from the needle exchange. Their apartment always smelled of the harsh alcohol scent of swabs. It felt good to sit in there, talking; when other customers arrived, we said hello, smiling. It was the bonhomie of complicity.

When I met Jake on my own, to score, he sat close, and talked low. I liked making him smile, caught by the implausible glamour of the man. Blushing when he complimented me, allowing myself to be flattered. His manner was a cross between lounge-lizard and big brother. With Jake I felt as if I were in a new world, but he made me feel safe too. Under the braggadocio, he was just a young man with a habit getting by on small-time dealing. Making the best of it. He tried to warn us what heroin would bring; but of course he had to sell his gear too. I never held that against him. I just liked his attention.

We saw less and less of Jodie and Sam; they'd moved in together, with Jodie's sister Abbey and her boyfriend, who was also using now and, though we were all bound by friendship and the drugs, I found myself infuriated by their blitheness and self-absorption, because they mirrored my own. James and I drew more and more together as the winter came down. I was busy cruising, not doing any art, not reading enough, idling and telling myself it was okay, this was my year off after uni.

'I love you,' we said to each other every time we slid the needle into the other's arm.

The drug fuelled us into one cigarette after another. After a taste we would be jittery with excitement and a feeling of power, talking rapidly, fluently. I hadn't expected it to be a stimulant. But most of the time it held us steady, serene. There was little physical thrill except for the first minutes, when I'd feel a glow that was as much psychosomatic as chemical. It wasn't quite the ecstatic swoon of the movies. We liked to lie back with a cigarette after the fix, but after a minute we'd sit up again. It was the doing of it, the equipment, the ceremony, the promise, that made my mouth water with excitement.

We still smoked pot from time to time but I liked it less now, on top of the smack; the two sedatives made me listless, and occasionally I would realise, dazedly, that I had breathed out but not in.

Again and again my journal described our resolutions, bright as epiphanies, that the drugs were no good, that we should quit; the raggedness of my nerves; the resolve to fix everything; and our failure. I wrote compulsively of being in love, and briefly of the drugs.

The light in the kitchen was high and fluorescent; one night I wandered in to get some water and, caught by my reflection in the window, I stopped and could not stop looking at my pale, lost face.

The band I played bass guitar in, a hard-edged indie trio, was

25

staggering by now. The friendship continued, but we all had problems which seemed very rock and roll; Mike suffered a panic disorder, Cass was driven and quick to tears; and here I was, in a black leather jacket, doing heroin in the toilets. Our music got darker, heavier, and the arguments more hysterical. In between we played the occasional gig and I still had the electric thrill of satisfaction—me, the shy girl, up there in the red lights, bashing out the sonorous chords of angst. But everything was unwieldy, and I knew that my band-mates were impatient with my tiredness, my crappy equipment I couldn't afford to replace and the way I turned up to every practice session late. I found it hard to come up with melodies now.

It wasn't long before we decided to take a break, and then the break turned into the end. 'Too hard,' said Cass. 'I'm sorry.' Later, I saw in the paper that the two of them were still performing occasionally. I said it was probably for the best. Sometimes James took my bass out of its case and played sad, jaunty songs on it. I just watched.

James was out seeing his parents, and I was alone in the flat. We'd scored; had some, and left the rest until later, for a bed-time treat. There was nothing to watch on television; I had no concentration to write or read. I fingered open the little origami packet of powder.

The packet, cut out of a magazine, revealed a shard of lipsticked mouth on glossy paper and a crease full of white powder. I held the little fold of paper carefully in my hands and tipped it into a spoon. I'd cleaned the spoon with alcohol first, with a swab from a small square packet with red lettering. The syringe punctured a plastic ampoule of distilled water; I drew up a centimetre or two of water, and then eased it onto the powder. With a pop the inner tube of the syringe came out of its casing and with the blunt end of it I stirred the powder until it dissolved.

In Australia heroin is not like in American or British movies, where a yellowish solution must be heated or mixed with lemon juice to break open the chemicals; our heroin comes from Afghanistan and Asia, and is pure white. What lay in the cradle of the spoon after a minute looked just like water.

I slotted the fit back together, dropped a tiny corner of the swab into the fluid, and used it as a filter as I eased every tiny drop of liquid into the barrel of the syringe. I peered at the fit to make sure there was no air. It didn't really matter—it was made with a lock to block any air bubbles entering the blood. But this was a fastidious matter. One took care with this drug.

Fixing up was one thing; I'd never injected myself. James's light fingers had always slipped the needle in for me. I set about learning how to do it.

In the back of a drawer I found an old tie. Tethering it tightly enough around my upper arm, one-handed, was difficult. It kept slipping loose. I gripped one end between my teeth and pulled it tight. I pumped my fist until I felt the veins swell; with my free hand I swabbed my skin. The needle-point closed in on me; inconceivably, it kept coming. Only a fraction of space between it being outside me, and inside. It didn't hurt much at all. At first I couldn't be sure I had the vein, then the needle popped into one with silent satisfaction. A tiny flush of crimson swirled into the barrel of the fit. And then I pulled my blood out of me, so fresh and bright in the chamber, until I had a proper conduit, the needle steady inside me, and I pushed the plunger in. My heart hammering.

Then I had to ease the metal out of me, carefully. I forgot to untie my arm first; blood spilled out of me under the pressure, down towards my wrist. I unwrapped my arm and stared at the wetness, the brilliant colour. I licked the blood off, captivated by what I'd just done. The proof of it, my blood, which I saw so often now, was almost glorious.

My other friends were busy with jobs. The house where Max lived had disbanded; that centre of my life was gone too. Never good at picking up the phone, I hadn't given my new number to other people and these days St Kilda wasn't as full of chance meetings and idle coffees. When I bumped into people something was awkward, and we'd wave goodbye on the footpath. No offers to duck into a café for a chat. *See you. Yeah, see you soon.*

In fact there weren't many coffees anymore. Money was difficult; even with minimal using, just enough to soothe the itch of want (and there was something about night time that confounded our resolutions to take a break), I didn't earn enough to support two people's habits, and pay my share of rent, and buy food, and go out. I worked four days a week in the bookshop and my wage didn't quite cover one taste each per day. On payday we'd have a drink at the pub, but most days we had to share a latte at City Books Café. I found an old credit card my parents had set up for me when I'd gone overseas a few years before. Every few days I'd withdraw fifty dollars, hoping I'd somehow pay it back before the account was sent to my mother. It was a nice clean number, fifty: discrete, dedicated to one deal from Jake. In a mad way it seemed irresponsible to take this money for food or bills; so we used, as conscientiously as possible, and one by one things dropped away.

We lived on porridge for a few weeks: at less than a dollar for a pack, it was cheap and filling. Then the phone was cut off, and then the gas, and we were reduced to cold breakfast cereal for dinner.

My sister called round and invited me to an afternoon movie. It had been a while since we'd caught up. On the tram into town I said I didn't have enough cash for a movie; would she lend me some? We'd always been at odds, with her quick-tempered decisiveness and my airy self-absorption. However, there was a cord of friendship between us as well, stronger as we'd grown older. She was younger than I was, but much more self-possessed. Now she gazed at me awkwardly. She said that one of our mutual friends had already told her I was using. 'Is it true?'

I made a face. I'd grown so used to the reality of drugs—they seemed normal. I'd forgotten the precious innocence of my family. My sister just looked at me and didn't say anything, bafflement on her face. I wondered if she actually knew what heroin involved. 'It's not what you think,' I said. 'It's okay.' I was aware of the elusive flickering of my gaze. From her face to the window, then to my own hands, resting in my lap. 'I don't have much cash, though.'

She saw my tiredness, and she was kind. She asked if I needed a loan. I blushed at her trust. I reassured her the money was for groceries and she gave me a couple of notes: sixty dollars. Later, on the way home, I stopped at a milkbar to buy something to eat. It was a cold night; I was weary and famished. At the counter I discovered the money was gone. It must have fallen out of my pocket. I put the bread back in the bin; the soup back on the shelf.

I got home feeling desperate; the time with my sister had reminded me of family and home, and our bleak flat with its empty cupboards was awful.

'It's okay,' said James. 'We've got 2-Minute Noodles.'

But when I put a saucepan of water on to boil I remembered there was no gas.

'Look,' he said, unwrapping the cake of wrinkled yellow noodles. 'We can eat them like biscuits!' I watched him open his tender mouth to take a bite of the harsh stuff, and started to cry.

'I can work,' I said to James one night. 'On the streets. Like Vicki.' I dressed up in my Anaïs lingerie: lace bra, suspender belt, French knickers. I coated my mouth with lipstick, made up my eyes. Just to practise. Dress-ups, like my thirties frocks. If I worked, we'd have money to buy nice clothes. I was scarcely thinking beyond the underwear.

'Look,' I said, coming out to show James. 'What do you think? Would you pay two hundred dollars to fuck me?'

The drugs were slow syrup in my mind. I didn't quite catch the depth of pain in the look James gave me.

'Don't do that,' he said. 'I couldn't bear it. I can't bear it.'

I stepped forward more slowly. 'But would you fuck me?'

'Yes,' he said. He clung to me. Long cool fingers on my warm bare skin. He rested his face against my belly. '*I* would. *Me.*'

JAMES SAID A FRIEND OF his had found a rehab for him to go to. I didn't quite understand. The idea that he might want to change things disturbed me, despite the hardship we had; as if I'd be left behind again, as if we weren't happy together. He said he'd be in there for a week. I couldn't visit. I couldn't ring him. He would send messages through the friend, a 'safe' person—someone who didn't use. An ex-girlfriend. I was simply numb with shock when he went off with his little backpack. That afternoon at work I got a call from her.

'He's fine, he said to say he loves you,' an unfamiliar female voice told me.

I was bloodless with rage. How dare she tell me he loved me? How dare she stand between us? I went home from work that evening to the empty flat, scored, fixed up and smoked a joint. I lay in bed crying.

The week was terrible. I was angry with James for leaving me, for being so selfish, for letting this other woman back into his life, for going somewhere I couldn't follow; I was bleak with loneliness. I rang the rehab centre to leave a message for him and the voice at the other end knew that I was the no-good girlfriend, that I was a user. It was the first time I felt that abashment. When the week was over I went to pick him up; a woman came to the front room where I was waiting.

'James has decided to stay a little longer,' she said. 'But he's worried about you, so we're going to let you come in and see him for a minute. We don't usually do this.'

The woman led me out through the building, to a yard with another building on the other side. She put a hand on my shoulder; I flinched it away, rigid with distress. A few people were hanging around, smoking and talking. I glared at them all. And then there was James, coming towards me with a shy smile.

'Hello,' he said, and wrapped his arms around me. He'd never said *Hello* before. A wrack of grief went through me; I started crying. His body felt thinner than ever, he smelled different.

'It's great here,' he said. 'I feel so good. New. I've been having massages and acupuncture and vitamins, they do Chinese medicine here and I had reiki, had this crazy vision and I saw Jupiter and the moon and—oh, hi Shane!' I couldn't bear it. It was as if they'd taken my James away and replaced him with a stranger. I hated his happiness. I wept and wept. He said he was sorry, but he was getting better, and he knew I was left alone, but he'd come home in another week and help me too, and he kissed me.

I dried my tears and went home blank, and the only thing I could think of to do with the empty afternoon was score.

He did come out a week later as he'd promised, and he sent

ahead a message to pack a bag and go to a doctor and request Doloxene, a medication to ease heroin withdrawal. The doctor studied me carefully as I made my request, impassive behind his glasses, and wrote out a script. Then I went to work and asked them to give me a week off. It was the fortnight before Christmas, the busiest time of the year, and they needed me but I said, awkward and humiliated and apologetic, that I was having some problems with a drug, and they looked at me with pity and care and said, 'Of course. Take as long as you need.' I could barely smile straight with the embarrassment.

The next thing was to tell my mother. My dad was away, and it didn't seem fair to leave my mother upset on her own, but there was no delaying it. This time I stayed the night; in the morning, I squatted next to my mother in the sunny garden and said, 'There's something I have to tell you. Please don't freak. I've been doing... something. Heroin. But it's going to be all right,' I said quickly. 'I'm going away and I'm going to fix it all up. Don't worry.'

My mother just sat there, and held my hand, and said, 'I knew there was something wrong. I knew it. Oh, darling.'

So when James came home to our flat we paused long enough for him to repack his bag and then my mother drove us to get a train to the country home of one of my old friends. On the way James said, 'Just tell me, you didn't bring any, did you? Because I know you might have wanted to. And you have to be honest with me if I'm going to help you get out of this too.'

'No,' I said, and I hadn't stashed anything in my bag, because I had my James again, and when he said he knew what to do I trusted him.

It wasn't so strange, after all, to have him back, and not to use. Jason's house in the forest was comfortable, and the summer was hot; we walked up and down the dappled rough road to town, sat around talking and scratching the ground with sticks. The tiny pink capsules from the doctor removed the physical suffering I might have had, but I didn't think there'd have been much anyway. I'd been using such small amounts. One pill fewer every day; we sat in quiet sunshine and made plans for a new future. I felt calm and blank. James's skin was hot under the arm I wrapped around him; he was as tender and loving as ever, we couldn't stop smiling quietly at each other.

Back in Melbourne after a week, we went straight to stay with my parents. The flat was too full of memories, and Jake was just across the road. James rang his own folks and after a couple of fraught discussions arranged for his brother to take over the lease. Christmas with my family was a mix of unstated strangeness and comfortable familiarity. My parents were happy to have me move home. Their static smiles told me they were still stunned by the idea that their precious daughter, the academic, the innocent, was a heroin user. But, as I said to them again on my return, everything was going to be okay now.

It was a muted summer. James went to stay with his parents for a while; then he got a room in a sharehouse not far from where I was. I went back to work at the bookshop, and that kept me busy; with no drugs to buy, slowly I paid off the credit card debt, and then the cash piled up. I missed St Kilda, but it was like a return to one's own country to be at my parents', where the fridge was full and the rooms lined with books. My bedroom was awkwardly stacked with all my belongings. I settled in, because this was really my home; I was twenty-four, but after my adventures, it felt right to be there again. We seemed to have agreed that I would stay until

I'd recovered my nerve. The days were full of dusty yellow light and quiet.

Then James and I started going back to Acland Street, for a coffee, for a wander. St Kilda was also a realm to yearn for, it was the place we knew together. We were always aware that just up the road, just a short stroll, was Jake's. And one day in February we took the walk. Back in his musty living room, back with the tough chat about the scene. The sweet sting of the needle in my skin. James and I looking at each other, mischievous with guilt. Afterwards we went to the park; we lay under dry trees, we felt great. It wasn't hard to tell ourselves it had been a nice thing to do. The other words, the words about the folly of it, were too hard to say.

The string of habit, slack, pulled tight. Days reeled together, the days when we'd decide, so casually, almost with speaking, that it was a using day. Once, then once a week; then the idea of waiting another week seemed unreasonable, and it was every few days. We'd go after I finished work: a tram ride, a stroll, a coffee after the fix. Like an outing. We were meticulous in our manoeuvrings towards suggesting it. The trick was not to be the one to say it. Heavy sighs, quick glances. It was crucial not to be the one seen weakening; through all the matrices of our shared knowledge of each other, we knew, each, exactly how to edge the other.

When we scored, we were full of love. Hours of talk, of voluptuous delight in each other's company. When we didn't, there was silence. And still we thought we would be together forever.

Some time towards the end of that summer we started trying the dealers in the city. Jake's supply was unreliable and it was getting more expensive. Everyone knew where to go in the city. There was a particular stretch, lined with amusement parlours and idle Asian youths. It was a different scene. Bruised-looking, rugged white guys

35

loped up and down, buying, scoping, yelling. At the backs of the parlours, or walking slowly up the footpath, were young men with bad teeth and alert eyes. The first times James and I went down there we hardly knew what to do, but it was easy.

A voice said, 'You chasin'?' in our ear, and we nodded, and followed a tracksuited back down a nearby alleyway. The guy pulled a tiny coloured balloon from his mouth. It was deflated, knotted; when I took it, there was a small hard bump inside. 'Forty,' he said. I dug into my pocket and dragged out two twenties. He nodded, and left. James and I walked away quickly; there were always a lot of police around that area. We headed to a café we knew in the next street; I took my bag with me to the toilet. I'd brought my portable drugs kit: a rigid sunglasses case containing a metal spoon and swabs and a couple of fits. There was a bottle of water in my bag. I had to rip the balloon with my teeth. Inside was a minute white rock, wrapped in foil. It wasn't powdered, like Jake's gear; I mushed at it in the spoon, and it dissolved into cloudy liquid. I remembered what junkies did in films; I took out my lighter and held it underneath, and the liquid cleared. When I withdrew the needle from my skin, my palms and soles prickled hotly.

The stuff wasn't clean, but it was cheap. I'd go around to James's late at night, after a day on my feet in the store; we'd scrounge our money together; and we, or increasingly just I alone, would walk to the station. I got to know the time of the last train home, the bustle of that street just before midnight, the way to nod at a pair of intent dark eyes, and duck into the back of an amusement parlour, among the clashing lights and bells and yelling boys; to pocket the deal, or hide it in the fingertip of my glove, and stroll off. I'd usually go straight to a busy bar, where an interloper skulking in and out of the toilet wouldn't be noticed. Sometimes the toilets were fitted with blue lights, supposedly to make it difficult for junkies to find their blue veins. I had only to locate the little hard bump of scar tissue in the crook of my arm, the small dark shiny circle where I'd punctured the skin again and again before it ever had a chance to heal.

A couple of times I was cheated. The rock was tiny, or the solution, when I heated it, remained cloudy with whatever it had been cut with. Once, amid the clanging arcade games, the boy I was buying from scooted off as soon as I handed over the money, and when I opened the balloon and the foil in a loud club toilet, there was only a flint of gravel inside. My sense of street cred was affronted. I wandered the street until I found him.

'You ripped me off,' I insisted, while his friends gathered around, threatening. The boy was showing me his wallet for some reason, perhaps to demonstrate that he'd never met me, that my money was not in there.

'What you want?' the others demanded. 'What you talking about mate?' I suddenly wondered if they had knives.

'All right, but you owe me,' I said with futile bravado, and walked away to try someone else. I too began to carry a small knife. Not that I would have known how to use it.

It was a surreal existence for months. During the day I was a mild, neat bookstore assistant, chatting with the local matrons and book groups, exchanging gossip with my colleagues, handling money, making phone calls, straightening my skirt. At home I was a nice, polite, middle-class girl living with her parents in an old haven of innocence. At James's, I was the awkward girlfriend, not quite cool enough for his housemates. And in the city, I was a swaggering junkie in dark streets.

Standing behind the counter at the bookshop I began to read

Holocaust memoirs. Something in me was almost consoled by comparison with the horror of the camps, by the radiant silence of tragedy. I read one after the other, turning my mind for a moment away from the trepidation in my own heart.

The money I'd piled so carelessly on my mantelpiece went quickly now, even with the cheaper gear. James was still on the dole. The idea of not getting on was enough to make us anxious and uneasy. I sold some cds and old books; I worked overtime if I could get it.

One last taste to say goodbye; one last taste to help out Jake when he rang needing money; one taste to get me through a difficult day; one taste to share with James. A taste to make me feel better; a taste to stop me feeling bad. If it was a grey day, heroin would brighten it; a sunny day was made perfect with a fix.

But it was no longer as simple as wanting heroin, liking it. Often now as winter came down I resented it. My body was tired; it was raining outside; the hour was late. Time for bed. And yet I had no choice. The drug took me out of the house, on cold bleak nights, on aching feet; it drove me to places I didn't want to be. There was a steely compulsion in me. I often wrote in my journal of how good it would be to be clean, how I was going to get clean, how fresh my life would be next week, next month, how resolved I was—but when it got dark, the thought of the drug muffled all else. I wrote of heroin as a scaly green lizard wrapped tight around my mind, blinking its cold eyes at me, blinding me.

In the meantime I was down to my last few dollars.

My parents didn't know I had resumed using, I thought. I was careful to hide my pinned pupils if I was home, or I would spend the night at James's. But there was hostility brimming in the house. Things went unsaid. As the first shock had sunk into my parents' minds, their fright curdled to something else. I had broken the innocence of our family and my cheer, forced, only made the atmosphere brittle.

And I could see that things were getting worse. I was more and more fixated on money, and on the single diversion of drugs. My old friends were out there, but already they seemed to belong to another time. A sense of humiliation scorched me; everyone had expected so much from me, and this was so little.

Another Christmas came and went. I worked hard, kept quiet.

There was a bowl of loose change in the house. Shiny gold two-dollar coins in among the dull silver. Late at night I scooped them out and put them, heavy, in a little bag; there were enough to score with. I thought, *no one will miss them*. Not yet.

Then my parents said they knew I was using again. I could only tell them that it was under control, that I was going to stop soon. They looked at me and didn't know what to say. Neither did I.

I was away from St Kilda, in the suburbs, in my routine of work and home and 'getting on': scoring. James and I were bound by the drugs, and love too. But we made love now less often. Heroin first blesses its users with enchantment and then parches them of sensation. The pulse between us was weaker. It was hard to come, hard to find the momentum towards crisis. But we embraced, still enraptured by each other's fragility, the poignancy of this grace amid the grime. We held each other close.

It was already a year since we'd left our little flat. Things were changing under the mist of drugs and at times I felt James grow cautious with me, drawn to his new friends and their common interests. I knew I was losing him.

We sat on the edge of his bed in the thin light of a grey afternoon and had nothing to say. I wanted to suggest we score; but we'd scored. I wanted to touch him; but I'd touched him enough. He was sitting apart, staring at his shoes. My beautiful boy, frail-thin and old-souled, full of thoughts he couldn't tell me, of a self-protective instinct I didn't possess.

He said, 'I think I can't do this anymore, Kate. I think I have to stop. I have to be on my own. You know I still love you…I still do. But this is killing me.'

And I sobbed and sobbed, because I knew he was right, and I wanted him well, and not shadowed by this dreariness, but I was so frightened to be alone, and I knew I wasn't ready for anything.

After we broke up I was numb. It was one thing to lose a lover from a fault in the relationship, or from having made a mistake, or even from loving too much. James and I loved each other, but this was emptying everything we had. It seemed a long time since the sarsaparilla on his porch back in St Kilda, and him running after my tram waving goodbye with his skinny arms.

He was stronger than I was. He went to his parents' place up in the hills and, without medication, without them knowing, without succumbing to the pain in his limbs and the torture of temptation in his head, he went through withdrawal and came back to his house and didn't use again. We talked sometimes on the phone, and when I cried he soothed me. But I was nostalgic for the early days, and he said, 'I don't want to think about any of that anymore.'

In bed at night I touched myself, clenching at the memory of James making love to me; the sweetness that we had forfeited. My face made the crumpled shape of pleasure, or tears. A huge grief yawned open in me, and then left me vacant.

So I WENT ON. AT HOME there were eyes on me all the time. There was little chance to do anything but go to work and return to the house. Now I had to find a way to score without the alibi of visiting James. I was feeling the effects if I didn't fix up regularly enough; I'd spend the morning in the store, dragging myself up and down the shop floor, limbs like sacks of mud, back aching, sweat acrid under my arms. It was hard to smile at the customers, to pretend I was fine, to run up the stairs to fetch books. Towards lunch I'd obsessively check the time. And then I'd dash out the door and hail a taxi. A mad drive to St Kilda, glaring at my watch; I had only three-quarters of an hour, and the drive took twenty minutes each way. A sprint up the stairs to Jake's door, a hasty chat, a quick fix in his living room, the bliss of relief and a few puffs of the post-fix cigarette; then back to the waiting taxi and the panting arrival back in the shop, ten minutes late. I did this every day.

My excuses about shopping and forgetting the time rapidly grew absurd; my nervousness was conspicuous. After a while I didn't even bother insulting my employers with these feeble lies, but just skulked back to the shop counter and knew that my deception was undoing years of friendship. But by that time I'd be cruising on the relief of drugs in my system, and it was possible not to care.

It wasn't as if I got a big rush from the smack by now, after a year and a half of using. There would be a heady sense of glow for the first five or ten minutes; my heart, racing with anticipation before the fix, would steady and I'd breathe cool and delicious air. I was aware that my physical pains had magically eased. Then I had the relief of having scored, of having achieved what I wanted above all else, of having managed it yet again.

Heroin is compelling, in the end, because it is satisfaction you can hold in your hand. Fulfilment, contentment, pride—these are feelings that a person can derive from being a good person, an able parent, a successful worker, an inspired artist. They are inchoate, invisible, ineffable feelings, for all their wonder. They are abstract. Heroin is a satisfaction you can pursue, it's concrete; you must get the money, find the dealer, arrange the equipment. Then you take the little grain of promise, and you dissolve it, and you draw it up into a needle; you hold it in your hand, and you push it into your flesh.

The further you get into heroin, the more it is the only kind of satisfaction you can imagine.

And heroin gives you permission to do terrible things. For the first time, I found myself behaving with all the ruthless selfishness and disdain of a real junkie. I told myself it didn't matter.

I was clear in my mind: I was a heroin user. Perhaps an addict, if I admitted it, though the word was frightening. A junkie was one of the hollow creatures I saw in the city or stumbling onto the tram, talking too loudly. Junkies had given up all their dignity. They had no respect for themselves, or other people. They did what they did without reflection, without a thought to consequences. They nodded off on the train; their faces were grey and blind-eyed. I was never, ever like that; I never gave up my composure. But inside I was skidding towards the single-minded obsession of need.

I stole money from work. It was so easy, with all the notes nestled there in the drawer. Even through the first year of using, when James and I were so poor in St Kilda, it had never occurred to me that every day hundreds of dollars passed through my hands. But now it did, and once I had the idea I couldn't let it go.

I didn't mean to steal. I would take the cash—a hundred dollars—and replace it later that day once I'd been to the bank with my pay cheque. Just a little loan. But the shop was busy; my after-noon break came too late to get to the bank; the money was spent and the drugs already simmering in my veins.

Standing behind the counter, counting the minutes before the till was reckoned at the end of the day, I became very cold and deliberate. It was a chilly April afternoon and the shop was quiet. The floor manager was down the other end of the shop. I could cover my tracks; no one need know that this had happened, that I'd slipped so far. I forged vouchers and adjusted receipts to hide the loss. My coolness horrified me and saved me.

My two bosses trusted me, they'd known me for years. I was like a niece to them. They were lovely. But they weren't stupid; they knew I was strange now, and a week later they told me to come into the office and they asked me to leave.

43

They were kind. They said they knew. They didn't want to punish me, but I couldn't stay. Their faces were tight with misery and hurt, and I looked back at them, buckling inside with disbelief that something so awful was happening, that I'd done something so horrendous and now they knew it. I started to cry. Messily I said that I was sorry.

'You know—you know I use heroin, don't you.'

One of them said, 'Yes. Yes.' His face was full of sorrow.

They sat there as I cried, and silently gave me an envelope containing a cheque for dismissal payments and sick leave. I knew I didn't deserve it, but I took the money, and got up, still crying, and left the shop where I'd worked since I was a schoolgirl.

It was the middle of the day. I didn't say goodbye to my colleagues, or the customer whom I'd been helping. I just left. Outside the sky was smooth and white with clouds. I went to the sea at St Kilda, and sat there, looking at the pale dirty sand.

I scored, of course; I bought several caps. I went home, and told my parents. They knew—that I'd been using, that I was desperate for money, that it was likely I'd steal eventually. The atmosphere was almost relieved, now that everything was open. My sister gave me a hug. We joked about what a lazy girl I would become without a job. I was still stiff with horror and remorse at what I'd done. But I didn't have to pretend anymore. I was out; I was turning into a junkie. Something was changed. And something had to change.

My sister got me alone and said, 'You don't know what happens when you're not around. It's so easy for you. Mum and Dad *cry*. We sit around talking about you, and we're all crying. You have no fucking idea how that feels.'

'I can't,' was all I could say.

The money my bosses had given me would last a while. It was a lot of money. My mother took charge, and suggested I leave it in her keeping, to dole out to me. We talked. It was agreed that I was allowed to go on living with them, even though I was using; there was no point in trying to fix things abruptly. My mother gave me enough money every day to score, and I stayed at home, trying to use less, trying to make sense of what I'd done, trying to envisage anything but this existence, and finding it almost impossible.

All the time people were telling me I *had to stop*. It seemed so simple to them. *You just have to stop.* Yes, I'd say. I know. But I couldn't, I couldn't. I could only try, and hope, but I felt that no one could understand the power of what was occurring inside me.

My sister, mother, father and I sat in the living room and they tried to talk to me. 'Do you see what's happening? Can you see where this is going? What you're doing to yourself?' They all looked at me, perplexed and injured. The more I tried to explain, the more insane I sounded; there were no words for what I felt. I sobbed in humiliation. There had never been sounds like that in this house before.

There were days of using, and days of struggling against it. I would slump around the house, ill and disconsolate, pursued by tempting thoughts. Walls curved in and over me. There was a whine of pure terror inside my mind. Reality hurt me like a sandblaster.

Heroin interferes with the chemical transmitters of the brain; it substitutes its own balms for all of these. And when there's no more heroin in a body, it goes into crisis, bereft. There are no endorphins to kill pain; they've all been disabled by the drug. The body feels flayed and raw. Mineral levels of all kinds are unbalanced; the brain works strangely. Deranged thoughts and crazed plans seem reasonable. And, through all this, there's the icy quiet knowledge that even if your chemistry readjusts, and the body battles through the

45

discomfort, and you give up the one thing that makes life bearable, then there are days and weeks and months and years of *resisting* ahead of you. As you lie there, hardly able to think or breathe for the fatigue, engulfed in the moment, this idea is impossible.

I couldn't keep it up for longer than a few days, and then I'd seek the solace of the needle. It was more terrifying than anything to actually be trying, with all my will, and not be strong enough.

My parents pressed me to see a psychiatrist. He was a dour man with a waiting room full of lace doilies and modern paintings. We'd sit in his darkened office, which was a little cold, and he'd set his thick face towards me and wait. There wasn't much I could say. I wanted to find out the mechanisms of my behaviour, and adjust the apparatus. But I had no idea how to go about that. I wanted someone to stop me dead, stop my agile mental justifications; someone to shove me against the wall with a hand to my throat and not let me go until I'd dug out some truth. But this man just kept saying he couldn't help me until I stopped using. And I couldn't.

'I get so depressed and frightened,' I said. 'Whenever I try to stop. The detox—trying to kick, sitting around at home all sick—it fucks with my head. Everything seems too big. I think I'll never ever make it past the fear.'

I left with a prescription for anti-depressants. It was true that they stabilised my mood; but, already numb with the sedative of heroin, I had little mood left.

All the pills did was damp down any feelings I still had. Swaddled, my little heart throbbed more quietly. The legal drugs weren't strong enough, though, to muffle the terror when it came to spike me.

I had no job now; no references, no confidence. I'd lost my boyfriend, my home in St Kilda. The respect of my family. My friends were busy. It was as if I'd walked into that pale sky—an empty, quiet place.

The love that my family still proffered embarrassed me. I could not tell them how little I felt I deserved it.

I sneaked out of the house and got caught coming back. I filched money. There were days when no one could bear to speak to me.

Night after night I plugged the needle into me. Its cool kiss.

Then my parents said that if I didn't get clean I couldn't stay with them. I had to sort myself out; what was wrong with me?

'I can't stand to see you killing yourself,' my dad cried, with a desperation I'd never seen in him. 'Please, please do something.'

So I rang the rehab James had gone to. It didn't seem like such a stupid idea now; they might know how to fix me. They said it was a six-day program, but if I wanted, I could apply to stay longer.

'Stay for the month,' urged my parents. I was to go in the next week.

'I'll just see how I feel.'

One last taste; I mixed it up in my room the morning I was to go in. Liquid ready in the spoon, the needle poised to suck it up; my mother knocked. I jammed my crossed arms over the tray on my lap, to hide the gear. My parents had never actually seen me shoot up. 'I just want you to know we love you,' she said.

'Uh-huh?' I was trying to smile. I was impatient for the fix.

'We'll take you down there when you're ready,' my mother said, and left the room.

I pulled my arms away from the spoon. It was empty. I stared. The edge of my borrowed dressing-gown had dipped into the spoon and soaked up all the liquid. I couldn't stop staring. Sucking at the

47

fabric desperately. Nothing. The shock I felt—my *last taste*, gone—
was beyond words.

I told my mother. She started to giggle. 'It just got sucked up!' I
said, and the stupidity of it hit me. 'Your bloody terry-towelling!' I
was laughing too. 'I have to score,' I told her. 'Before I go in.'

'But you'll be late!'

I looked at her, reason ready and sly on my tongue. 'I have to.
One last taste. To say goodbye. Otherwise I won't have finished.'

So my mother drove me to Jake's, and waited outside while I
had my taste in the living room there. I got back in the car.

'Ready?'

I was full of heroin and relief. 'Ready.'

It was an old church building, with the day-treatment out the front,
a yard behind, and at the back the residential building, sealed from
the outside world. The centre was a holistic healing centre: they
offered massages, acupuncture, reiki. The front rooms smelt of
perfumed oils. The back building smelt of household cleaner and
detox sweat.

In the lounge of the residence there were a dozen people
making sandwiches at a large table and sitting around on old
couches. The person admitting me, a brisk middle-aged man, took
me up to my room. Three beds.

There was no chocolate, sugar or coffee allowed. The diet was a
healthy, detoxifying one. We would be in bed every night at ten.

He was kind, evidently accustomed to the blank look I had on
my face. He put a hand on my shoulder. 'You'll be fine here, Katie.'

I went downstairs and outside to have a cigarette under the
green plastic portico. There were mud-splashed plastic chairs in a
circle around an old fruit-juice can used for an ashtray. Some people

came out and sat with me and lit up smokes.

'I'm Danny,' said a round-faced, dazed-looking young man. He spoke slowly, and tugged at his long jumper. 'Everyone knows me here. I'm always here, aren't I?' he asked another man.

'You're like the house mascot,' the man said. He had a rough, lined face and a beanie on his head. 'You're our fucking totem.'

I sat and smoked. People smiled at me, and asked my name. 'You been using long?' one asked.

'Nearly two years,' I said, and found myself almost proud. 'About a hundred bucks a day.'

'Right,' he said. The feeling was almost of school camp, except that here faces were pale with sweat, or rugged with life's experience. Jeans were ripped, jumpers were saggy. There were some young women, timid or loud; a couple of clean-cut young guys, a couple of Asian faces, a lot of men. I gathered almost everyone was here because of heroin.

The afternoon went on, and already I felt comfortable. I knew enough of the scene, and Jake's assorted associates, to know how to mix with this company. Jail terms, comparing of scars; a blokey humour. 'You're a bit nice for this kind of thing, aren't you?' someone said.

'Not too nice.'

'Hah!' He grinned and offered me a cigarette. 'Me neither.'

I heard that people would arrange drops of chocolate bars over the fence. Forget drugs; heroin users are addicted to chocolate. We dreamed aloud of ice-cream and cake.

There was a good feeling there. The staff had shifts, but after only a few days there were familiar faces. Three times a day we were called, one at a time, for our meds, and some traditional Chinese medicine as well if we wanted; black and bitter mouthfuls of liquid,

49

to soothe the nerves or help the detoxification process. I took everything they offered. The little pink Doloxene pills familiar from the country detox with James helped too; I managed to sleep every night. Others didn't; there was one young man, Andy, who said he hadn't slept for fourteen nights. He was pale and aggrieved. 'Every time I do manage to nod off during the day they fucking wake me up!'

'It's all about getting a routine,' the staff said. 'Regular meals, regular sleep times. You've all been all over the place, you have to get some order back.' Andy scowled.

The days were tightly scheduled. Breakfast, then a swim at the public baths down the road. At first I just paddled around one end of the pool, shy in my bathers and weak in the muscles. Then I tried some laps. It was humiliating. In the next lane the local patrons ploughed up and down—young women and Russian grandmothers slogged, never pausing in their slow heaves towards each end. Our gaggle of young people flopped arms towards the rim of the pool, out of breath. It was so obvious what we were.

'It's a terrible thing, that heroin,' said an old man to me. He was white-haired and one-legged. 'Lost it in the war,' he said. 'You young folks. You're all getting better now, aren't you?' He smiled at me.

'We are,' I said. 'We are.'

There were tensions, but mostly the atmosphere was cheery. People seemed to like me. I was happy to talk to everyone. I made jokes with the men and chatted with the girls. I made friends with my room-mate, a sallow, gentle girl who wore a silver bell around her neck. My old friends wrote me encouraging letters which I received with surprise and gratitude. Cheered once I got over the first week of withdrawal, I was jaunty in the mornings, surprised at my energy, and starting to discover a zeal for improving myself. The group therapy classes were almost like university tutorials; it seemed that there was a science to the understanding of addiction. And each acupuncture session, each massage, seemed like a limbering of something I'd allowed to stiffen in myself.

Being treated embarrassed me. A guided meditation class had me in tears, trying to visualise the correct shade of magenta spiralling through my body. Reiki made me giggle in the awed hush of the room. But I persisted, and I found that just taking it, taking the kindness, wasn't as dangerous as I'd thought. I let my limbs loosen and my body be gentled. I felt better every day.

Still the thought of heroin hummed in the background. I was in a strange mood; removed from the life I'd known, safe in this small, enclosed world; but surrounded by the issues of drugs, by those who understood what it was like. We'd wake some days to find one of our number missing. 'Jumped the fence,' we'd say, although whoever it was had simply asked to leave, and gone. It was as easy as that. I could feel the pull of healthiness, of hope, but also the tug of heroin and its promise. Recovery, as we were told every day, was hard work. Long work. It took years. The prospect of such struggle was so exhausting that it sometimes seemed as if it would be simpler just to use.

One night this all got too much. Dazed in bed, desperate to sleep in a prickle of thoughts and dread, I got up and went to Becky, a plump, motherly staff member on night duty. She was watching television in the lounge. The room was cast in blue and black.

'I'm afraid,' I said tiredly. 'I'm so afraid I can't do this.'

She smiled at me. 'But the thing is, just because you're afraid doesn't actually mean there's anything to be afraid of. Perhaps you can do it, even if you're afraid. Have you thought of that?'

I hadn't. Maybe I could puncture the bubble of panic, maybe I could just try it anyway. What was the worst that could happen? I thought, *I can always use when I get out, if I still want to.* And so I stayed.

Tim, a handsome, lithe boy with dreadlocks and tattoos, didn't. He walked right past a staff member with a bar of chocolate in his hand. He had to leave. 'He'll go out and use,' we protested.

'But he's broken the rules that keep you safe,' the worker said. 'It was his decision.'

A few days later there was a whistle from behind the tall wooden fence that separated us from the outside world. Tim's head appeared. A few of us stood and chatted to him. But his face was pale, and his speech and eyes slow with drugs. It was horrifying, and we understood how different we felt inside here.

In my diary I wrote, *I can do without heroin for now. I feel good like this. But I shan't say 'never again'. Not just yet. It's out there. I can wait. But when I leave…*It wasn't that I didn't believe in recovery, or see the need for it. But there was a hushed voice in me that said what I wanted, I would get. And while I was happy now, I couldn't shut that voice up. The drug had its own psyche, embedded in mine.

We all had private counselling sessions. Mine was with Cassie. It seemed hard to believe she had ever been a user; she was so groomed, so calm. She sat there, facing me, and said, 'You're always smiling, Kate. Are you happy all the time?'

'I guess not,' I said. 'I can't be that happy if I'm using, can I?'

'No, I don't think you can be happy all the time. What do you feel when you're not happy? When you're sad, or angry? Where do you feel it?'

I touched my belly, my throat.

'And what do you do with that?' She was looking at me serenely.

'I just try to deal with it. I try to keep going. You know?'

'You're smiling. Can you stop smiling a moment? Just—stop smiling.'

52

There was silence. She watched me. I blinked at the ground.

I thought of how much pain I'd been through, and how stupid it was always to be smiling when my throat was aching with misery, and I sat there, and I couldn't get the absurd little curve off my lips. This woman could see right through my bravado; she knew I was a faker. She knew I wasn't all right, and I knew that, but I'd done so many stupid things, and I was trying to be brave, and all I could do was hold on. She was beautiful and composed. I was sitting there, having fucked it all up.

'You're still smiling,' she said. I couldn't stop. I had a stupid grin on my face and my eyes were full of tears.

I stayed the month in rehab. I grew clear and vibrant. I was a veteran to the new arrivals every day. The staff winked at me as I bounced past, as I ran around the yard playing ball, as I tried out the boxing bag up the back. I spent time alone, thinking, trying to work through what I'd learned in therapy about myself and my self-esteem and my family and the perverse behaviours I'd identified. Clarifying things. I felt better than I ever had in my life. This was like a home. On my last night I made a speech at dinner, about the wonder of surprising yourself. My room-mate came and gave me her silver chiming bell. 'To remind you,' she said.

But my time was up. 'You've done really well,' Cassie said. 'Don't be too confident, though. I mean, there are a lot of pitfalls out there. It's a long road.'

'I think I'll be fine,' I said, and there was a huge smile of hope on my face, and in my deceitful heart a little sneaky wriggle. Because the afternoon I walked out, instead of going home to where my parents and sister were awaiting me, waiting to see their healthy, happy daughter, I turned left at the gate rather than right, and went to Jake's.

Just one. Just to say goodbye to it. Just as a reward. Just because I'd waited, and I was confident I was changed. Because it was there.

I rang home, on the way to Jake's. I told my parents I wanted a night of transition before I came back. They were bewildered when I said I'd stay with an old housemate in St Kilda, and see them tomorrow. I knew they were expecting me, with a special dinner and proud faces. It was too late for me to think of that, to allow even one flicker of their hope to enter my heart. I found my coldness all over again. I thought that meant I was strong.

The taste was too potent for me. I'd been a month without heroin, and my tolerance had fallen. This was the kind of situation where people 'dropped'. I didn't overdose, but I was sleepy and dazed when I arrived at my friend Matilda's to beg a bed. She was surprised to see me, but let me in. My dazed eyes must have told her all she needed to know. I sat up to keep watch over myself late into the night, and through the thick haze of the drug and the numbness I wept a little because I knew I'd already failed. The humiliation was raw to touch. I flinched. Like a cord the addiction had pulled me, against all the tethering of my reason and support, pulled me right back, and I'd followed. My fear of losing control made my heart race like a drug did; only the drug could calm it.

I went home the next day, still pinned, still stoned. My parents' smiles wavered when they saw me, when I wasn't the cheery, hopeful girl they'd talked to on the phone at rehab, their daughter restored, the nightmare over; when I averted my face and said I was tired and couldn't face their company. They didn't say I was stoned. I didn't say, I've blown it. I just crept into my room and told myself it didn't matter. Of course it did.

I TRIED. I TRIED SWIMMING at the local pool, to keep up the fitness I'd gained, but the school children there crowded me. I tried drinking herbal tea; coffee was tastier. I did improvised yoga in my room, but there wasn't space. I tried to keep busy, but I didn't know what to do. And I tried not to use again, but I did.

My tolerance shot up again. When you stop, you dip your resistance to the drug. But a few tastes and you return to exactly where you were. The drug is a constant lover.

It was as if rehab had changed me, but it hadn't stuck. Out of the safe environment, away from the talk of psychological patterns and the company of those who knew what drugs were like, I felt like I'd walked out of a dream. That silver chiming bell hung around my neck but it didn't help. Now it was just me, the house in the suburbs and my disappointed parents.

I was alone with my terror. And I clung to the cord of heroin, because at least it tied me down.

The days at home strung out. One shallow breath after another.

There was a silence griming the spaces between our words to each other, the falsely normal interactions of daily life. Since I had lost my job, I was home almost all the time, walking carefully, sitting in my room, avoiding my parents. I didn't like them to see my pinned pupils, the harsh signs of my helplessness.

I marvelled at the unmarked skin in the inner arms of everyone I saw. Not a nick, not a bruise or scab. Those people turned their palms upwards, reached across a table without a thought.

I needed another job. I had no references, no particular skills beyond bookselling. My classics degree was useless. I was exhausted. And the drugs seemed like enough work.

It was still bizarre, using drugs in the same house as my parents lived, where I had once been innocent. My room was much as it had always been, with the pale green paint I'd chosen when I was fifteen; with my own name scrawled on the chest of drawers in my childish hand. It had the dustiness and quiet of a museum. My piano remained mostly closed; to play Beethoven's grandeur now, when I felt so humbled, seemed ridiculous. I skulked through the familiar spaces of our house.

When I walked up the hall to my room, what did my parents think? I would fix up, furtively crouched behind my bed. The laws of bad luck would inevitably have my father knock and enter at the moment when I had the needle poised against my skin. Shoving my tied arm out of sight, shaking with the reflexes of shock, I'd mumble replies to his conversation, humiliated and impatient. I had no idea what he knew, or guessed. My lies

56

were always less successful than I thought.

Obviously, they knew I was using. When I went out, it was to score. I was trying to stop, and they knew that too, and upon that they fixed; this time, with encouragement, with attention, I might break through the crucial five or six days of major detoxing and out to the stage where I could think lucidly, where I would see the disaster of my life.

A few days on the gear, a few days off. I was either ill or stoned. My diary entries were fastidious, loquacious, repetitive. It was a stumble from one jerk of fright to the next, eased with drugs in between. I was never so certain of getting clean as when I was dirty.

My parents had to believe what I said, though they knew I was a liar. They loved me so much, and their love sustained me and enraged me and broke my heart.

We experimented with systems. We tried pretending nothing was going on. We tried being jovially honest about it. We tried giving the money that I still had left from the book shop to my mother and having her drive me every two days to my dealer to score, hiding my little packets in her wardrobe to dole out to me three times a day. I crept in, found the stash with the unerring instincts of the needful, had my fix before I was meant to, and pretended I was going along with the program. That system didn't last long.

My father made paternal chat, as if nothing were wrong, with a disquieting, tremulous hope in his eyes. My sister had moved out. When she came to visit us she was taciturn with me. Her smiles were emptied by the apprehension in her eyes.

We tried locking me in the house. I found new ways to sneak out late at night and score. Edgy with nerves as bedtime approached, measuring my mother's dallying in front of the television against the time of the last tram to St Kilda, fingering my bank card from its safekeeping in her wallet and replacing it later in the dark. The next morning my parents hugged me and said, 'You're doing so well, we're so proud of you.'

I turned my not-quite-pinned eyes away and said, 'Yeah, thanks. Thanks.'

A week later and I swore I was going to get clean, but I had to pay Jake back some money first. It had been three torturous days of detoxing and I said he would come looking for me if I never went back to pay him off. All my funds were gone now. 'You won't buy another one?' my father asked.

He fetched a fifty dollar note. I took it smiling. 'I won't.'

I did. The repayment was a lie. The deal was hidden deep in a corner of a pocket. 'Gotta go,' I grinned at Jake in his living room. Outside my mother waited in the car. She'd warned me, driving there, that she'd search me. It was for my own good. I thought she was joking. I sweated with the anticipation of a fix. Only half an hour more, and I'd have it, I'd have it.

'I'm sorry,' she said once we were home, as she told me to raise my arms. She rummaged in my pockets, paused. She was out the door of my bedroom and stalking down towards the toilet before I could stop her.

Too late; she'd thrown the packet down the flushing drain. It was gone. The water roared. I couldn't believe it. Something animal and raging came up in me; I slapped at her arm, as hard as I could. I smacked it again, in spite. She was too close to me. '*You fucking bitch*,' I heard myself shriek.

'I don't believe anything you say,' she shouted, appalled; there was horror in her face. 'If you say the sky is blue I think you're lying.'

'I'm not always lying,' I protested, wounded. 'Sometimes, sometimes—' I was crying. 'I'm still me. Please believe me. I'm still me.'

The mortification was complete. I couldn't do the right thing; I couldn't admit what I was doing; I could only lie, and have my lies recognised, and keep on lying because there was no other way of getting what I needed. Or protecting the ones I loved.

'I don't ask you to care about me,' I said. Their care was the rope around my neck and the thin thread to which I clung. Without my family I would have nothing except myself, and the drug.

And yet I simply could not stop. There was something in me, even beyond the torture of detoxing, beyond the shame of using, the anguish of causing my family hurt, that insisted that if there was an opportunity, I should take it. As if I were still making up for my tentative adolescence, leaping into adventure. An adventure of dreary predictability, but edged with the glamour of a sharp silhouette moving through a ragged world.

The scar on my arm was clotted with tissue now, and sometimes it was butchery as I tried to find the vein beneath, digging into flesh, racing to beat the blood thickening in the syringe. But at night, sick and sweating, or even when I was coasting easy and already stoned, the drug nagged at me. *More.*

We all watched television together at night. We ate dinner. I rambled around the house, reading, keeping to myself. But I noticed that when I tried simply to make conversation, it was met with a kind of perplexity. It was hard to know what I should say instead.

A week later and we had fallen back, in exhaustion, to letting me out of the house unaccompanied. There were errands to run, friends to catch up with. I came home in the afternoon, weary with the effort to resist St Kilda. I'd been holding back all day. At the end of the street my house was in sight, only a few metres away. I paused and thought, *I could go back out for one.* I could get some smack, and I could have it. Surely it was only a matter of time until I used again. Entering the house meant giving up my chance. I stood, wavering, tormented, for ten minutes. I knew what it meant if I went back; it meant I was turning away from this safe house, from the ones waiting in there for me, from their concern and their love. If I went to Jake's, I would have to wait till night to return, when they were all in bed, to hide my give-away eyes. Me in the cold night, waiting for shelter. I stood there, with my head resting against a tree in the bleak grey light of the afternoon, gulping down pain. Until I walked back to the tram stop with my emptied heart.

I made a 'will', a letter to my family, just in case I overdosed. *Don't be sad. Don't be angry. Thank you for everything. This wasn't your fault. I had a good life. I'm so sorry.* I scrawled it in my diary, where no one would have found it anyway.

As I grew more and more frightened of myself it seemed a good idea to see a counsellor again. I was escorted to see a woman with a snug office in a day rehab centre. She had a short haircut, a realistic smile. Juliette was good for me. I could tell her what was going on; we talked about practicalities. She didn't let me bullshit too much. I couldn't talk about everything, of course; I was ashamed. Even to this sanguine woman I couldn't admit the whole reality of my deviousness. The absolute cold will to destruction and the disregard for others. I chatted, and ruefully admitted to many faults, and charmed her with my jokes and cleverness. And I knew I was forfeiting a chance to have been honest, if only I'd known where I could find honesty in myself. My soul seemed glassed with ice.

Juliette, however, was good company. She knew the scene but was not of it; she had seen girls like me before. I wasn't the worst case she'd met. I don't think she knew what to make of my prospects; I had all the factors for a good possibility of recovery, but equally I had the intellectual shrewdness to obfuscate. I had the single-minded, absorbed self-destruction of the privileged child.

We began to meet for each session in a café, drinking iced coffees. Around us couples smoked cigarettes in the sunshine. The stereo played Cuban jazz. Juliette said, 'If you don't stop, I reckon you'll be dead within a year.'

That made me pause. 'I don't think so,' I said, and snickered at my own arrogance. Charming, disarming. 'I'm too clever for that.' I didn't think she believed what she'd said.

'Clever,' she said, challenging me with raised eyebrows. 'That won't save you.'

Sometimes I pretended to go to see Juliette and instead took her fifty dollar fee and skipped off to St Kilda. At Jake's I sat on the floor, being witty. Vicki was slumped on the couch, dozing; Jake made coffee. It was a nice afternoon but the curtains were drawn.

'Vicki's having a busy time on the streets,' Jake remarked. 'There's some festival in town, lots of tourists. It's mad.'

'How much does she make on a busy night?' I sipped my coffee. He made it strong and sweet.

'A few hundred, usually; more at the moment. They're so easy to please, her mugs. Most of them just want a chat and a cuddle. She's really popular,' he said, looking at her sleeping face with affection.

She seemed exhausted. I could imagine why.

'The cops are out, too,' Jake added. 'They're all over town. I'm keeping my head down.' We sat in silence for a moment.

'Better go,' I said, and scrambled up. 'See you soon.'

I went home and told my parents how good my chat with Juliette had been.

61

Most of the time I did go to my counselling appointments. It felt awful, letting Juliette down. She urged me to try a group session, where she introduced me to Mandy, a frail girl aged about twenty. 'Mandy's from a nice family like yours,' Juliette said. 'She's been using for a couple of years. Next week she's going to prison.'

I looked at Mandy. She was pale, haunted, morose; I compared myself to her, and I thought of jail, of how I'd be beaten there, how I wouldn't last ten minutes, and I thought how impossible it was that it should ever happen to me. I was still cruising on confidence, on my own preciousness. I had ways to get by, I would always get through. Mandy smiled at me sadly. I twitched my lips politely, not identifying.

Juliette was no fool. 'So. Tell me. Have you been thinking of working as a prostitute?' she asked a few meetings later. I'd begun talking to Vicki, when she was awake. She'd answered slowly, in a pragmatic voice edged sometimes with savagery, sometimes with pride. Jake watched me. Vicki warned me of how tiring and dangerous her work was. There was another police blitz on, and a girl had recently gone missing.

'Maybe,' I said to Juliette.

'I knew you would be. And I'll tell you, I've met a lot of pros, and if you start, within a year you'll be *screaming* to get out. I'm telling you. It's not what you think it is.' Her face, broad, roughened, was beautiful amid the clatter of the café. She had recently asked me to compose a passage to be read at her wedding.

'I'm sure you're right,' I said. Juliette's smile was rueful. She cared for me, but she knew a trajectory when she saw one.

There was a boy I knew from the bookshop. He had been a customer, and he was very beautiful. He'd asked me out, and now, months later, I rang him and said yes. I thought some affection might cheer me up. Richard's skin was golden, his eyes were dark and serious. He was only nineteen.

We sat in a café and he ordered drinks. Hot chocolate. He smiled at me. We were both nervous as we chatted. Then I crossed my arms on the table and leaning over them said, 'There's something I should tell you. You won't be expecting this.' I paused. 'I use drugs. I use heroin.'

He gave me a kind of skewed smile. 'I thought maybe you did.'

'Are you scared of me now?'

'No.'

We kissed in my room that night. He was lovely, and he offered me company, offered me admiration when no one else did. I kissed him, but he was too young. Abruptly I felt monstrous.

'I don't care if you're six years older than me,' he mumbled. 'I just really like you.'

I fixed up drugs, sitting at my desk. I made him watch.

It was only two months since I'd been in rehab but it felt like my life was skidding fast. I no longer knew what to expect, and that gave me a kind of freedom. One cold winter afternoon I met an old man on a tram. I was on my way out of St Kilda, and we started talking. His name, he said, was John.

He was a classic old guy: tweed car-coat, hat, kindly smiling wrinkled face. We were talking so easily—about St Kilda, about life there—that he invited me to stop for a coffee. We had one, still chatting happily; then as I walked him back to the tram stop he said, 'Would you give an old man a kiss?'

I bent to his cheek. He turned it and kissed me on the mouth.

His mouth was warm and it was a good kiss. That was another

surprise. People passing looked at us, as we kissed, and this scrutiny, if nothing else, made me defy the reflex reaction of repugnance. I thought, so what if he's old? Does that make a mouth less warm, an instinct less powerful?

He asked me to his place for dinner. Why not? I was up for anything that day, bored and stressed. And I'd already slipped out of respectability and its rules; I loved to test the expected. We got to his old-guy flat: overhead lights and piles of magazines and dusty cheap furniture. John made soup from Promite and boiling water; we sat at his old laminex table. A glass of warm milk and Weet-bix with jam for dessert. He told me that since his wife died twenty years before he hadn't found anyone else, but he still had plenty of sex drive. Porn and peepshows weren't to his taste. Masturbation was boring. I kind of knew what he meant.

I thought, *I might be his last ever lover.* He was young and full of sexuality once, he might even have been handsome. *Will it hurt me? No. Will I make him happy? I think so. Can I do it?*

We moved into the living room. He laid me on the couch and took off his hat and jacket, which he'd kept on through dinner. I was surprised to find his silver-haired head bald on top; suddenly he looked a lot older. His body was white and spongy. But I kept thinking, *It's just flesh, it's not beautiful or ugly, it's a body. It wants me.* I undressed. I caressed his body, I sucked his tiny old nipples. His penis was small and shrunken, the musty scent of old man in the hair around it. I told him he had nice legs. He wasn't getting hard, but he said, 'Just lie there and touch yourself.'

He embraced me, he stroked me with warm hands, tender hands, we kissed; then he stood and made himself come. There was only a little fluid. I came back to reality, wondered what I was doing in this flat with this old guy; remembered. We smiled at each other and he went off to wash. I pulled my clothes back on.

More than anything, I felt like I'd done something good, something kind. As he walked me back to the tram stop he told me he was eighty-three. For some reason this made me feel even better. I had done something unusual, I had had sex with an eighty-three-year-old stranger; how free I felt. Perhaps he regularly seduced young women, with his kindly manner and impertinent kisses. It didn't matter. I couldn't think of anyone I knew who would have done this. I wasn't hurt, I wasn't soiled, I had crossed a line and having done it for amusement I now felt I could do other things for need. I knew the days of need were coming.

A WEEK AFTER JOHN, ON A winter's night, I asked Jake and Vicki to take me out on the streets. It was time. As far as I could see, it was the only thing I could do. I was living on borrowed money, and hardly any of that. It was a choice between giving up heroin or taking what seemed like the most responsible, independent option. I knew I didn't have the strength to beat heroin away. It owned me.

I couldn't do street crime. I couldn't imagine knocking old ladies to the ground and pelting away with their handbags. I wasn't smart enough to run scams. And I'd hurt enough people already; I didn't want to hurt anyone else.

This way I could make enough money to pay my way. No more selling off my little possessions at pawnshops, no more days terrified about having no cash. I could make money out of nothing, out of my body. The work was right there on the side of the road, driving past every night. I could work, and be my own person, and extricate myself from the nightmare of lying and having stolen from those who loved me. I could be as honest as possible.

The voices of my feminist upbringing might insist that prostitution was a form of enslavement, that it objectified and demeaned women, women who whored were to be pitied. I guessed that this was very often true, but I didn't like simple judgments. Novels and a couple of first-hand accounts I'd read, flipping through the books in my bookstore, suggested that perhaps it needn't always be so. Perhaps it could be a route to independence, to empowerment. It would be a new kind of adventure. There was a kind of glamour to it, too.

I had simple images in my head of what prostitutes were like. Blowsy blondes, with cheerful bosoms and scarlet lipstick and cackling laughs. Svelte brunettes in plush hotel rooms, wearing suspender belts above long thighs. The stoic girls I'd seen in St Kilda, standing glumly against walls in the street. I thought of prostitution in colours and textures. Red, black and cream; lace and skin and nylon.

In my reasoning I recalled the soulless fucks of my youth. Sweating and gasping beneath a boy I liked, but didn't want to have sex with—surely everyone had had bad sex, out of politeness, or greed, or convenience. It was how things were. If I could do that, then I could do it and get paid as well.

I already knew the dark St Kilda streets by then, knew the unshaven, sweaty face of the underworld. I had met jailheads and murderers, I spoke the argot of smack. I had a tough face I could put on over my gawky shy smile.

But first I had a date with Richard. He took me to an early dinner. I was awkward, knowing that he thought we were starting something. I knew I was going places he couldn't follow. In the street outside he went to kiss me; I flinched out of the way. We were both embarrassed. He was looking at me so bashfully, with tenderness and the preparation for hurt.

'I'm going out tonight,' I told him. I said this as cheerfully as I could. 'Starting something. Tonight's the night I learn to be a hooker.' The word had a kind of bravado.

He said nothing.

'It'll be okay. I'm going to make some money and then I'll be home.' I put my arms around him, breathed into his neck. I wished him to know how grateful I was for the sweetness he'd offered me. 'Wish me luck.'

At home I threw his number away. I didn't want to hurt him any more.

I dressed that night in black, with eyeliner and a determined red mouth. Here we go.

It was Jake, in fact, who took me out. Vicki was sick. 'Stand here,' he said on the footpath, up on St Kilda Road. 'I'll wait for you in the pub over there. When you get in the car, tell them it's fifty bucks for oral and seventy for sex. Come over when you've got some money and I'll keep it safe for you. You'll be right.' He strode across the road and I stood there, my heart going fast, my thoughts stalled.

The streetlights were white and the road was glossy black. There were no other girls around that I could see; it was a nasty, chilly night. I wondered if there were bitch-fights over territory, like I'd seen in movies. Fishnet stockings and big hair and yowling.

I needed a fake name. I knew working girls used fake names. The only thing I could think of was the one I had used to tell drunks in pubs. My fingers trembled as I lit a cigarette. It was very cold. I was glad I'd just had a taste.

My parents thought I'd gone out with Richard again. It occurred to me, stupidly, that some of my old customers from the bookshop might drive past and see me. The thought amused me.

I watched the glaze of headlights, the windscreens of oncoming cars: a series of trapezoids with the silhouette of a single, male driver. One pulled up in front of me; I reached over and opened the door, slid in. The smell of an unfamiliar car. A woolly-haired, middle-aged man looking at me. It was happening.

'Hi, I'm Lucy,' I said. 'How are you?'

'How much for a headjob?'

We pulled out into the traffic and he drove us to a side street. Winter-bare plane trees shaded us from streetlights; the air outside was foggy with cold. With the engine off, everything seemed very quiet. All around us, houses were full of family lives. The lights were golden down here.

I got out a condom from the handful Jake had given me. The man looked as nervous as I was; he abruptly lifted his hips and pulled down his pants. He was hard. I started to bend across to his lap, got caught on the seat belt. 'Just a minute,' I tittered. *Jesus, I sound like an idiot.* 'Okay.'

Down I went. Condom on. It didn't take long. I remembered I'd been told I was good at this. I hoped I was giving value for money. *What if he bashes me? What if he…Shit, Jake told me to get the money first.* I kept on tonguing; the unfamiliar smell, the sense of this man's face above me, looking down at the back of my head, the sound of his breathing.

A gasp, a pulse in the flesh between my lips, a sharp scent; it was over. *I've done my first job,* I thought, as I pulled the condom off him and wrapped it in a tissue. What to do with this? I stashed it in my bag. He handed me money.

'What's your name?'

'Ken,' he said, smiling a bit now.

'Ken, you know, I've never done this before. Was that okay?'

'Me neither. You were all right. Where do you want me to drop you?'

I found Jake in the pub and gave him the money with a smirk. And then I went back out into the street and picked up another man. This one was an Indian guy in a small beat-up lorry. 'Hey, mate, what are you after?' Mugs, Vicki called them. A mug. Another blowjob. And again.

Time went fast. It was so easy: stand, wait, look; get in, drive, suck. Pocket the cash. The men seemed shy, friendly enough under the nerves, their desires basic. There had been four men. They all asked for oral. I wanted to keep going, the money a wad in my pocket when Jake, tired, insisted we go. He didn't ask me for a cut but I gave him forty. It seemed fair. I went to his place, scored and fixed up. Took a taxi home; the news-screen we passed said the time was half-past midnight and the temperature was zero. The lights of the house were off, everything was silent. I got into my bed in this other world, the soft lights of home, the softness into which my hardness no longer fitted. My heart was blank, my veins full, my mind gloating.

I'd found the way to make this work.

I had no qualms about sex for money; none that I could feel. I'd always sworn not to screw a dealer for dope, that was tacky. But this was work. I'd earned my money honestly. Fuck the law. I had no boyfriend to 'betray'. There was nothing of my heart involved in this. It was just skin and flesh, action, touch. My mouth wasn't soiled,

I hadn't been hurt. I was already thinking ahead to the next night.

Part of me, if I'd un-frozen enough to examine it, was still shocked. I'd crossed another line. I batted away the significance of what I'd done. Or was it so significant? I'd opened my mouth, I'd let someone put their flesh inside it. As any girl might do at a party, going home with a man. I'd taken cash; that was a good thing. I wasn't sure where the line was, really.

When I woke the next morning, my room was just the same as it had ever been. I showered, I brushed my teeth, I went out to say hello to my parents. My pupils had dilated again. They thought I'd been on a date. I felt stronger, knowing that instead I'd been out— out achieving something that would make me less of a burden, that I could apply myself to; something that would make everything better.

There was no point in regretting or doubting. I treated it lightly; giggled when, a few days later, I mentioned it to Max on the phone. I thought I was so cool, so tough. I wanted to prove myself, out there on the streets; I wanted credibility. Finally to shuck off the old, timid scholar whose awkward totter through social scenes made her blush. I had a new stride, loping along fearlessly through the dark, daring anyone to try it on. The thought that I had perhaps just done something momentous slipped off me as smoothly as the needle glided in.

I didn't go out every night, though, and I still tried not to use; tried to go as long as possible without. A day, or two at the most. Every time I thought about using I wanted to do it, and had to beat back the thought. *I don't need it. I shouldn't want it. Someone will notice. It's not possible to get away. I'll do it later.*

The first sex job, the first time I allowed someone to fuck me for money, wasn't a big deal. I knew that sooner or later a guy would be

71

prepared for more than just a blow. When the time came I was so excited by the prospect of the money that I didn't heed that I was passing yet another frontier. To me, already, my body was skin, surface. Penetrated by a needle or a penis, it would seal again.

He entered me—clumsy, in the confines of a car backseat; hurriedly, in the exposure of a side street—and I wasn't prepared.

'I need lube,' I said, but I had none. Hurriedly I moistened my fingers.

'All right there?' he asked, and thrust in again.

'Fine.'

It never occurred to me to pretend pleasure; we were fucking in a car. He was paying me. All he wanted was a vagina. It didn't take long—four, five minutes. I lay there with my head braced against the arm-rest, smiling up at him encouragingly or blank-faced, waiting for him to finish. The guy was a friendly fellow—young, affable—and he meant me no harm. Afterwards he said he hoped it hadn't been uncomfortable and gave me the money. We had a nice chat about backpacking as he drove me back to Carlisle Street.

A couple of weeks went by like this. At home and mild by day; going out a couple of nights a week under various pretences to score and work. I was trying to hold off, but I'd set up a way to make scoring easier, not more difficult. There was a constant, weary struggle going on. Yes, no, can, can't. Want, refuse. Want. Want and capitulate. I was exhausted.

My parents had started going to a support group which advocated setting boundaries. I thought this was fine, and was relieved to see their anguish lessen as they realised that my drug habit was not their life. The main philosophy, as far as I could tell, was that the family could support me but quitting was my own responsibility. It was about boundaries and respect. They would tolerate my addiction as long as it didn't interfere in their lives. I supposed this was 'tough love'.

'It's killing us,' my mother said simply. 'We don't have lives anymore,' and I looked at her frightened face, her tired mouth, her expression fearful of hurting me, and for a moment I understood, and went to my room, and cried in secret for what I'd done to them.

They set me a contract agreement: to stop using for a week, to be honest with them. The contract said that I couldn't go out of the house alone. I must respect the rules of the house. There never had been any 'rules', it wasn't that kind of upbringing. But I supposed they meant being clean and polite and considerate. I should eat breakfast. Help with the housework. I had to ring the old rehab centre about going back in. I was expected to stay clean for at least a week, or until I could get into rehab. If I broke these rules, I would have to leave immediately.

I agreed to sign the contract. For all my crazy, sly scheming on how I could make money, make the whole thing viable and support my habit and not make trouble for anyone, still I knew that these people were trying to help me. And much as I didn't want to need help, I thought perhaps it would be easier, and it would stop the arguments. And if I didn't, I'd have to leave anyway. I signed. An actual piece of paper, with our signatures.

It wasn't so easy, though; one night, about halfway through the week when the cramps and the aches and the fret–fret–fret of hanging out were making me wail aloud, I crept out through a window once more and went to St Kilda. I got gear on tick from Jake, with a promise to pay him back later. As if I would, of course, be seeing him again. I was too nervous about leaving the house to stay and work on the street that night.

My purchase was enough for the next day too. In the morning, after I'd greedily been unable to delay taking some, my mother noticed when I stumbled in the hall.

Walking into my room she went with her sixth sense straight to my stash in a small decorative pot. She held up the remaining tiny packet. She looked at me. I stared at her.

'You've blown it.'

'I've blown it,' I said at the same time.

I had half an hour to pack. There was no acrimony. I knew I'd broken my pledge and had to leave. I abandoned my room, my books, my warm bed, the stocked pantry. I took tight, black clothes and make-up with me. There was ten dollars in my pocket.

My father was out of the house. My sister had been staying over for a few days but she wasn't there either. She'd left me a note that morning, saying *Don't bust. Please don't bust. Stay here. I love you*, that had made me sob and sob before I had my hit. Now I was numb. There were tears held back in my mother's eyes. She gave me a shaky smile.

'Don't think we don't love you. We just don't trust you. We love you *so much*.'

'I know,' I said, and walked down the concrete path to the street.

I had been using for two years and one month.

I arrived at Jake's that afternoon with a suitcase and tired resignation on my face. The only way was forward. I'd set my trajectory already; in a way it was a relief not to deliberate any further. After another hit I went out to work. Then I worked every night. A couple of mornings sleeping on Jake's couch, a fortnight in Matilda's spare room, and then a month in a cheap hotel. I didn't ring home for four weeks, reluctant to cry. My body was taut with determination and my heart was slick as ice. I stopped taking the anti-depressants; there was nothing to feel. In my hotel room I would make up my face, pale with scarlet lipstick, I would fluff my hair into a sexy urchin mop and pout into the mirror. I was twenty-six years old and I was going to start my adult life.

I took a photograph of myself every day. In the photos my face is serene, my expression sardonic, my mouth under the lipstick is tremulous.

The nights were cold and they were all I saw. Daylight crept away from my waking hours; I saw only the bleed of winter sunsets as I opened my eyes in my little hotel room. In bed I ate comfort food, full of sugar, and I read fantasy novels in the lamplight. Finally I'd get up and go out into the black.

It was my bad luck, or inexpertise, that after only a couple of weeks on the street a car pulled up and, when I walked forward, I saw it was a woman behind the wheel.

She held out an ID card. 'What are you doing?'

It took me a second to realise what she was. 'Nothing. I'm waiting for a friend.'

'Don't be fucking stupid. Where's your friend, then?'

From the passenger seat of the unmarked car her male colleague got out. He came to stand next to me. I was unsettled by having to talk to her, still in the car, with this large man standing so close behind me. They were both wearing jackets; I was in a singlet, my arms bare to the freezing night.

'She's—she's just around the corner.'

'Look. We have to know who's who. Then we can keep an eye on everyone, right? Tell us you're working, and your name and address, and then we can leave you in peace.' The policewoman's voice wasn't harsh, but I didn't like the way she was looking at me. Cynical and tired and contemptuous.

75

'Okay. I'm working. I've just started.' She was already getting out a pink note-pad.

'Name and address?'

I gave it to her. The hotel where I was staying, the room number, my real name. The scene felt unreal.

'Right.' The man got back in the car, I stepped back, and they drove off. I just stood there, and lit a cigarette. Then I waited for the next mug. I was shaking for quite a while but I wouldn't be stopped.

It was more than a month since I'd left home and the time came to see my mother. She met me in a café in St Kilda. We sat over hot chocolates. My heart, racing as I'd waited for her, quietened. She didn't seem angry.

'Where are you staying?'

'I'm at a hotel.'

'That's good. I wasn't sure where you'd go.'

'I've got my own kitchen there.' Not that I ate much.

We sipped. There was sad acoustic guitar on the stereo. The coloured lampshades threw gentle light. My mother smoothed the table surface with her small hands.

'You know we—'

'It's okay, Mum. I know I broke the contract. I'll be fine. Time to grow up, you know?'

She looked at me and we shared a smile. 'You're doing it the hard way.'

'I know. I always do, don't I?'

David, an old friend from uni days, found me by getting Jake's number from my parents. He offered me an empty room at his place on the other side of town. 'Seems a shame not to use the room,' he said. David worked in the daytime, as a lawyer, a normal person, and I would scarcely see him. He was patient and unshockable. He told me years later that he had been terrified the whole time. 'I used to peek through the door when you were asleep in the mornings,' he said. 'Just to make sure you were alive.'

'I wasn't afraid,' I said.

IT WAS WINTER WHEN I started. It was winter for a long time.

I would wake late on David's floor, in my bare room, in my stinking sleeping bag, on my lumpy pillow. Grey light, old paint on the walls. Freezing air. My waking mind recoiled from the dullness ahead of me this day—yesterday—tomorrow. It would grope and seize the promise of the taste I'd saved from last night. Fifteen mils of clear liquid ready to sink consolation into my veins.

Huddling again in the sleeping bag, curled up in my own warmth. I thought of the cardboard box I'd hidden in as a little girl. I wished I'd never come out. The dim light through the drawn curtains was almost like the shadows inside that burnable box.

Drowsy again, and wanting to linger in the no-world of dreams, I smoked and read, focused only on the page, the other lives there.

My mind filled with the candlelight and rich crimson walls of ancient worlds, with the smooth landscapes of fantasy realms. Quests and heroes. Nothing contemporary: my life was all too urban and grim. I let these gracious days swell in my mind until they pressed against the drabness before my eyes.

The afternoon would darken slowly; at twilight, shivering, I'd wash and make myself up and go into town. In the middle of the city I waited for the St Kilda tram, sourly observing the fortunate burghers of Melbourne heading home to their warm living rooms and kitchens. Five dollars in my pocket. Not enough for cigarettes, but a coffee at the Galleon was two bucks, while I watched other people eating and wrote my diary. Page after page of strong handwriting, fragile feelings. It seemed important to keep chronicling my life now. I wondered, if I died, whether this would be the only thing to tell people what I'd been.

I miss the family. I miss talking science with dad. Hanging out with the sis, watching the mad dances and girlie stuff, mum's cuteness. I wish I didn't feel like a different person to the one they know; wish I weren't so apprehensive of seeing them.

Washed hair, then smeared sticky goo in it, wonderful. My sticky-goo-urchin look. Windy outside. I was rained on last night as another girl and I stood on the corner screeching with laughter about the absurdities of our clients. 'Yeah sure I'll go back to your place and do everything for just thirty bucks and let you waste my time and I'll be so honoured.'

Saw Jason the other day, down from the country. All my friends are worried about me, he says. They all have faith in me, I know, but doesn't anyone believe that I might know what I'm doing? Or enjoy it? Or be able to tell occasionally if I'm fooling myself? Jason said he was sorry for making me cry, he hugged me.

Met an old Bulgarian man last night, he was so nice. He took me home to his place and we did the job, it was all right. Lots of talking. He said he thought I was beautiful. He seemed to really like me. I told him I'm a user and he gave me a long talk—the usual stuff, but then he said that one day my face will change, and my mind will change. That was something I hadn't thought of. He gave me his phone number and told me to ring if I ever need help. I was with him for ages and I really needed to work to make enough money so he gave me extra. He made me feel good.

I'd close my diary and pay for the coffee. Smile at the waitress. Off on my rounds. Out into the chilly black streets. Out to walk the block. Carlisle Street, Barkly Street, Inkerman Street. Walking against the tide of cars, walking stiff and alert, alone, walking all night, walking to keep going.

It was a job. I never had a night off.

A time of firsts. The first time I had sex with someone whose name I didn't care to catch. The first time I had sex in a lane, in an office, in a hotel. The first time I had anal sex. The first time I was with a black man, an Asian man, an Arab man. A fat man, an ugly man. Different skins, different accents, different types of penis. Cut, uncut, thin, bent, thick. White pubic hair, black, curly, straight. All the different smells, all the different cars. I was curious, and in a way I was glad of the experiences. It was like an education. I didn't remember most of the faces.

The work was always the same thing, but every mug was a bit different. Some men took me back to their place; sometimes we just parked by the side of a road and got on with it. Most wanted oral. Some asked me to pull my pants down so they could inspect me before they agreed to take me. It was just perving. I did it resentfully, but I couldn't really care. Occasionally, in desperation, I would take

80

a small, easy job for only ten, enough for cigarettes, sitting in the car next to a guy jerking off under a jacket over his lap. Maybe I'd pull my shirt up for his inspiration. Bored, looking out the window. I always had to supply the tissues for afterwards. But one proper oral job might make me enough to score one taste. I could head up the weary slope to Jake's flat and rest in a cosy lounge room, talk tough and relax for an hour, listening to Jake's tales and trying to coax some words out of Vicki. Then the rest of the night's work would begin.

One taste wouldn't satisfy me for long. I needed to make enough cash every night to buy a few more, cover the taxi home—unless I had a job with a driver, and got a lift as part of the price—to buy myself a toasted sandwich and a packet of cigarettes from the all-night café near David's, and have a couple of bucks left for tomorrow's tram and twilight coffee. I lived on a frugal budget. No new clothes; rare meals; no entertainment. I bought books, because I needed them still.

I bumped into Cass, my old drummer, on the street. 'Hey, what're you up to?'

'Oh, you know, this and that.'

She observed me thoughtfully as we walked together to her tram stop. I told her briefly what was happening. Everything sounded so tawdry when I mentioned it.

'Is there anything I can do?'

I thought, all I need is money. But I didn't think that was what she had in mind.

It wasn't the work that was most tiring, or even the perpetual toiling around that damn block. It was the fight to be paid, the inevitable haggling and cheating. I was guilty of lowering my prices out of need, which encouraged the mugs to barter shamelessly—but how angry I was that these men could see my desperation and use it to halve my asking price. Usually I settled for half or even a third of the going rate just to avoid having to get out of the car, sometimes a distance from the block—wherever they dumped me—and walk back, to start the whole trawling process again. The night would pass, the busy hours dwindle, and still after hours of walking and arguing I was short. Even on a good night it was hard to get ahead. Exhausted, forlorn, I would simply buy more smack.

I endured the weather. Heroin insulates against sensation; I could stand in a short-sleeved top in the middle of the freezing night and not feel cold. Rainy nights, when my umbrella blew inside out and the mugs wouldn't stop to let a wet girl in the car, were worst. The rain blinded me and the jobs were few. I walked against the wind, hoping for the warmth of a car, went home soaked and sniffling. Nights like that it was a push to make the money. But I had no choice.

I worked through illness and pain. Somehow—perhaps it was the scouring of the drug in my system—I rarely got sick. But my teeth were getting bad and I had no money or time or energy to get to a dentist, and so I worked with my face swollen from toothache, eyes tight with headache. My feet were sore from the walking; my vagina was chafed. I fell and bruised my chest; the men pressed on it and I bit my lip. I had a semi-permanent urinary tract infection from the rough sex.

Shoulders rigid with tension, I made myself stride on all night.

Running against time. Only ten hours or so until I'd be too sick without heroin to be able to get some. By the time I woke, the drugs would have seeped out of my system until I was watery-eyed, fever-hot, stiff, aching, nauseous; my eyes dry, my skin clammy, exhausted and restless at the same time. I'd have to go out—get the tram across town, set off around the block, trying to disguise my illness with facepowder and a hopeful smile. It didn't matter how sick I was, how trembly; if I didn't go, I'd only get worse. I pictured myself sprawled on the floor of my room, undone, helpless for days. I made myself go. To stand sweating and dizzy, waiting for a car to stop, take the meagre payment offered—anything, just enough, please, gagging at the condom nudging the back of my throat—do what I had to do, and somehow force my failing legs up to Jake's place. Ringing at the phonebox, no answer, waiting, ringing again. Thinking, *I just can't wait another second, another second, another second.*

Sometimes I'd go out before dark, to catch the late-lunch trawl: truckies, tradesmen on their way to a job, business guys heading back to the office after a nice lunch. Parking was harder in the daylight; we might drive for half an hour, inspecting carparks and alleyways. At least the truckies, with their snug cabs, could tug the curtains over the windows as if pulling over for a nap. The other guys yanked down their pants furtively, in bluestone lanes, while I bent over their laps.

Down at the needle exchange on Grey Street—passing the even more bedraggled girls who worked down there—I could get my brown paper bags of clean fits and condoms. I would stuff a few condoms and lubes down the sides of my bra, stash my bag of fits under a bush, and set off. I battled to make my clients use condoms, especially for oral. So many of the girls, they said, didn't use them; why should they go with me?

'Do you really want me, if I've been with other guys without protection?' I'd ask.

They'd shrug, then wheedle: 'I won't come inside you'; 'I'll only put it on the outside—' Depending on how desperate I was for the job or how little I cared about my health I would agree or refuse. At the very least I tried not to let them ejaculate inside me. Thankfully there were few full-sex jobs and they usually agreed to protection. In my rational mind I knew this was important, that I had to be smart and stand up for myself. But I was almost too tired to care.

I set myself to ignoring the stench of penises that had nestled inside trousers all day, unwashed. I became adept at surreptitiously wiping them clean with my palm before I went down, at spitting mouthfuls of come out the car window. I watched as the men tucked their messy cocks back in their pants without even wiping up. Some men tried to kiss me, forcing their wet tongues against my clenched teeth. I had saliva on my face. My fingers stank of sex. I grew not to notice it.

My legs ached as I pounded around that block. The streetlights were stark, the parking lots and nature strips as I turned onto St Kilda Road were littered with old tissues, condom wrappers, the occasional discarded fit, instantly recognisable to me with its orange cap. I passed girls I knew, stopped to chat a moment—to pass on warnings, relate disasters, speculate on what the cops were up to that night. We all appeared to be heroin users, at least the young ones. There were a couple of old chicks. I was a bit of a curiosity, since most girls stood—not always in the same place, and I never saw the proverbial cat-fights over a spot—while I tramped around and around.

I'd been doing this for months now. The weather began to warm. From time to time the police put on a blitz to keep all the workers on their toes and the residents of St Kilda happy. I'd learned to double-check for undercover vehicles every time I approached a car; I'd learned how to walk quickly past any girl I saw talking to uniformed police.

I learned that I'd made a mistake that first time I was stopped, by admitting what I'd been doing. My friend David, being a lawyer, was able to tell me that the police required an admission before they could charge me. 'Just say nothing,' he said. 'Be polite, and stay calm, and don't tell them anything. They'll try everything, you know—they'll threaten you with this and that bullshit—just keep quiet. Then they can't do anything.'

I was already in a car with a mug, just another job, when the flashing lights came on and instructed us to pull over. My mug held his head in his hands before we got out of the car. Three detectives in plain clothes.

They tipped my bag over the footpath. Keys, lipstick, hairspray, loose change and my holder for cards, all over the asphalt. 'We saw you, you were walking down Barkly Street and you got in the car. Don't give us any fucking shit. You're busted for loitering.'

'Loitering? I was walking! Now I'm in a car!'

'We saw you. Loitering is *being in a place*.'

I suppressed the urge to say that, in that case, existence itself constituted loitering; they'd found my expired student card.

'A smartarse, huh?'

I said, 'No comment, officer,' and raised my cigarette to my mouth. My hand shook violently. The big guy next to me stepped very close, puffed up his chest and folded his arms.

'We've got a list down the station,' said the little one. Behind him the female detective stared at me. 'We put girls like you on it when they're not honest with us. And every fucking time we see you, we're going to pick you up. You understand?'

I blew smoke. '*No comment.*' They glared at me, but let me go. I was in Albert Park, two suburbs away from St Kilda; the mug and his car had already vanished. It was a long walk back to my rounds.

The cops trawled the block all the time: easy pickings for their arrest quota. I heard they divvied up the score: one night, they'd get the girls. The next, the mugs. The next, the boys who loitered in the park down by the beach. It was all regular, and I gradually came to understand the deal. You had to let them hassle you a bit, break you in, charge you a few times; so you paid your dues. Then they'd be friendly—they'd look out for you, warn you of 'ugly mugs' around, stop and chat about business. It could get easier.

I wasn't prepared to be charged. There'd been that first time, when I'd just started working; but no charge sheet had ever arrived. It had probably just been a warning. I didn't want a record; I didn't want to give up hope of getting a job, of having a life that might be, after all, still left unmarked by this experience. So I kept an eye out for the blue and white cars, the sleek unmarked Commodores, for undercovers posing as working girls. I kept my eyes very sharp, and kept walking.

Getting in another car, turning to another man's face, I concentrated on my relief that I had a job, there'd be money, I was out of the cold and rain. I carried hairspray in my bag to zap attackers, but I'd never had any trouble. We drove into the back streets of Elwood, or down to Albert Park, or up into Balaclava's lanes. Oral in the front seat; they unzipped and down I went. Roll down the window, spit, wipe, smile. Sex in the back, my legs silhouetted through the window. Or in the driver's seat, the elbow rests and gear stick digging into my knees as I straddled.

The men were often sweet, middle-aged guys in aged cars with rust around the doorhandles. Or young ones, nervous and awkward. They were all sorts. Union officials, truckdrivers, travel agents; students, plumbers, businessmen. It wasn't always the cheapness that drew these men down to St Kilda; some of them liked taking their chances. The rest of the time, they really were just cheap.

And almost always, they paid less than I asked. The anger inside me grew familiar. There was always another girl further down the block that would do it for twenty bucks less.

Slowly, I was becoming that girl.

Turning the same dingy neon-lit corner again and again. Past the slatted windows of an expensive restaurant, past the grass-grown car yard, past the closed mechanic's. Rubbish on the footpath and scruffy people in tracksuits. The soft lights of living rooms in art deco flats. A takeaway joint, a vintage furniture shop. A family out for a stroll averting their eyes from me. I dressed in tight but not slutty clothes, I carried a backpack, I walked with my head down, my eyes looking up.

And so I walked, on and on all night.

I STILL CALLED MYSELF 'Lucy'. A nice name, simple and sweet. Easy to remember, easy to forget.

A taxi driver eased confessions out of me one melancholy night as he took me home. I wasn't sleeping well, and there were few jobs on the street; all I'd had to eat was a chocolate bar. Jake was annoyed with me. The gas crisis was on, there was no heating or hot water to be had in Melbourne, and the freezing rooms at David's were colder even than the street. Everything seemed dark all the time. Alan talked to me, and listened. 'You're like a flower in a hurricane,' he said. He glanced across at me as we drove. 'You don't belong here. Darling, you shouldn't be here.' I nearly wept for his kindness, but I couldn't allow that. If I started, I might never stop.

Almost all my interaction now was with my clients and fellow users. Every few weeks or so there would be a brief visit to my parents, for dinner. I'd walk in and the familiar scent of the house was disconcerting. Fresh, chilled air evaporating off my clothes as I warmed up.

They didn't ask what I was doing for money, but I thought they must have guessed. 'No, I didn't hear the rain this morning,' I said. 'I sleep all day.'

'Do you need a loan?' asked my mother.

'I've got money.' I didn't want to say it; I couldn't bear to think of them knowing I was out there in the wet, cold streets not so far from this house; I couldn't imagine how they felt, if they already knew. But I was weary of lying to their faces. It was easier to keep quiet.

'Take a fifty,' said my dad, and I took it.

I couldn't stay long after dinner; there was business to do on the street. Leaving the house and slamming back into the reality of my life was the worst part. My parents watched me thoughtfully while I was with them, and we made little jokes, but they didn't say much. It was an awful kind of comfort to see them and sit cosily in the safety there, and yet I would be eager to leave too.

I'd see Jake and Vicki, to score. They had a lounge room. And they were friends. Occasionally I'd bump into someone I knew from rehab a year ago; we'd shoot the shit, taking the rugged stances of those who knew something secret, and hear the gossip about how other ex-residents were doing. It felt as if there were a little community of us, eddying all over town. We'd laugh and joke in slang. But I was wary; I hesitated before I trusted anyone to take my money and score on my behalf. A person mild and generous in the kitchen of the rehab centre might be a dog or a thug outside and desperate for drugs. Sometimes we'd fix up together, and I was startled by offers to shout me a taste. There was generosity, too. When I'd see burly jailheads I knew hanging out on boardinghouse steps with their cronies, there was a pride in strolling up and getting a pleased grin in response. I did think I'd made something in this harsh life. I wasn't no one.

I had regulars, if they could catch me. Some of them were bland and straight, others were more eccentric. Fred, in his fifties, dusty and worn, liked to massage my feet, be masturbated with both feet while I twisted his nipples as hard as I could—a difficult balancing act—then lick my feet clean and give them another rub before he tenderly put my socks back on. He could only pay me twenty dollars. I chided him every time; he'd say, *I'm sorry, it's all I have.* Barry was white-haired, genial, and he liked to cuddle and fuck in the front seat of his tiny Morris. George drove me to his empty deluxe office and fucked me front and back after I gave him head, kneeling on the thick carpet in the dark, listening to the idle computers hum. Abdul gave me a lift home one night and asked me to be his secretary. Willis, with scratchy wild hair, parked in the grey concrete bunker of an apartment carpark and said, *Tell me you're a slut, tell me to fuck you.* 'I'm a slut, fuck me, fuck me,' I droned. I wondered what the students in my feminist university classes would have thought.

The sight of a familiar car, the knowledge that a man had come looking for me, the warm greeting, was almost like comfort. We would joke and chat; the drive to and from the parking place was companionable. They were on the sly, too. There was a friendly complicity to the business. Most of them were nice guys, after all, even if they cheated me. I chose to overlook that disrespect; at least they remembered me. With my face always in the shadows, that meant something.

Every night with my clients we searched for discreet places to park. There were many lanes in the residential streets around; I couldn't understand why they weren't more often used by the other girls. Perhaps they were too obvious, or perhaps they were well-known by the police. No one ever busted me, but as I bent over a mug's lap I would have an ear out for a neighbour squawking protests, or the approach of a car that would mean someone had called the cops. Some nights my instincts told me to direct the driver further away: down to Albert Park Lake, or into side streets in the next suburb. Now that spring was coming the leaves rustled above the car and we undressed in the flickering light of the streetlamps. Cul-de-sacs, canal-sides, back lanes, the parking spots of empty office blocks. It could take a long time to settle on a place, but we always found one. Time was running past, my system was draining out the drugs; one job could take an hour by the time we went and returned.

Very occasionally a mug would pay for a hotel for the night. They didn't want a furtive screw in a parked car. I was embarrassed, when they stopped their cars and asked if I had somewhere, not to be able to offer them a room. It felt unprofessional. We drove around St Kilda, to the usual dives, and sometimes further out. Concierges were suspicious, even when the man went in alone to ask. But I eventually learned which hotels would rent out by the hour. There was one down by the sea, where a grizzled old man in Room 23 would hand you a key and take twenty bucks off you for fifteen minutes. When I walked into the shabby little cell there was the scent of semen in the air, a used condom on the floor. I only rented that place if the mug said he didn't mind slumming it. I thought sometimes the men liked the glamour of a little rough trade.

Another time a moustachioed family man took a room in a nicer place. He said he'd booked it for the whole night so I could stay on there after we'd finished. We did the job, enjoying the large bed and the bathroom and the privacy. He left before midnight; I had enough money from this to score for the night and so I did, and returned with chocolate and juice to spend the evening indoors, watching television, the street girls passing the building outside.

When I woke in the morning it was to the manager opening the door. 'Who the fuck are you?' he asked as I raised my blurry head. 'The guy who took this room said he'd be gone by five and it's past seven. I've got people coming in half an hour.'

His contempt was obvious, although I knew a few working girls lived in the hotel. Stumbling half-naked out of bed I groped for my clothes on the floor. 'I know what you are,' he said. I dressed and gathered my bag and reeled off into the morning without even putting my contact lenses in. St Kilda was different in the daylight. I shrank from the gazes of its ordinary residents. I took a tram ride, my eyes closed, straight to David's and back to sleep until it was dark again and time to go back to work.

One night a truck driver picked me up. The truck lurched to a halt beside me; it was a huge bound to get up into the cab. I perched there on the grubby vinyl seat and checked him out. He asked if I'd go with him to a hotel for a few hours. He'd pay me well. I have to score first, I told him. He was a truckie, he wasn't shocked. He drove his roaring truck up the quiet, narrow side street to Jake's, gave me some money in advance and kept my silver rings as collateral while I rushed in to buy, terrified that I'd take too long and come out to find my beloved rings and my mug gone. The truckie, Greg, was thickset and coarse, with dirty hair and oil-grimed fingers. We drove and drove, along a dark freeway, and stopped at a motel. He took a bag with him.

Inside the room, he settled himself in. First I fixed up. 'Try this, go on,' he said, and after I'd injected myself he laid out a line of white powder. I said no, but he insisted, and I clumsily snorted it up. It was speed; I was immediately giddy with restlessness and a prickly joy. The two drugs in my system—one slow, one fast—clashed and fizzed. When I got out of the shower he dribbled baby oil all over me. There was a spa, too, and after we'd mucked up the bed—his thick, rough body delightful on my intoxicated skin—we soaked in warm water and talked.

'You know what it's called when a truckie takes off all the gears? When he's at the top of a hill? You'll like this,' he said. 'You get to the top of a big long hill, and you just take all the gears off, and down you go. The most amazing fucking feeling. All the weight of the rig behind you. It's called "angel gear". Like an angel, right? Fucking *flying.*'

'Mate, that sounds like my fucking life,' I said.

We spent the whole night playing, snorting speed, giggling sex-talk. He opened his bag and brought out handcuffs; I figured he was okay, and I let him put them on. He fucked me, as I squirmed theatrically and gave him coy looks over my shoulder, and then to my relief he took them off. I enjoyed the seedy idiocy of this scene. At dawn he took me back to David's and I went to bed feeling like I'd had some kind of stupid adventure.

I found myself in crazy situations, the type to make me laugh in disbelief at how far I'd come. Naked but for socks, bent over the lap of an equally naked fat man on a park bench late at night. Both Doug and I were alternating chuckles with low sexy murmurs. He would smack my bottom until it glowed with heat in the cold air, a sensation I'd never had before. 'Is that okay? I don't want to hurt you,' he'd murmur, and I'd say, 'I can take it harder. Come on, harder!' and he'd grin, and I'd bend further over, loving the ridiculous porniness of it all as he whacked at me. *Slap, slap.* When a man passed us with a takeaway pizza box in his hand we just stared back at his astonishment and chortled as he walked quickly on. Freezing cold, our breath coming in white clouds, our flesh pearl-pale under the lights.

Doug would drop me off and hand me an extra five dollars. 'For a hot coffee,' he'd say.

Other times I convinced men to jump park fences. 'Just pretend you're a horny teenager,' I'd cajole when we were desperately searching for somewhere to fuck and they had no car. I'd lead them up to a high wrought-iron fence, and we'd scramble over and find ourselves in a huge, silent dark space. Possums hissed in the trees and we crunched over gravel paths to the rose garden. In the pagoda in the centre of the formal rose beds I'd take down the man's pants. He'd be smiling, startled at finding himself in this setting. The odd sensation of skin naked to the outside air. All around us would be the scent of trees. Above us the sky pink with light.

And once there was a storm. My mug, a loud, bragging type, insisted we lie on the grass. The wind rose, cool, and the grass underneath pricked my naked skin. The man's face above me was ugly, but there was a din of thunder, and the dazzle of lightning; raindrops fell in my open mouth. I lay there, feeling wild, feeling something at last.

A few guys were even attractive to me. I discovered that it was possible to be aroused by a mug—by his stubbled cheeks, the tautness of his belly, by the fervent look in his eyes. There was one young man, who turned up at rare intervals; he'd drive us down to the beach-side carparks and with the blackness of the sea before us we'd kiss, passionately, and he'd look at me with dark, intense eyes. He was quiet; his moans when I made him come were rewarding. I wondered, sometimes, as he took me back to the block, if I might have a crush on him. It was almost like being with a real man.

I wondered if I'd ever have sex for my own sake again. Whether anyone would want me after this. How could I go back to innocence? It wasn't worth thinking about.

A mug dropped me off in the city one night just past midnight. Turning a corner into the main drag, steering past all the young men loitering around on the footpath, I ran into James.

'Hi!' I said. He looked just as he always did: thin, dressed like a ten-year-old boy, and very startled. It had been a long time since I'd seen him.

'Hello,' he said. 'What are you doing here?'

We started walking together. He was glancing sideways at me, quickly and cautiously. I could see he was nervous. 'I—I'm working, now, James,' I said. 'On the street.'

His footsteps continued. I didn't dare look at him. 'It's not so bad! I'm pretty good at it—' I was smiling, probably strangely. 'I know you never wanted me to do it when we were together, but— anyway,' I said. 'How are you? How's life clean?'

'It's good.'

'I tried—but I wasn't ready. I'm getting by.' I hoped he saw my smile.

The night was full of well-dressed people going out to expensive entertainment. We jostled our way through the crowds. James relaxed, talked about his new sharehouse, his job. He told me Jodie and Sam, from the old days, had got clean. I gabbled on, about staying at David's and how tough I was now, how independent. I told him about Jake, and the girls on the street, and a boy I saw nearly overdose at Jake's—

'My God,' said James. 'Is that what your life is like now?'

My smile skewed on my face. The expression on his was aghast. Then he was veering away into the doorway of a club.

'I'm going in here,' he said, already metres away. 'Stay safe, Kate. I miss you.'

There was still time for thinking. I wrote my diary obsessively. Some things haunted me. I wrote a card to my employers at the bookshop. *I'll never forgive myself,* I wrote. *I just wanted you to know.* Barely anything made me feel shame anymore. But the hot stench of that remorse was sickening. Nothing would rinse it from me.

And I got a tattoo. It had to be something to give me strength. Something to mark my body which would remind, and recall me. I knew where I wanted it: in the hollow between the round of my shoulder and my collarbone, a tender, sheltered place. I told the tattooist I wanted a white rose. I'd always liked white flowers; to me, in my dreamy adolescence, they'd represented something lovely and pure. Now I marked myself with this symbol to remind myself of that naïve girl with her head full of fantasies. The flower was just a bud.

The pain and the blood didn't bother me. I was already familiar with both. In bed, after I had it done, I caressed the raised skin, the firm outlines of bud and leaves. On my tattoo there were no thorns.

THE STREET, JAKE'S FLAT, the toilets in cafés and pubs where I fixed up, the bare room I had at David's, my books, the needle next to my pillow. These things were my life now. The sky always darkening when I woke; the pewter glitter and hazed streetlight of the night.

Each night's earnings were only just enough to get me through. There was never anything left to use for levering myself ahead. I honed myself down to the essentials to find out how strong I could be, how brave.

I was brave. I turned the fist of my heart until the knuckles showed.

If I dared think of what had happened to my life, how all the promise people had seen in me had been abandoned, I found myself curling into a ball, swallowing down the panic greasy in my throat.

Seeing people I knew was unbearable, full of awkward silences, nervous glances. I felt they could hardly bear to look at me, from their own embarrassment and my own. Occasionally I did bump into old friends; they asked after my health with either a careful intonation or a happy obliviousness of what had happened to me. When the front door of my parents' house closed behind me after a visit I'd relinquish the strained cheerfulness of the past hours. Back out into the streets where at least I was not out of place.

There I knew people, a few familiar faces amongst the constantly changing rota of women in shadows. A girl in a red scrap of silk on the corner, a blonde matron by the milkbar. As I passed on my rounds of the block we'd say, *Hello, how's it going? Watch out for the blue stationwagon, he's a fuckwit. It's cold tonight. Where are all the mugs? The cheese are down at the corner, don't go there.*

And I knew other users, from rehab or from Jake's. I walked out of Jake's with a boy one afternoon, and fixed up in the park with him. He took me home to his bedsit and he was sweet and he kissed me. It felt almost like the beginning of something, but when he was going down on me I asked if I could have a cigarette while he was busy, because I was bored, and I knew I couldn't find pleasure like that now.

He was leaving town to get clean, anyway. He gave me two tiny paintings he'd done of the sea, one bright, the other dark. I kept them, and stuck them on the bare wall behind my makeshift bed at David's, but I never saw him again. I just went on, forgetting.

'Have you heard about—' someone would say when we bumped into each other in the middle of the night. Those words were never good. I heard that Tim had died, the handsome boy from rehab. He'd overdosed in front of his friends and they didn't call an ambulance until it was too late and he was dead now. I sat down on the dirty footpath. I thought of sexy Tim's beautiful tattoos and how they were rotting in the ground. Something that felt like tears came up in me; but I never cried anymore now.

Faces in the street, a ragged community passing through. You never knew who'd vanish next; left town, cleaned up, busy, dead. I drifted along like a dry leaf in a tired breeze.

But I wasn't completely unmoored. I struggled every week or so to counselling appointments with Daisy, a woman who worked out of the rehab centre. Tiny, unkempt, witchy-wise, with tufts of white hair sticking up from her pink scalp, she was old and tough and droll and when we sat together she'd get down to brass tacks. 'I don't care if you're stoned off your head, as long as you can think,' she'd say. 'I'm more interested in why you use, and how you're living.'

I felt that I'd identified some of the reasons why I used—lack of self-esteem, a wish to obliterate myself—and yet had no idea how to approach fixing them. You couldn't just buy a kit of self-esteem at the supermarket. It was hard to come by, when you were considered society's lowest. Confronting my own pathetic perversity distressed me.

'Come on,' said Daisy. 'That's bullshit. Don't get yourself down.'

'It's—I don't know, something in me doesn't want the responsibility of living. I wish you could fix me, Daisy.'

'Fix yourself,' she said. 'Slow and steady, chickie. Every user's story has a beginning, a middle and an end. You'll get there. Whether you end alive or dead is up to you.'

And so we talked about how to get by, how to stay healthy and the problem of where I was living. 'You've got a good friend in David,' she said, 'but you can't stay there forever. The poor boy probably needs a break. You too.'

It was good advice. I could feel the edges of my survival fraying. I was wearing out from this relentless life, working every night. No movies, no outings with friends, no music or joy or ease. It had been months since I'd done something just for fun. My skin was pale from never seeing daylight. Men observed that I was yellow around the eyes.

I wanted to go back into rehab but the waiting list was months long. And so I came up with the dramatic idea of moving to the country. Somewhere simple, far from St Kilda, where I could unpack my books and find myself again. Using—well, there were no dealers there, were there?

Daisy stared shrewdly, but didn't discourage me. 'What will you do with yourself?' she asked.

I said, 'I'll do stuff.' As if determination were all that was needed.

Somehow, miraculously, I made it happen. I thought of a town where I had a couple of friends already living, a nice town, full of young people and artists and cafés. My old school mate Jason said he'd live with me; he found a house, and I went up for the day to inspect it and sign the lease. It was a huge effort—travelling four hours each way without sleep after a night's work, looking the estate agent in the eye and handing over the bond money I'd borrowed from the government housing agency. I walked into the creaking, lopsided old weatherboard place, imagining a new life here for myself, a life full of afternoon sunlight and books and serenity.

'Okay?' said Jason, smiling from a doorway.

'Beautiful,' I said.

I moved in, with my parents' help. My mother took a photograph of me and my dad that day: he's hugging me tightly in my new back garden, a thin, pale me in my furry hooker's coat, my eyes looking at the ground, a childish, abashed smile on my face.

I had that house for six months. And in that time, I spent probably three weeks there altogether. I had my books and my desk and my bed waiting for me, all laid out, all ready. It was terrifying.

Every time I arrived at the house I felt tired, already coming down after the journey from Melbourne, already wondering what I was going to do there. I had no television; the shops were a hilly walk away and in my state of weakness there was nothing I wanted to do but lie down. My friends there seemed embarrassed by me, and I couldn't blame them; the last time they'd seen me I'd been ostentatiously shooting up with James. I hated our encounters.

I just lay around the house, baffled by the complexity of normal life. Even cooking was too much hard work. I had little money to buy groceries, having spent it all on as many tastes as possible before I left Melbourne. There was no fridge, and we had to buy drinking water. I was too sick to eat. All I could manage was to lie on the couch, making frail conversation with Jason. I reeked my way through the house, poisoning it with the stinking smell of my skin. And in my head, every second, the thought that I couldn't bear this, that the night would come and there was nothing to do, another whole night of wakefulness in a chasm of time, my body screaming, *intolerable*, and the last bus back to town was leaving in an hour.

That house wasn't my home. My home was a dirty bed on a bare floor. My home was my parents', from where I was exiled. My home was Jake's living room, where I could sit and chat with people who knew my world. My home was somewhere cold and comfortless.

I'd gaze at my books, with my burning dry eyes, and I couldn't imagine opening them. The desk where I hoped to write stayed

101

half-unpacked. The place was horrific in its reproach.

So I'd dither, and believe I was determined to get clean, and promise myself that I'd be back in my retreat in a couple of days. I'd dump clothes in a bag and run off, suddenly invigorated, to the bus.

Back to St Kilda and Jake and the gear. To another night on the street.

There was a regular I called Boris. He wasn't Russian, but with his thick black moustache and strong accent and dark eyes, he had an affability that let me nickname him. He picked me up in his gleaming new car, waving out the window at me and I ran over and we drove to his apartment down by the water. He was witty and warm, thickset and easy to cuddle, and he said, 'You can stay here to sleep if you want.' I trusted him and stayed. He was gone to work when I woke up, so it seemed he trusted me too. After that it became a routine, that I would stay, and he'd give me ice-cream or a cup of coffee, and I'd let myself out in the morning. I found that I made myself at home when I was there, and he didn't seem to mind. I liked him, his company and his kindness; his eyes were sad. He always paid me the full rate and gave me a chocolate bar.

One night I confessed that I used. It couldn't have been much of a surprise to him. He looked at me with his sad eyes. 'If I can help you with anything, Lucy, you tell me.' I felt secure enough, after that, to fix up in his bathroom. He didn't mind.

It had been six months of life on the street. The country house wasn't working, but I thought perhaps it would, if I did a supervised detox at rehab first. Miraculously, when I called there was a bed going; I could get in straight away.

I lasted all of the first day and a half, and then in the middle of the night, the drug fretting at my mind, I left. Walking out into the cold night, already horrified that I'd been so weak, I rang Boris. 'I'm out on the street. I'm frightened.' I was crying a little. The world, in its blackness and emptiness, the silent street, the phonebooth glare, all appeared so forlorn. All I seemed to do these days was make mistakes. There was no right move.

'I'm coming to get you,' he said.

And so I went to stay with him.

It was a strange time. We were like lovers; but the sex was my payment for his hospitality. He was divorced, estranged from his family and angry about it. When we had sex, it was always the same. Hard. We were like friends: he and I talked all the time, shared confidences, jokes, pet names. We were like an old married couple: he went to work every day, long hours, while I slept and waited for him to come home, and cooked dinner for us. We were like a man and his kept woman, but at the start I still went out to work, and it was strange how uncomfortable I felt leaving him to go fuck other men.

I lived there for almost two months. He was very kind to me; he bought me expensive ice-cream every day, because I liked it. He had a motorbike, and we drove—me exhilarated, fearful, proud on the back—around St Kilda in the summer nights, and down the coast. He gave me driving lessons and took me out to dinner, and we went to see movies. He let a woman thirty years younger than himself come into his life and live with him, and he gave me money to score and paid all the bills until he was running out of cash. He joked me out of bad moods and kept me entertained. Sometimes I was in love with him.

I felt my life was stabilising; by now I was rarely going out to work. I was remembering the comforts of a proper home, a kitchen, a television, a partner of sorts. It was summer now, and all around me was the clamorous joy of St Kilda: people sitting late at outdoor cafés, going to see bands, walking dogs, wearing new clothes. Boris was my ticket to a better life. I knew, of course, that I was exploiting him; but he needed me too—for sex, for companionship, for affirmation. Sex was a currency: even a wife might have opened her legs in return for a nice home, a steady man, the solace of security. Perhaps that's how everything worked. One needed; the other needed; you exchanged.

I lay in his bath one night. The candlelit room was dark and quiet in the steamy fog, and I watched my body slip in and out of the shining water. I looked at my body: its imperfections, its tenderness, its specialness. It was mine, this body. I imagined it dead.

A scalpel slicing a Y-cut up my torso, parting the flesh. My scalp slit above my blue overdose face, and my skull opened for a pathologist's cupped hands to receive my brain. I imagined what a mortuary attendant would make of my tattoo, of the length of my fingernails, of the stubble under my arms. All the little details that would remain for another to see. Would they feel pity for me? Would they notice the fragility of my skin? I remembered James stroking my breasts, noticing a mole on my back. This strange body that I disdained so much. In the bath I wept for how I might die.

I decided, yet again, to try getting clean. This was the best chance I'd had in months. Daisy the counsellor said, 'Try.' So I planned it with Boris, who said he'd support me. I'd get medication from the doctor, and we'd sit it out. Boris took me to the video library and I rented all twelve episodes of 'I, Claudius', a historical melodrama I'd loved as a child. Itching, sweating, squirming, I sat there with him and we watched those tales of deceit and family betrayal. As long as I was absorbed in the drama, I could ignore the discomfort; when an episode ended, I'd blink back to the reality of my aching bones, my hot eyes. Twice I was fighting my way out the door when Boris picked me up and held me down in a chair. He withstood my complaints, my feeble rationalisations that one taste, just one, would allow me to go on detoxing more easily. He knew nothing about drugs or addiction; it was like the early days with my parents, but I was hoping that this time the 'tough love' would work.

I ended up convincing him to let me score at intervals. Once every two days, then every three, then every four and so on. Every time I used again, I had to start withdrawal again, but it seemed worth it, and slowly the severity of detoxing began to lessen each time. When it was the day to score I'd be relieved, energetic, house-cleaning and going out with Boris for dinner and walks in the soft summer twilight. We'd run across the road from his building and into the sea. Swimming; I hadn't swum in the sea for years.

Mostly, however, I was listless. Boris would try to interest me in a stroll, and I'd creak down the beach path and back again. I was sullen; tempers got short. He was kind, but he was quick to anger and baffled by my behaviour. The nymph he'd invited to live with him had turned into an intractable child. And I started refusing to have sex.

It wasn't only that my body ached. I could feel myself drawing in. The integrity of my body's bounds grew more important. I couldn't convince Boris that having sex with him reminded me of the life I was trying to escape now, that it made my sensitised skin crawl, that I needed to seal something around myself, my apertures, in order to nurture the strength to believe in myself. He would tug at me at night, and when I locked arms and legs and clenched my body tight, he would lie there in a simmering fog of resentment. I couldn't let him fuck me, but I knew that, if I didn't, I would lose my haven. It was a terrible tension.

'*Get out*,' he said one dawn when he finally got up to go to work. 'You can just get out of here.'

'Fine. But I can't believe you're kicking me out for this. You fucking bastard,' I said, shoving my clothes together into a bag. He said nothing as I slammed the door.

I went back to David's. I still had a key to his front door. But that night, when I was out on the streets again and stoned, I saw Boris's dark car pull up and his sad face look out. I ran over and got in.

It was Christmas. I arrived to spend the night with my family, and my mother said, 'I've got a message for you, and we'll take care of it, and then we don't have to talk about it anymore.' She was very tense. 'The St Kilda police rang. They said you weren't at the hotel where you said you were, and if you don't go in tonight there'll be a warrant for you. They said you'd been charged with working on the street. Are you?' She stood there, shorter than me, looking up, trying to keep it together.

I just stared at her. 'That was fucking *months* ago! Of course I'm not at the hotel! They rang you to tell you there's a *warrant?*' I wasn't a frail girl anymore. Now I was a woman on the streets of St Kilda. Now I knew what was what. 'And they rang you *tonight?*'

My mother said, 'I'll drive you down there.'

The pink sheet I was given at the police station said I was charged with soliciting. I was taken into a room and asked to make a statement of what had happened. After all these months on the street my conceit made me almost chummy with the officer who took my statement. There was a date for a hearing at the Magistrates' Court in six weeks. I stared at the flimsy paper, and put it in my pocket, and walked out.

'So you are working,' said my mother who had waited in the car. 'Daisy rang us and hinted. Just to let us know you were all right. Once, when you hadn't rung for a while. Are you safe?'

'It's not like you think it is,' was all I could say. 'I can look after myself. It's fine,' I said, because I had to. 'I'm not in any danger.'

She looked at her hands loose on the steering wheel.

'It's fine.' I had to hug her. 'Don't worry, Mama. Don't worry. One day this will all be over. I promise.'

'Do me a favour?' said my mother. 'Keep your ID on you all the time. Just—in case.'

The next day as usual we had a Christmas lunch with the extended family of cousins and their children. Most of them knew what had happened to my life; some didn't. I sat there, aware that my pale skin, the shadows under my eyes, were being assessed. An outcast, a prodigal daughter, returning for one, fake day of normalcy. I kept smiling. And when everyone left I went straight to my stash, to fix up. My parents pretended not to notice. Later that night Boris picked me up.

He stood outside the front door to meet my father. I was so fond of him, and grateful, that I didn't see how awkward it was for both of them. I assumed my parents were grateful that someone was looking after me. Boris and I rode off on his motorbike and my dad stood on the verandah, waving us off.

January was spent detoxing and ill, chemicals seeping from my pores, peering through Boris's high window at the healthy, happy, beautiful people of St Kilda as they ran alongside the beach, roller-bladed, chucked frisbees, had picnics, swam, enjoyed life in the sun. I envied them so much. It seemed impossible that I would ever be able to run again. Or gather with friends. I sat there mucky with rancid sweat. My bones were pumice; my veins were lead. It was an effort just to breathe. Time was very slow.

Again, I dreamed of my house in the country. Surely this time it would work. Boris said he'd drive me up there in a fortnight, when he could give me some money. He might even stay with me for a few days. I knew he would be forlorn without me.

I was still going to counselling with Daisy. One day as I left I bumped into a young man I'd met on my last stay inside and a couple of times out in St Kilda. We'd shared cigarettes and laughs and he'd read me some of his poems. He was a slim guy with an impish face, long curls and a country boy's long lope. Now a few of us lay on the sunny lawn outside the centre and Robbie joked with me, complimented me, delighted me.

'I'll steal your heart one day,' he said, smiling at me from his freckled face and broken teeth.

'We'll see,' I said.

THE NEXT TIME I WENT TO see Daisy, a week later, Robbie was there again, and we walked down the street for coffee with another guy, Charlie. I was feeling the restlessness of my temporary release from Boris's apartment. Halfway through the drinks Charlie said, 'It's my dole day,' and there was that distinctive ripple in the air around us.

'I've got a number,' said Robbie.

His smile was gorgeous. And so we called the number, and we scored, and I swaggered off with the two of them to fix up in a park, feeling the old life, the comradely nonchalance of the user in company.

It was a nice afternoon; we lay around dreamy. I mentioned that I was going to the country and Robbie said, 'Can I come?' Benevolent with chemicals, I nodded. I wandered back to Boris's, expecting to beat him home before his return from work, and somehow hide my pinned pupils by staying in bright lights. But he was already home; he looked at his watch, and my skittish gaze; he knew.

'This time you can stay out,' he said. And because I was stoned, and I had somewhere else to go now, and I was sick of him and his reproachful looks and his middle-aged complacence and the claustrophobia of his apartment, I didn't apologise, or protest, or tell him calmly that I appreciated all his kindness but it was time for me to leave. I just took my stuff and left with a cold heart. I left him to his anger and his empty place and the silence when he came home from work every night. And I didn't ever see him again.

I worked on the street for a couple of hours, then went that night to my family, who took me in. I stayed over, camping as I'd done occasionally on the lounge room floor and mixing up furtively in the bathroom. It was home, but it wasn't a place I could stay. Already I was looking forward to making a new start—again—in the country.

I arrived off the country bus the next day to surprise my housemate Jason. He was a cheerful person, and didn't seem put out by me suddenly appearing. He was used to my haphazard plans by then. I stocked up at the supermarket; not having scored before I came, I had some cash. The weather was warm, I was feeling good.

My attempts to get clean at Boris's hadn't worked, but nevertheless I'd reduced my usage dramatically. Even the taste the day before, while it had jerked me back to the early stages of detoxing, had left me only with a mild version of the aches and sweats. Gradually, I'd diminished the effects of withdrawal, and I had some medication left, and I thought that this time I could make a go of it.

I had no place at Boris's to go back to. My pride prevented me from begging forgiveness. And David was moving out of his house.

There was nowhere for me to run back to in Melbourne. I was here to stay.

I was sitting in the garden three days later, nursing my tired bones and reading a book, when the phone rang. It was Robbie, saying he was at the bus stop in town and asking directions to my house.

He'd said he would come, but I hadn't expected him to. I barely knew him. He had a dirty sports bag with him, and a sneaky, pleased smile. Part of me wasn't horrified when he pulled a tiny foil packet from his pocket.

'I know you're getting clean,' he said. 'But I thought you might appreciate this.'

I took it from his palm. It was a sunny day, and I felt cheerful; some smack would make everything sparkle just that little more. I had no clean needles, but there was a hard yellow plastic jar in my bag, designed to store dirty fits and still containing a few. I smashed it open on the kitchen floor with a rock. Washing out an old fit—the darkened blood rinsing out gradually, the delicate weight of the thin plastic cylinder in my fingers—mixing up in my room with Robbie crouching nearby, the wicked glances between us; it was all easy. My heart was beating fast. And then, sitting outside in the buttery sun, with the trees all around and the long sweet grass and a charming boy next to me, it beat more slowly with the ease of contentment.

Robbie stayed in my bed that night. We didn't have sex, but we kissed. I said, 'I don't want to fuck you because I can, I want to mean it.' And he said he knew that, and kissed me again with his cool freckled lips.

The next day we went for a coffee in town, talked and looked in bookshops and felt our bones creak but not too badly. I liked Robbie, with his cheeky sense of humour and iconoclastic take on

111

the world; he could discuss politics and UFOs and antique furniture and street life, a loose arm slung around my shoulders. He was pale and soft-skinned, with a bewitching laugh, and for the first time since James I felt like I cared to kiss someone, sleep next to them, and feel safe.

We could get clean, we thought. This was the life. Up here, in the country, with my books and Robbie's plans for furniture restoration and making crafts and gardening. He was full of grand designs and it sounded so easy. I was simply delighted. Everything seemed possible suddenly.

Robbie had to go back to Melbourne, though. Did I want to come with him? He had a room in the Gatwick on Fitzroy Street, an old boarding house full of crazy characters. He said, 'I get the dole tomorrow, we'll be right. Come back with me while I get my stuff.'

St Kilda was still cruising in summer. On Fitzroy Street people were sitting beneath the plane trees, drinking beer in the late afternoon sunshine. I'd sat on the bus from the country watching the side of Robbie's face and falling in love with his clear skin, his sunburnt neck, the firm line of his jaw. People greeted him as we trod up the stairs: old alcoholics with bilious faces settled in armchairs on the landing, a tiny, scrawny woman with bleached hair and black gothic clothes who whined out his name with affection. His room was panelled with wood, dark and old-fashioned, and the floor creaked with every footstep. I was enchanted with all the seedy cinema of it.

We were going to get clean, but first things first. We were back in town, and we had money. I rang Jake. He greeted me with his usual knowing smile. 'Who's that?' he asked me as Robbie waited outside.

'That's my man,' I heard myself say.

In our creaking old bed Robbie and I ate cream cakes for breakfast and read *Alice in Wonderland* to each other. I couldn't believe I was lucky enough to find such a beautiful man. 'Be mine,' he said. 'Be mine forever.'

It took two days before the money ran out. Then, of course, we didn't have the cash to get back to the country. 'I can work,' I offered, and Robbie didn't like the idea, but it was all we had. His previous girlfriend had worked in a parlour. 'I'll spot for you,' he said, and so as I strolled around my block he followed a little behind, to take down licence-plate numbers and wait until I returned safe from each job. Once, I looked around and he was veering as he peered at the pages of a book of Baudelaire's poetry I'd given him, reading by the orange streetlights he passed. I loved him for that, and I was proud to be able to make the money, to match him in street-smarts. We were a tough team, for all the tenderness between us.

So there was a new routine. Of course, there wasn't as much money now I had to split my earnings to support two of us. We bought from Jake, but there began to be times when I needed to get it on tick, and couldn't pay him back when I'd said I would. I lied, and said I'd thought Robbie had done it already. 'He's going to be trouble for you,' Jake said. 'You're already different.'

When I came home at four o'clock now it was to the always-busy Fitzroy Street, with its ragged characters, its screaming in the street and all-night takeaway joints and sleek bars. I loped up the stairs of the Gatwick greeting the regulars still ensconced on the landing. Robbie and I made friends with two gay boys upstairs, pretty young men who welcomed us in to share joints and giggle and try on clothes. One was a transvestite, even more exquisite in his stockings and heels, and he worked down at the park near the beach, where the boys loitered.

Robbie said, 'I feel bad that you do all the work. I'd like to give it a try.' He wasn't bisexual, but he thought he could suck a dick. So one of the pretty boys took him down to the park one night. I left him there, smoking cigarettes with the others under the palm trees, slouching on the grass; it was a strange feeling to walk away and off to my own block. Like a married couple setting off to their respective offices in the city. I did my business, and came back to get him hours later. He was squatting by the side of the road, slightly apart from the others. He looked upset.

'How was it?' I asked.

'I freaked out,' he said. 'I don't think I can do this.'

'It's okay,' I said, and hugged him and took him home and we fixed up. We lay in each other's arms in the dim light of the old lamp. He didn't try it again. It was understood that I could take it; he couldn't.

It didn't seem so strange that I was working again. Now I wasn't alone, now I had a proper room, this life seemed almost manageable.

We kept it up for a couple of months. The thought of my house in the country was there, but we hardly mentioned it, and there never seemed enough spare money or time. Every now and then I'd put money in the bank for Jason to pay our landlord in the country. It was a shame to leave the Gatwick when there was still some of the rent week under our belt, when Robbie's dole day was coming up, when we still owed Jake money. The problem was that we couldn't actually pay the rent here. We had to run up the stairs now, quickly passing the manager's office, ignoring the notes left under the door. The deals from Jake were getting smaller as our credit worsened.

Down to our last ten dollars; down to our last ten cents. I jiggled the coin in my hand. It wasn't the first time I'd been reduced to this. Robbie said, 'Wait here,' and I saw him approaching a stranger. He came back with a begged cigarette to where I was standing, abashed and fidgeting. 'I've been thinking,' he said. 'We should buy a car.'

I looked at him in disbelief. Held up the little coin in my fingers.

'I know,' he said. 'But a car would be good.'

I started walking fast. We were on our way to Jake's, to wheedle some gear on tick.

'You gotta have your dreams, Katie,' I heard him say lightly behind me.

My court date came up. David said he'd defend me. 'No make-up, wear your hair up, find a skirt, take your nose-ring out,' he said. 'Just sit there and let me handle it. You'll be fine. They don't want to break you, they just want to get you out of the way.'

It was terribly early in the day to appear looking respectable. The courtroom was a little sleek chamber, windowless, upholstered in smooth grey. In the back row of the public seats was a group of schoolgirls on an excursion. David directed me to sit next to him, in the front row. The magistrate peered at me briefly. He was an older man, with white hair and a pert expression, and a laptop on the desk in front of him.

'Look remorseful,' hissed David.

The police prosecutor, a solid woman in her blue and white uniform, conferred with David. He came back to me looking annoyed. 'That bitch, she's going to read out all the details of the charge. She doesn't have to. It's just spite.'

I sat there, prim and awkward with my too-clean hair falling in my eyes, as the prosecutor relentlessly enunciated every detail of how I would solicit my jobs, how much I charged, how I would use

115

the back seat of a car for sex. I kept my knees together ('Don't cross your legs') and my eyes on the floor. Behind me I was aware of all the schoolgirls listening. *I don't care*, I told myself.

David made an articulate defence, describing how I'd been an academic success who had unfortunately fallen in with bad company and gone astray. My counsellor Daisy had written me a client assessment. David mentioned the rehab and the house in the country. The magistrate regarded me impassively. 'I will say in closing, Your Honour, that my client has excellent chances for rehabilitation and recovery, and that a penalty will only jeopardise this.'

A small flurry of consultation with the prosecutor and tapping on the laptop. 'Miss Holden,' said the magistrate, and David nudged me to stand. 'I understand your circumstances, and they cause this court much regret. But I will use you to make an example to this community.' I cursed the schoolgirls. 'And in order to dissuade you from falling further into a life which is clearly causing you damage, I will issue you with a good behaviour bond for six months. This means that if you are arrested again in this period, you may face severe consequences.'

'Thank you,' I said, and sat again.

David bought me lunch afterwards. I had to excuse myself for a moment while I retrieved my box of syringes and spoons from under a bush where I'd stashed them while I was in court.

'It could have been worse,' he commented, once I'd fixed up in the restaurant toilet and sat down to eat some salad. It was too early in my day for the heavy meals on offer.

'It would have been a lot worse without you, mate,' I said. He held my hand across the table, looked at me sadly.

'That's what friends do.'

His hand was warm. The tears behind my eyes were warm too.

This meant that working on the street was now even more fraught. That night I could barely bring myself to approach the cars that stopped for me, out of fear that the police would see.

I'd moved from one side of St Kilda to the other; there was a different tone to life now. Robbie introduced me to queuing up for food vouchers. I'd never considered charity before; that was for poor people, and I didn't think I deserved it, or had the energy for it. But I watched Robbie plead emergencies, and walk out with an advance cheque for fifty dollars. It was a lot of work; crossing from one side of St Kilda to the other, gathering paperwork, cajoling rent receipts, getting medical certificates. But at the end of it was a needle full of juice.

All the time I felt more and more that I was one of those people on Fitzroy Street whose eye a nice person wouldn't want to meet.

One night at the beginning of March I was picked up by a young, preppy guy who called himself Scott. Glasses, tidy shirt buttoned up to the collar, nice new car, snappy manner. He told me he wasn't after a girl, but the brothel he worked for needed extra ladies for the night, and he could guarantee me a good night's earnings. This guy looked clean and bright; he even said he could organise some smack for me if I wished. I said I'd come, just for a try, just for something different. Just another, more unusual, booking.

WE ARRIVED AT AN ELEGANT terrace house, on the other side of town. The brass plaque next to the front door said *Cherie's*. Inside, Scott introduced me to Juanita, a middle-aged blonde woman behind a huge desk, and left me standing there. 'Enjoy,' he said as he walked out. The woman asked me my name; I told her it was Lucy.

'Okay.' She gave me an ambiguous half smile and went back to her magazine.

In the lounge room, beyond the entrance hall and the desk, was a black leather couch occupied by half a dozen girls, either asleep or hypnotised by the television on the opposite side, and a dozing man, slumped into the cushions. No one gave me more than a glance.

Along one wall ran a faux-marble bar, with a mirror and a sink and coffee cups behind; the lighting was low, so I could see a court-yard illuminated beyond the rear window. Facing the front desk was a staircase. The whole place was quiet, except for the buzz of the television turned down low.

The girls were all in sexy dresses or lingerie and high heels. I was in jeans and a tight singlet, my little backpack on my shoulder. I hovered awkwardly, ignored, until ten minutes later Juanita at the desk told me to go upstairs to room five. I knocked on a door marked '5' in brass, and opened it. There was a young man lying naked on a bed. He was good looking, with black hair and blue eyes; he smiled at me, but didn't say anything. The room was nice: a big bed, big mirror, expensive linen, soft lighting, and a toilet and shower hidden behind a partition. On the bedside table were tissues, and a small basket of condoms and packets of lube.

'Hello?' I said. I felt very grungy in this clean ambience. 'I'm Lucy.'

'Hi Lucy,' he said. 'Sean.' He shifted lazily on the bed.

As I undressed Sean met my chatter with silent smiling irony; he just lay there and watched me as I got more and more unsettled, and then he yanked me up to sit on his cock.

He turned over for a massage after the sex, and I rubbed at his muscles for a bit; then he jumped up for a shower. I followed him, grateful for the chance to wash off the grime of sex. The dirty towels, what to do with them? I left them on the bed in a clump. A phone buzzed. 'Answer it,' he said. A voice on the other end said, 'Time's up. You can come down now.'

I grabbed my bag and we went down the creaky stairs. He went over to talk to Juanita and I sat on the edge of the couch. Later that night I noticed Sean whispering in clients' ears, suggesting this girl or that, fetching orange juice or coffee for them. He was apparently some kind of host. I caught his eye; he winked, and said nothing. I guessed I'd been tested and approved. I went upstairs with the next client I was given, and ignored Sean leaning sardonically on the banister.

It was strange, to have a room. It was more formal here than the occasional hotel rooms where I'd taken my street mugs. Now I was conscious of my body under the lights. For the first time since I started working I wondered, with an old sense of chagrin, how I compared with other girls. I hadn't shaved my legs but at least I could shower after each booking. And every single booking, I realised, involved sex. By the end of the night I was sore. But I had had the chance to ease myself into techniques I'd barely used in my working career so far: different positions, different expressions on my face. Already I felt more performative, more self-conscious, more aware of some responsibility as a worker.

The men, too, behaved differently. They had come not for a furtive blowjob in a parked car, but to experience something more than just intercourse. There was a stagey intimacy here. I had to be charming; I had to satisfy, in a new way. My nervousness became a desire to prove myself.

When the shift ended at four in the morning, Juanita counted out my earnings carefully. Out of habit I stuck the money down the side of my bra.

'You can come back tonight if you want. Be here at seven,' she said.

'I might,' I said, still wary of commitment.

I'd rung Robbie at the boarding house, to let him know where I was; I was looking forward to going home. I'd worked hard, and it was exhausting trying to guess at the protocol of the place; no one helped me out, and I'd had to fumble my way through with several bemused clients. The other women gave no apparent signs of resentment when I sat on the couch, and a couple had given me careless smiles. Mostly I'd been ignored. The money was better than I'd made on any night on the street, even after half of it was kept by the house; the warmth of the lounge and the relief of not looking out for the cops had lulled me. I decided to come back.

On my second night I was told to take over a booking after the client had complained about the girl he'd taken: I was instructed to make him happy. I walked into a darkened room. Only a little light came through the painted-out windows. There was a large bulk on the bed. I could smell alcohol and hear wheezing.

I walked over and lay down, saying, 'Hi there, sweetie, I'm Lucy. Do you need some attention?'

Massive hot arms swept me in tightly. He was drunk, sweaty, disgruntled and still very horny. His tiny fat prick jutted from the corner formed by his belly and thighs. His flesh weighed on me, his stink choked me, his clumsy hands ripped at my hair.

'Just wait a minute!—Just wait, sweetheart—' I gasped as he missed his aim yet again and I wondered how long till I could get out. I fumbled for a condom. His hands were grasping at me, his stubble was scraping my face. I didn't dare complain. I lay there and held on and moved my face fretfully from side to side, evading his, feeling the chafing of my skin under his dragging touch, the weight of him crushing me.

Inside, I felt myself become cool and determined. *I have to manage*, I thought. I didn't show how he was hurting me. This was part of the discipline I had learned.

The buzzer went and it was over.

I let myself get hurt a lot. I had been trained in the bookshop to be patient, forgiving, tolerant of customers, and I thought the same rules would apply here. I allowed men to maul me, leave

121

finger-shaped bruises on my arms and hips, burns on my skin from stubble and harsh holds. I pressed my lips together and was polite. They were paying, it was my business to endure. They weren't always brutish; sometimes it was awkwardness from inexperience, sometimes it was alcoholic clumsiness. I was strong, I could take it, it was a matter of pride. I needed the money; I wanted them to be satisfied.

I began to feel at home at Cherie's, to have regular clients, to observe the workings of what I later discovered to be a brothel known for recruiting young women who'd never worked before and giving them access to heroin. It probably wasn't in fact as evil a house as the unlicensed joint a few doors down, into which sullen Asian girls were whisked by minders and where, it was whispered, anything at all could be arranged. The girls there were prisoners. Cherie's was more subtle. Half the guys who attended were normal clients who simply liked the atmosphere, and never knew what was going on. The other half arrived on the scent of girls in need of money who might be cajoled into dispensing with condoms.

There was something called a full service, Juanita told me. Massage, oral sex, and sex. This is what the client paid for at the desk, and that's what he was entitled to. Bookings were half-hour, three-quarters, or an hour; customers could elect to extend as you went along; some girls were in the rooms for hours at a time.

We were given half the fees at the end of the night. Beyond the duties of the full service, what was arranged between client and girl (or client and host and girl) was their own business and the money passed between them was the girl's. The extra fees were tricky to negotiate when I didn't know what the other girls were actually charging; as on the street, my prices sagged as the need for money rose, but at least here clients could resort to credit card if they didn't have the cash, and often at the end of a night I'd have a fair bit

122

extra. Occasionally even a tip. The wealthier clients were the stingiest.

'Optional' extras, often demanded, included sex between the breasts (Spanish), kissing, the client giving oral sex to the woman, and dirty talk. The common 'fantasies', which cost a fee, were Greek (anal sex), using a vibrator, twins or doubles (two girls attending to one man; two girls attending to one man and each other in simulated lesbian acts), dress-ups, if you had your own costumes, and golden showers (urinating on the man's body). I'd encountered several of these ideas on the street, but the confines of a car had restricted what was possible. Here, in the privacy of a room, face to face and with a whole double—or triple—bed to spread over, men wanted more.

I offered kissing, but baulked at having someone go down on me; many girls felt that was too intimate, and saved it as their partners' last prerogative. I had no vibrator or nurse costume, but I was game to try the rest. I needed the bookings and the money, but there was also a part of me that was curious to master these disciplines. I wanted not just to compete for the money but to be successful here, to be wanted, to learn. The hints I picked up from the other women's conversation, or even from friendly clients, I tucked away as I'd once tucked money into my bra.

'Sure, a golden shower, I love doing that,' I murmured the first time someone asked me, panicking to myself about how to produce urine on demand.

'Three glasses of warm water, quick; then when you get to it, just think of waterfalls,' said a girl who called herself Lily, when I was getting ready for the booking. The client was already in the room, having his shower. Lily poured me a glass from the kettle in the kitchenette. 'You put the guy in the shower first, right? Lay him on towels in the shower, and then just *concentrate*. Most of them don't really know what they want, it's just one of those porn movie things.' She was proved right; the young guy under the bright shower lights didn't seem aroused by my desperate stream of liquid over his masturbating hand; he said, afterwards, 'I just wanted to try. I'm glad I tried it. Now I never have to do it again.' I tried not to be embarrassed by having just peed all over a stranger; after all, he was paying me for it.

'You want me and Nikita together? Who's a greedy boy?' I said, faking delight in the lounge.

I was self-conscious at the idea of being naked in front of another woman. 'I'm a bit—I've never done this with anyone,' I whispered as Nikita and I entered the room ten minutes later.

'God, just don't look at me,' she said. She was lovely, small and lithe, with long, dark red curls. 'I've had two kids, I've got stretch marks like you wouldn't believe.' We giggled together over the man's belly, acting it up as we each sucked on a hairy nipple, inciting each other's delirious 'moaning'. Our complicity made it bearable. I observed her, as discreetly as possible; she had some new moves I hadn't seen. It was the first time I'd watched other people fucking in front of me. I hadn't even seen that many naked women in my life, but somehow, with Nikita catching my eye from time to time, I wasn't embarrassed by my own body. I instead I relished the sense of shared power we had over this helpless man. He loved it, of course. 'I feel like I'm in a porn movie,' he exclaimed at the end of the session. This diminutive Japanese guy with his slim penis, smothered in beautiful women: it made his night. We laughed at and with him, and I felt the beginning of the conceit that I could make someone happy.

Every night there was something new. Slowly, I worked out

124

some tricks. I was learning to be clever, to use my wiles to protect myself. 'Here, baby, between my tits,' I said, squinting at the danger end of a pink penis, desperate to get it out of my chafed body for a while. And so I did Spanish.

I was a quick learner.

I'd always shied away from the idea of a brothel. Giving up half the money; being cooped inside, waiting passively for the men. It had seemed a claustrophobic trap. I'd been apprehensive of the other women I'd have to work with, in the same way as I'd been nervous of other girls in school. Street work had been confronting, but I'd felt a kind of self-possessed agency in it.

Now I wondered why it had taken so long to get here.

It all seemed so much more professional and stabilised than on the street, and it was legal. With a regular stream of clients coming through the door instead of having to be landed like fish, I had more energy. Rather than three or four small jobs a night I could manage five or six, if I was lucky enough to get the bookings. My body was sore, from the shock of repeated penetrations and the longer friction of half-hour sessions, but I wasn't exhausted from trudging the block and watching for the cops, and we sipped coffee between each booking.

But it wasn't comfortable in every way. Juanita was not motherly, she was not kind; she sat, thin and sly behind her big desk, an enormous Fragonard print gilt-framed behind her, and watched us with cool eyes while her scarlet mouth smiled at the clients. Sometimes Bruno, the other 'host', would come and sit with us at the dawn end of the shift, and make smutty jokes in his eastern European accent, and his face seemed like the face of a nice man, except for what he urged us to do. Sean remained enigmatic; he was rumoured to be Juanita's lover. He and I rarely spoke; one night, tottering down the steep stairs on my borrowed high heels to where he was chatting with a client, I stumbled and lurched forwards into space, grabbing at the railing; as I collapsed abruptly at his feet I saw him break into a laugh.

A few of us noticed that every girl (and every one of us was a heroin addict) made only just enough money to last the twenty-four hours until the next shift. There was no contract: we weren't bound to return by anything but our need. We didn't know how Juanita had gauged our habits so well, but she seemed capable of such calculation. A couple of tall Vietnamese men would pay a visit during the evening and be followed out of the room by sweating, anxious girls who returned from the back rooms eased and languid. I didn't try their wares; I was too shy to approach them. The local vice squad guys came in and sat with Juanita at the desk, chatting and smoking. The parlour was licensed, and regulated as part of the Victorian legal prostitution system; it had a registration number and the permitted six rooms, and so ostensibly it was covered by the law. What went on there, however, with the unprotected practices and the drugs, was obviously not always strictly legal.

Not that any of us was in a position to complain. Using an illegal drug is disenfranchising in many ways: not only have you become a second-class citizen in society, but you forfeit your dignity under other laws. None of us could afford to lose our job there unless we were on our way to another house; with a daily habit to feed, the risk of ending up with no money was too great to indulge our disgruntlement.

Little by little we were tempted into various indiscretions. It wasn't long before a man simply pushed my legs apart and went down on me, despite my protests, and I was too apprehensive to argue about it. Then there was the rest of it. First you lowered a

126

price for a fantasy; then you promised to kiss in order to secure a booking; Bruno would instruct you to let just one man get oral without a condom for a price; then no extra fee. And all the time you were aware that other girls already offered more than you, that the drugs had to be paid for, that it was all too easy to end up sitting on the couch all night. It was humiliating, but no more so than on the street. Or so I told myself. I was more disturbed by the way these decisions were taken out of my hands. Here, I was told when to risk my health.

The most tragic person I met was Sammy, a young blonde with a tired, mocking face below tizzy blow-dried hair. She said she was going to jail after a completely fucked-up life, abused by her father, beaten by her husband, her children taken away, and she didn't care anymore. Whether any of this was true or not, she gave anal sex without a condom for fifty, or free, to get a booking. She was only about twenty-five, and there was bleakness on her face in repose. The rest of us simply suffered the whispered chats with the hosts. It seemed all the more vulgar that Juanita had herself been a working girl once and knew what we were facing. No one ever said that to her, though. And she said nothing at all.

Compared with the streets, however, this was comfort itself. A warm room to sit and watch television, free coffee, company, and beds to fuck in—even showers afterwards. We would order in takeaway meals and talk, and I grew fond of several girls. Emma, a tiny, pretty Vietnamese girl, worked to look after her two younger brothers, both addicts too. Poppy wore only lingerie to show off her gymnast's body, and heavy make-up to disguise her sulky face. Charlene, a lugubrious blonde, told me she had suffered a complete personality severance from job stress and become, so she said, two distinct personalities, although I only saw the one. Come down from

127

the north in search of work, she lived in the house, sleeping in one of the rooms in the hours between the end of the night shift and the beginning of the day shift at ten.

We would talk easily, but I found myself growing cautious with information. The sense of competition was strong. And there was always the smoky tang of lies in the air.

Just after I started at the brothel, I had a message, through my parents, from Jason. We were being evicted from our house in the country. I'd slipped too far behind with the rent. Jason wasn't as angry as I expected; for me, the news was a relief. It had been a couple of months since I'd been up there. Now I had to get my stuff out. I was too busy working to do such a huge job. Finally my parents and Robbie spent a day recovering all my belongings before the bailiffs cleaned the place out. My old room at home, I heard, was stacked with boxes.

The week after, Robbie and I had to leave the Gatwick. We owed a month's rent, and had no money to pay it. The landlady was understanding. 'You can come back when you can pay the debt,' she said. We weren't the first tenants to default. We lurched out of the wood-panelled gloom of that strange old relic, waving goodbye to the mumbling spectres on the landing, and hobbled with our bags to the tram stop. The day before, we'd been to the government housing agency, and they'd given us a voucher and recommended a place on the edge of the city, on Spencer Street. It, too, was old and rackety but with none of the Gatwick's charm. The place stank, and we lugged our stuff up four flights of stairs and down several dark passages to a room that opened onto a concrete light-well. The bedspread was stained and charred with cigarette burns.

'So, here we are,' I said, and Robbie looked at me. We already didn't want to be.

At midnight a few days later I said to my client, an affable man with soft breasts and a black moustache, 'It's my birthday!'

'Congratulations,' he said. 'Let me give you a massage to celebrate,' and rubbed his hands over me, well-meaning, but too rough. I lay there, pondering.

In the afternoon later the same day I woke to the sound of rats under the bed. The room was cold, Robbie had gone out, and the bleak light came in through the furred turquoise curtains along with the sounds of Spencer Street and the city churning obliviously through its day. I knew I should get to a phonebox and call home. It had been weeks. But there was no way I could take a night off and see my family; there was no way my twenty-seventh birthday was going to be any different from any other day. Suddenly a horrific vertigo came over me. This was not what I imagined twenty-seven to be like. This was not what I'd imagined any of my life to be like. There were rats under my bed, and the most I had to look forward to was the white powder on its way, and the chocolate bar next to the bed. I took the book I was reading from the table; I turned on the lamp. I shoved my face up to the pages and started reading as tears ran down my face.

WE LASTED A WEEK IN that place. Then we couldn't stand it—the degradation, the shabbiness, even after what each of us had already lived through—and we found another boarding house, this time in Fitzroy.

Fitzroy was the across-the-river equivalent of St Kilda. Another ragged, working-class suburb that had become bohemian and then been discovered and slicked up. There was plenty of scunge left, however; in the back streets the smell of dope wafted from the houses. I had sometimes come to Brunswick Street, the main strip, to shop as a teenager. Now the first places Robbie and I got to know were the café near the new place, the needle exchange down on Smith Street and the pawn shops.

Our new palace was an old thirties maze of dank carpet and half-finished renovations; but it had a large room, with a saggy double bed, a dressing table, and the rumour of a fridge available to buy from another tenant. Through the frosted window I could see sunshine and shade. There was a shared bathroom down an outside alley and, allegedly, a communal kitchen. The rent was a hundred and twenty a week and there was no sound or stink of rodents; we took it. One more awkwardly laden tram ride, me blinking in the daylight, and we were settled in.

We collected the clean, harsh white bed-sheets from the man at the desk with pride, made the bed, and put our clothes away. With quiet hands I set out our belongings on the dresser: books, make-up, swabs and fits, some trinkets, and a handful of coins.

Every day, apart from a few afternoon hours of hanging out with Robbie and exploring the new neighbourhood, and the times I went with him on the expedition across town to score from Jake, my waking hours were spent in the brothel, still learning my way.

There appearance mattered in a way it hadn't on the street. I borrowed some shoes from the lost-and-found cupboard and learned to teeter on high heels for the first time in my life. I was loaned a dress, too. Red velvet. I'd never worn such a thing. I smoothed the fabric over my curves and saw how the high heels pushed my body into a new, insolent posture. I smudged dark eye-shadow around my eyes and put on lipstick, and learned how not to leave it on during a booking and walk out with a cock-sucker's ring of pale red around my mouth. I leaned in as I shook clients' hands in the lounge so they could see my cleavage. I would need all the girly wiles I'd disdained my entire tomboy life if I were to make the money I needed. I compensated by not simpering or acting foolish, by using my wit, and by striding as boldly as I could in my heels.

I found I liked some of my clients. As with the mugs on the

131

street, even in this sleazy place they weren't all bad. Many were normal joes who came for the friendly girls. They seemed oblivious to the smacked-out zombies on the couch, the calculating glances of the hosts. Within a week, I had acquired regulars. One of them was a jovial bikie, who would give me a back rub and tell me how beautiful my breasts were. A giggling eastern European fellow booked me one night and kept me for three hours lying on my front while we discussed history and politics and he admired my arse, stroking my buttocks in rapture. An Indian student sat on the bed, trembling with nerves and need.

Other clients were coarser, come in search of girls who'd skip the condoms and offer cheap anal; they weren't interested in looking us in the eye, except to assess our compliance. Their bookings were usually arranged with the management and, once a host had sidled up to one of us and whispered, we would go up to the room and find the gentleman already sprawled on the bed, greeting us with a blank stare. It wasn't that they didn't make conversation: they'd joke and chat. But there would be a heaviness in the air, in their humour. Their hands would hold us less forgivingly. The awareness of our need for money brought a tilt to their thoughtful smiles. Perhaps the joking was in the way of apology as we bent our heads to their naked cocks, took the cash they held out for the privilege of our other entrance, as we stared at the ceiling in determination and they grunted on top of us, mauling our skin.

Two weeks into my time in the brothel I was surprised to see a familiar face: a girl I knew from the streets, who also occasionally scored from Jake. She'd disappeared from the St Kilda scene and now I knew where to. She was striking: a delicate, almost antique face, framed with lush black hair and animated by her irrepressible spirit and smile. Esmerelda, she called herself. She leaped up to hug me, and from that time we were comrades in the house. It was a strange thing, to have a friend, a female friend again, and one from whom I didn't have to obscure the realities of my life. We talked about working, and the street, and keeping our boyfriends' habits. She paid for her partner's drugs, but refused to buy him cigarettes, a particular scruple; she'd collect butts from ashtrays and bum cigarettes off clients, keeping a little tin full to take home. She convinced me that Cherie's was the place to be and she loved Juanita, who seemed to dote on her.

She gave me advice. Don't think you have to kiss them. It's at least fifty for anal. Did you see the panic buttons in the rooms? Just next to the lightswitch. Bruno will come up if there's trouble, though it might depend on who you're with. Watch out for Brandy, she's giving fantasies for free these days. Do you do twins? I'll try to get you into one if anyone asks me—we can do a booking together! Make sure the clients behave themselves. When they're behind you, always reach around and pretend you're squeezing their cock tighter, or play with their balls—so you can feel if the condom's still on. Never, ever, tell anyone, not even the other girls, your real name. Or where you live. Or how much you make.

I didn't know her well and I had long since learned to be a little cautious with everyone, but she already knew my real name. Esmerelda and I sat on the couch every night, close together and holding hands like twelve-year-olds in a camp dorm, giggling and talking, and I think she was as glad of me as I was of her.

She told me she'd found a better dealer and drove me after the shift, just as dawn broke, to a carpark. A stout Vietnamese man in a tatty sports jacket stuck his head in through the driver's side window and Esmerelda grinned at him.

'Lucy, this is—what's your name going to be today?'

'Plum,' he said, smiling like an idiot at the ridiculous name he'd invented. His face was merry and his accent thick. 'Plum! I give you phone number. You can ring me. I come to you.'

The deal was good, much bigger than Jake's, and when I tried it in the thin light of my room, Robbie sleepy and waiting, it was stronger. New place to work, new place to live, new dealer, better money; in one big heave, I'd finally left St Kilda behind.

Only three weeks after I started at Cherie's, when I'd mastered the high heels on the stairs and the routine of slipping out to fix up in the dark alley around the corner, when I had my coterie of friends and was thinking I was set fair to stake some ground, Robbie's ex-girlfriend Serena saw him in the street. She was a prostitute too.

'She's working where? That place's fucked. Tell her to get out. No, I'm not kidding. She can go to the place I've just quit. Here's the address. Tell her.'

I knew Serena had been working a lot longer than I had. Maybe she knew what she was talking about. Cherie's did have some dubious customs. So I got up early the next afternoon and went round to a house called Mood Indigo.

How did one go about applying for a brothel job? I'd ended up at Cherie's by accident. Did you need references? Did they want to know why you were leaving the last place?

The woman at the reception desk was bent over some paper-work and warbling away to the radio when I walked in from a long entrance passage. The building was like a bunker, without windows, and with low ceilings, but there were rose bushes out the front and a wrought-iron fence. A tidy place, similar in décor to Cherie's: faux-marble counter, flowers in a vase, an Alma-Tadema nude on the wall in a gilt frame. Opposite the reception was a small nook with black leather couches. There were no girls sitting there, but I could hear the sound of women talking down a short passage opposite the desk.

'Hi, I, um, wanted to ask if you had any jobs going,' I said.

She looked at me. Dark hair, hyperthyroid eyes, a small mouth with a droll expression settled permanently in the lines around her lips. 'Have you worked before?'

'Yes. I'm working at the moment.' I wasn't sure if I should have said that. I was flustered with the awareness of having things to hide. Like the drugs. I hoped the light was bright enough to disguise my constricted pupils.

She came out from behind the counter and said, 'I'm Nora. Let's go have a chat in one of the rooms.' She led me into a bedroom.

She asked me about having worked, and I managed to evade telling her where exactly; she didn't ask. She said Mood Indigo was an 'intro-house'. Ladies had their own lounge, and came out to meet clients individually. This sounded good; it was tiring being on display to men all the time. What services did I do? I said I did a good straight service but I was pretty open to learning.

Nora took me in to meet the girls. Their room was quite large, windowless, with a kitchenette in one corner, a television on a bracket, a large table in the middle, a make-up counter with a mirror and fluorescent lights, and a row of lockers along one wall. There were a couple of women sitting at the table, flicking through magazines and watching 'Days of Our Lives'. At one end sat an older woman, small, with dry blonde hair and an encampment of magazines and rolled cigarettes spread out in front of her.

'This is Lola, and that's Briony and Camille,' Nora said. They

135

looked up and nodded. 'This is—what's your name?'

'Lucy.'

'Lucy, that's okay, we don't have any Lucys at the moment.'

The girls went back to their desultory entertainments. Nora took me through to the desk again.

'So, what nights do you want to work?'

'All of them.' She looked up at me. There was something kind and shrewd in her eyes. I dropped mine to stare at the counter. There was a little gleaming smear of what looked like lube along the edge next to a bowl of mints.

'Seven nights? All right. We're a bit low on girls at the moment. You won't get too tired?'

'No, I like working hard. I like to concentrate.'

She filled in a roster-sheet. 'Phone number?'

'I—er—I don't have one at the moment.' In my mind I saw the stained carpet of the room Robbie and I shared at the boarding house. 'I'm living in a hotel. I'll bring in the desk number next time.'

'Right…Well, can you start tonight?'

I hesitated. I really had come to enjoy my little corner of Cherie's. I had friends there, and regulars. I knew the drill. But this place looked nice, and I was happy not to see any hosts around. Perhaps this was a step up. The receptionist was friendly, and that made me feel better than I expected.

'Sure.'

So I ditched Cherie's with a phone call, saying I had to take the night off—thinking, *hedge your bets*—and went home to score. At seven I put on my make-up and got on the tram back to Mood Indigo.

When I arrived I realised that I had no dress or shoes. The costume I'd worn at Cherie's had almost come to feel like my own, but now it remained in the locker there for another girl to wear.

There were clients walking out of rooms with rumpled girls wearing dressing-gowns, and a change-of-shift stir as women in street clothes came out to get their pay. Nora introduced me to the other receptionist, Bea, an older woman with crimson lipstick on a tiny bow mouth, a halo of carefully frizzed red curls and thick eyeliner around her enormous eyes. I was blushing as I explained my lack of costume to Bea.

'Not to worry, sweetpea, we've got some spares. But you might want to get some of your own pretty soon.'

In a locker I found French maid and policewoman costumes and children's plastic doctors' kits, and a long black dress and too-large high heels, which I strapped on. The other women in the lounge watched me as I slunk into a chair and gazed at the television.

I'd already learned that there's a kind of quiet bristling when a new girl starts: some women figure that more girls mean more custom; others see only new competition. And new girls usually do well. I needed to be successful—successful enough for four tastes a night at the very least—but I didn't want to step on anyone's toes. The girls' lounge was too small for enmity, and I didn't like not being liked. I'd already discovered that the company of the other women provided a warmth I'd been missing for a long time.

Before I could do any intros, however, it seemed I needed to be checked. As it happened, that night there was a doctor in the house—she came once a month to check all the girls for sexual health. I'd never heard of this at Cherie's, but Bea told me it was a legal requirement. I was shown into the little room where Nora had interviewed me, and a pleasant-faced young woman said hello. She asked me to lie on the bed and she gave me a physical examination, then asked the usual questions about safe sexual behaviour. I told her about my permanent cystitis and she wrote me a script.

'When's the last time you got your period?' she asked.

'I haven't had it for about two years,' I said. A quick glance at me. 'My last doctor said it's because my body knows it's not a good time to be fertile.' It was also because of the heroin.

'Stress,' the woman agreed. 'This can be a stressful job.'

She wrote out a certificate with my working name on it and told me to give it to reception. I was now cleared to work. 'You can ask me anything,' she added. 'This is a proper medical examination, just like at the surgery. Speaking of which, do you have your Medicare card on you please?'

I fetched it from my locker and gave it to her. It felt strange to sign my real name on the slip. She handed me the receipt. 'How are you finding the place?' she asked.

'You're the first person to see my vagina here, so I can't tell you yet,' I said.

She laughed. 'I reckon you'll be fine. I visit quite a few places, and this one's good.'

Back in the lounge things had settled down and everyone was watching the evening news.

'Girls! Intro!' Bea trilled from the door. We all stood and shook out our hair.

The routine wasn't so different after all. We took turns to stride in a suddenly confident lope to meet the man, who was tucked around the corner in the little nook. In the corridor as we lined up to wait our turn a couple of women asked my name. Carmen, an elfin-looking woman in an ornate bustiere and flowing skirts, told me I should make myself at home. A tall blonde with lanky limbs and emerald eyeshadow made dry jokes and muttered that she was

Valentina. The others ignored my tentative smiles. I was glad, in a way, not to get the first booking. I got the second.

The men I met that night seemed more genteel than those I knew on the street or at Cherie's, though I couldn't say exactly how. They were the same mix of ages, races, professions, attitudes; but there wasn't the same brittle atmosphere. There were a lot of Greeks and Italians, office workers with briefcases, older men in jumpers and slacks, as well as a couple of tradies with canvas caps and young men in runners. I wasn't sure what to say, marching up to them and jumping straight into business. At Cherie's the intros had often been on the couch, acting as if we were in a bar to pick up these delightful men. In the corridor I tried to eavesdrop on the other women's spruiks, but I couldn't hear. Used to making chat before getting into details of my service, in this new formal context I fumbled through a few nervous conversations. I was aware of taking too much time and was startled when, cutting off my questions about his evening, the client would simply say, 'So do you let guys go down on you?'

Bea gave me a look as I came out and later took me aside. 'You don't have to give them a long talk, honey. Just walk in there and tell them what you do or don't do.'

I tried that. Phrasing an attractive list of services was hard. Carmen demonstrated hers. 'Full service, extra fantasies available. Oral sex, twenty dollars. Vibrator on me, twenty dollars. Vibrator on you, forty. Dress-ups, fifty. No Spanish. Greek, one hundred. I do twin service but not bi. I don't kiss. If you give me trouble there's no refund. Any questions?'

It seemed a bit blunt. I wasn't yet sure what my extras were but I could see that it was possible to charge for some things I'd been giving away free. This might even be my chance to stop doing some things; I could be one of those girls who said, 'I don't let guys give me head. That's special for me. No, no Greek. I don't kiss.' On the other hand, Cherie's had taught me all about competition. You still had to jostle for bookings, after all. I didn't think I could risk being too precious when I needed so much money every night.

I experimented through the night with variations on a spiel. 'Hi, I'm Lucy, how are you? How's your night going? Are you looking for anything in particular? I offer the full service, and I do some fantasies. What's that? Can you go down on me? Well…Are you any good?'

My tone was somewhere between comforting and coquettish; it depended on what I had to work with. Most men were dour and their questions were basic: do you do Greek, do you kiss, do you let guys go down on you? For now I said yes to all of them, and made my eyes sparkle a bit, as if I were doing it only for them. They stared dully back, and maybe chose me, or didn't. None of them asked me for service without a condom.

I relaxed a little. A couple of house regulars came in, and booked me after Bea had a word to them and they'd checked me out: genially, they helped me tidy the room. In the girls' lounge, the other women started to include me in the conversation, although I kept quiet and took a corner chair out of the way. I missed Esmerelda.

There weren't many girls on that first night, only five of us, and the place seemed busy with a regular stream of clients. The rooms were nice, with gilt mirrors and showers in a corner. I learned the new rooms, each one decorated slightly differently, and their numbers ('Half hour with Peter, Lucy, in room four'). I was shown where to dump the dirty towels in a back room, and how to take a selection of condoms from the counter basket as I went in to my

140

booking. There seemed a bit more housekeeping procedure in the place: a routine for disinfecting the shower with antiseptic spray, tidying the moisturiser and talcum powder bottles on the bedside table, spraying room deodoriser, filling out a small form at the start of each booking, with the length of the booking and room number. There was a particular way to arrange the towels in decorative folds at the end of the bed—we spread them across the sheets during the booking—a special pattern for the many pillows on every bed. At the end of every shift we changed the bedlinen. Each room was equipped with speakers for whatever top forty music was playing, and a television, on which porn movies played.

The building was a Victorian-era single-storey cottage. At the end of the corridor was a large room, with yellow silk draped across the wall; the room across the hall had a slightly creaky bed, a cold greenish light that made for rumours of ghosts, and a spa. The next room had a double shower and a king-size bed for large bookings; then there was a smaller, cosy-feeling room, with dark green and blue decoration and a pesky shower head too high for adequate cleansing of genitals. There was a tiny room, where Nora had first interviewed me, with a narrow bed; this was mostly used as an ancillary introduction lounge where we would find clients perching awkwardly on the edge of the mattress, sitting right on top of the little towel rosette. Occasionally we busted them pinching the talcum powder from the drawers. The sixth room was comfortable, tucked away from the others, with a spa and shower and warm yellow wallpaper. This was usually appropriated by the top girl and it was months before I got a booking in there.

I wasn't entirely dumped in without a clue, as at Cherie's; still, it was weeks before I learned I was meant to wipe down and dry the glass shower walls after every booking. Each room had to be kept impersonally tidy in case another lady needed to use it and, of course, it had to look immaculate for each client. The air was dense with the scent of deodoriser.

I liked the place. It had more cheer than Cherie's, and the clientele here appeared safer. No drug dealers came skulking through the lounge. I couldn't tell if the other girls were using, but, overhearing a scornful reference to 'junkie girls', I guessed most weren't. I pressed down my thoughts, closed my lips and bent over a crossword. Obviously this was a place where, as an addict, I'd have to be careful.

Already I found myself walking with my arms slightly crooked up, fiddling with my fingers or holding a coffee mug as an excuse. The tiny dark marks in the crook of my arms felt exposed, even under the paste of make-up I'd applied. But no one seemed to notice them. I had never looked stoned, with the wall-eyed blunder of a user who combined pills with gear to wipe themselves out. Only my tiny pupils gave me away, while my composure looked normal. I learned to look at the floor while I talked to people, to hide my eyes.

The only awkward moment was towards closing time at four, when I used the payphone in the corner of the lounge to call Plum, the dealer. Aware of the other women listening, I said, 'I'll have a *cup of tea*. No, make it two,' although I knew this was ludicrous. I decided to force the pretence through; there was no other way. 'Pick me up at work, yeah?' I gave him the address, unsure from his sleep-thick accent whether he'd understood.

'My boyfriend,' I said to the girl near me. She nodded, not looking at me.

That first night, I made slightly more than I would have at Cherie's. I collected my money at the end of the night—a newly complicated business, with the little forms and a signature to confirm that the numbers were right, and a nice handful of cash. Bea said, 'See you tomorrow Lucy,' and I waved a shy goodbye to the other women as I walked out. Plum was, miraculously, waiting for me in the carpark. I got into his car, cold in the dark night, pulled the wad of money out of my pocket and bought an extra deal.

WORKING EVERY NIGHT, I soon got to feel at home at Mood Indigo. Having a private lounge for ourselves made the atmosphere more familiar and relaxed—girls spent the free time plucking their eyebrows, slumping in chairs with their feet up, drinking coffee and talking together. We could stagger back from difficult or amusing bookings and relate the drama, or return from an intro to make snide comments amongst ourselves. In the long quieter hours after midnight we watched television, picked over warmed-up takeaway or fussed with make-up. It was a homely, womanly ambience. This relaxation was all new to me. I had a locker in which to store my make-up kit and my bag, without fear of my wallet being stolen; but in any case, the other women didn't seem the type.

And they were just normal women. It was a long time since I'd met any. We shared the collusion of prostitution, but the rest of our conversation was about domestic things: kids, clothes, television. Most of them were down-to-earth, practical types. We didn't speak much about what we did when we weren't at work, but over time I found that Nicole had children, and tuck-shop duty at school; Carmen was studying to be an accountant; Monique ran a craft stall once a week. Alexia was a security guard. Others were saving to buy a house, or did a lot of shopping. No one really talked about why they needed this kind of money; everyone wants money. I wondered how these women happened to be here, how they'd started, what had made them decide to cross the line themselves. But I couldn't ask. There was a delicacy around that kind of thing.

It took a while to meet all the women, and to get to know them. Some were inscrutable, or formidable. Lola presided over the group on her nights. A tidy small woman in her fifties with great legs— enhanced by a short dress, nude stockings and glittery gold heels—and a hacking cough, she had an acerbic eastern European sense of humour as she ruled the television remote and kept a stern eye on everyone. Lola was rumoured to be the management spy; and you certainly didn't want to cross her. She liked working, for the money and the entertainment and the chance to swear loudly; at home she was a genteel divorcée with two grown children and a grandson. There were nights when she never got a booking; but she'd saunter out with her Tina Turner legs and her large bosom perked up, and for every week of nights with no bookings at all, there was a boom shift for her. She did particularly well with men of her own age and confident youths in tracksuits.

There was another older woman, Sandra, a bloated, purple-faced blonde who said little in a finicky, mannered voice and heaved herself around the room to systematically steal everyone's seat. She had a way of staring at me, rather spookily, for hours. Sandra didn't

145

get many bookings. I would have pitied her but for her truculence.

It was easier to warm to Heidi, a woman in her forties. She had a straight-up, strong personality and the precious ability to laugh at herself. Late to work every shift, she'd yank on a long dress and set about making up her wise, ordinary face, joking that she needed at least three hours to become as beautiful as the rest of us. She was a lesbian who'd only recently started working; she said not being attracted to men made her a good worker, free to enjoy the men's company without being emotionally engaged. 'Besides, I like dildos so a live cock's almost as good,' she remarked. She looked out for me, gave me advice about life and had a way of loosening the lounge's atmosphere with her jokes and her common sense.

Most of us were younger, ranging from one cheeky redhead of twenty-one to a couple of women in their mid-thirties. There were some brothels specialising in young girls, but this wasn't one of them; to her chagrin, young Renee wasn't as popular as she expected. The patrons here wanted normal, substantial women, not fantasy Lolitas; a few of them told me that young girls weren't experienced enough. I was beginning to appreciate that professionalism was about more than just washing your hair and opening your legs; many of these men valued a woman who was a person, who had experience and knew what she was doing in bed, whose personality might make up for slack flesh, who might talk as well as moan. The younger girls seemed contrived by comparison, with their saucy talk and pouts.

I came to believe that there were three main types of working girls. How we had fitted ourselves into each type I wasn't sure, but you could almost pick a type from the kind of working name a girl used. Women with names like Gypsy, Scarlette, or Crystal were 'sluts', wearing skimpy dresses, heavy make-up, and tending to offer

146

a raunchy, no-holds-barred service. Their appeal lay in the tawdry Route 66 fantasy of a motel room, a naughty girl, a wanton minx. Cherie's had been that kind of place.

The glamour girls had names like Chanel and Lana, and they were a man's fantasy of a model companion, a princess, a dream that they might purchase for an hour. These women were better looking, more svelte, and possessed an aura of chic exclusivity.

Then there was the mid-range. The 'girlfriend'. Women who were pretty enough, and glamorous enough, but not ideally perfect. Women who dressed better than the men's own wives and girlfriends, who wouldn't say no to a bit of naughty play, but weren't terrifying. Women with names like Nicole and Briony and Heidi. Or Lucy. In Cherie's raunchy atmosphere I'd tried to compete with the other girls, but now I was happy to fit into this milder stratum. My clients, too, spanned the mid-range. They weren't as likely to be arrogant or intimidated by me, though I met with both reactions.

On Friday and Saturday nights the mood changed. The glamour girls came in for their exclusive shifts and their scheduled regulars. They all seemed taller and bolder and rushed in and out of bookings to fix their make-up and get instructions from the receptionist. Valentina was one of them—tall, impossibly beautiful in her long body, with gleaming blonde hair, an outer-suburbs drawl and a scoffing kind of wit. And Monique, whose impish face, hairpiece and spectacular catsuit-encased body gave her a Barbarella cuteness. She'd get a break only rarely and sit with us, giggling hoarsely and telling jokes against herself. 'So I was there just now, with my arm halfway up this guy's bum, and I accidentally turned and saw myself in the mirror on the wall. And I'm like, *how did I get here?*'

Angie was the most startling. She was slim, with a boob job and transparent dresses, great legs, and the loudest, filthiest mouth I'd ever heard. You could hear her braying from the men's lounge. She'd start the shift by swaggering in and saying happily, 'Cunt! Cunt! *Cunt cunt cunt!*' and then tottering over to the mirror to mash make-up onto her face. She never stopped talking, aided by the diet pills she took for stamina, and the men loved her. 'Get a mouthful of that, dickhead,' she'd say to an intro, shoving her bum at him. 'What's that? You're scared? I'm scared too, sweetheart, that's why I talk such shit.' Everyone adored Angie, although we force-fed her Minties from reception in order to glue her jaws shut occasionally. She was a mother from the suburbs who was a genius at crosswords; in real life she wore twinsets and never said anything worse than 'damn'. Work seemed like an excursion for her, until the end of the shift when, exhausted, she'd sag in her chair, finally silent.

These girls weren't frightening or haughty; they were confident in their work, long familiar with their shifts and their clients. The hectic atmosphere of weekend nights was almost like a strange party, as more extravagant costumes were yanked on, the air was scented with facepowder and a dozen types of perfume, and women dashed about giggling. I watched these expert women, and studied what made them popular. It wasn't that they were all tall and lovely—Tara, a quiet, witty blonde girl, was almost dumpy. But they had confidence, and a kind of sparkle. They were like the cool kids at school. I was somehow thrilled if I got to talk to them in the midst of the rush.

And they worked only one or two nights, and were booked solidly. Working every single night, I wondered if perhaps cutting back on my shifts, becoming less available, might give me the same

148

advantage. But I was too afraid to go a night without earning. First I had to build up a clientele.

The glamour girls showed me something to aspire to. I was nowhere near achieving that. My work was for my habit, and Robbie's. But when I heard these women speak of buying furniture, clothes, holidays and houses, I felt a little longing start up.

Sunday nights were quiet after the frantic rush of the weekend. Friday and Saturday nights were boozy and blokey, as office men clamoured for a good time. Sundays were an evening for men to treat themselves. The clients took longer bookings, and might want a spa, or just conversation after the sex. Regulars came in. The feeling in the lounge was relaxed. Fewer girls worked, perhaps only four or five of us. There'd be a movie on television, and takeaway dinners ordered in, and time to talk, paint our nails, sit around. It was a night for the 'girlfriend' girls; a good shift, but not the most racy.

Right from the start I became friends with Asia, a voluptuous girl with an exceptionally pretty face. She had a kind of cruising confidence beyond her years, and something about her that told me she knew drugs. She was full of amazing stories: how at the age of twenty-three she already had four children, how she'd worked as security for a club frequented by gangsters she called by first names, how her ex-husband had smashed her about. Her teeth were all broken in her pretty mouth. She was amusing and kind and somehow different from everyone else. She didn't get many bookings. We sometimes did sessions together, bent like black-haired twins over the man's prone body: her luxurious flesh and my skinny flanks. We each thought the other sexy. And one night, when everything seemed too much for me, when I wasn't getting booked and I didn't know how I was going to afford the drugs and she found me

149

alone in a bedroom crying, she lent me fifty bucks, knowing without being told. The next day she gave me a little box containing a silver ring, some underwear and a small vibrator. On bad nights we exchanged a lot of quiet glances. She was my new Esmerelda, a person with whom I could share things.

It wasn't as if we didn't need friends there. I caught the name of one girl before I met her. It seemed Stella was a popular subject of conversation—discussed in outraged, exasperated tones. She was a bitch, she was dodgy, she was up to all sorts of tricks. 'Did you see what she did the other night?' was the usual hissed beginning when her name came up. To my ears, she sounded like some of the women I'd known at Cherie's, and I thought I could probably handle her.

'You're new,' said a soft voice one night towards the end of my first week. I turned. 'I'm Stella,' said the young woman next to me at the make-up counter. She had an aristocratic face, sharply defined, and a soft, compact body in a thin dress she was pulling tight with her hands. 'You're so pretty. I'm sure you'll do well here.' She smiled. Stella was a charmer.

But it didn't take long before I understood what the other ladies had been hissing about. She was a piece of work. Not the best-looking girl, she maintained an impressive roster of regular clients. Rumours flew about what she did to get them: she did oral without a condom; she wore no underwear and flashed the men in the privacy of the men's lounge; she gave them a quickie handjob in the intro; she offered anal sex for free. She bullied her regulars into staying with her; she was heard shrieking at one when he tried to book someone else. Clients related stories to us about the offers she'd made them. We noticed she always sat nearest the door, so she was first to 'accidentally' walk out to see the receptionist and find a

new man just strolling in. We overheard her whispering calumnies about the rest of us to the receptionist, to the clients.

'I was just doing an intro,' said Valentina, 'and I saw the guy looking at something over my shoulder, and I turn around and there's fucking Stella, standing by reception, writhing and rubbing her fucking tits! I can't take it, I'm going to stab her.'

'Last Christmas,' said Chloe, 'we had tinsel all over the place and she did that to me. I looked around and there she is, with a piece of tinsel, fucking *skipping*. And no undies. Of *course*, he went with her.'

'She doesn't shower after bookings. So she can run out and get another one straight away.'

'That's why she's always putting on more perfume.'

We all glared at each other. 'That slut.'

Stella was awful. But she could be so charming, and soft and disarmingly generous at times. Bringing in a magazine someone had mentioned wanting, offering food around. Giving kind advice which may or may not have served her own purposes. Her demeanour seemed calculated; there was something opaque in her calm, disdainful gaze. But I noticed, over the months, how much pleasure the rest of us took from hating her; how alight with outrage we became in our endless complaining sessions; how, when Stella finally left, another girl was fixed upon as the pariah. To me Stella seemed very alone; she told implausible stories about her life, her parents and their careers, her child and her husband. She must have felt our loathing, and yet she fronted up every shift with all the self-possession in the world. She damaged me, trying to set me against my friends, stealing my regulars, sabotaging my confidence with casual remarks, but even so I had an almost-admiring fascination for Stella.

*

At Mood Indigo I kept the drugs and the boarding house quiet, though no doubt people guessed. After a couple of months Asia told me, 'We all thought you were a junkie when you started. Lola said, "She's got black bruises under her eyes." Then we saw you come in one night without your make-up on and put black eyeliner under your eyes!'

'I *am* a heroin addict,' I said, but she already knew that by then. So we laughed.

I had to be careful what I revealed about myself, because it was clear that junkies were despised and mistrusted, and so I listened to the vitriol against them, and gave noncommittal smiles, and invented vague stories about the 'hotel' I lived in and the 'debt' I was working to pay off.

Everyone told lies to the outside world about what they did. Receptionist, croupier at the casino, night-cleaner, data-entry. I didn't care what the outside world thought; I was happy, even, to brag. It was part of defiance. But inside the house, that's where I had to deceive.

Humour was the currency of the lounge. I heard myself making hearty jokes, inventing nicknames for the other women I liked, catching the strands of deprecating wit and scorn and flinging them back with a twist.

'If you pull your g-string straps higher, it makes your legs look longer,' suggested Monique.

'Shows off the stretch-marks nicely,' said Heidi.

'As if I have stretch-marks! I've got *texture*. My men *lick* them.' I pouted. 'I should charge extra. *And* I can talk for bloody hours about medieval art. The perfect woman.'

'Lucy, you bloody wish.'

'I know. But I do get my men to sleep through the bookings once I get talking.'

It wasn't so much constructing a personality, for me, as extrapolating one. It was as if we all enlarged ourselves; not quite different from who we were in real life, but exaggerated. A halo of personality to shield our too-accessible flesh. All my humour, all my impudence, my candour, and especially the sexuality I'd muffled in my younger days, I now wore proudly—self-consciously at first, as I developed Lucy's character, and then more comfortably. Lucy was me, but more so. It was a surprise to find myself confident, once I had territory to be confident in; raunchy, once I felt that raunchiness wasn't embarrassing; witty, once there was an arena for wit. I marvelled at how I could adjust my character; from gauche to coy, from ingenuous to dominating. Never ceasing to be myself, but shifting aspects as the face of the person across the room changed from hour to hour.

I realised my figure, too, was changing. I'd always hated my body and shrouded it in over-sized clothes. Now I drew gazes towards my breasts, my curved waist, my legs. For the first time in my life I began to consider my body something to glory in. I stood taller. And when I bought a new dress, it was tight.

IT WAS A NEW AND enthralling experience to keep myself looking lovely all the time. I would rush in every evening from the street, bare-faced and barely woken, and for ten minutes sit there constructing Lucy. Enhanced, composed and reconstituted, I was ready to go out and conquer a man. It was new to shave my legs every single night—dashing into an unused bedroom for a shower, since the bathroom at the boardinghouse was filthy and cold—to pamper my skin with moisturisers. Having seven or eight showers a night with the antiseptic soap in the rooms made my skin very soft but dry; the girls' room was always full of women smoothing creams onto their legs. I watched the others: how they applied their make-up, how they styled their hair. My eyebrows were plucked thinner. I began to grow my hair long. I bought more cosmetics, I experimented with glittery shades. My locker filled with sprays and bottles;

at the start of the shift each one of us would stake out her own place on the counter beneath the fluorescent mirror, like a surgeon's tray. We'd come out smeared and rumpled from each booking, but be presentable to the next intro, perhaps only a minute later. There was a ritualistic pleasure in sleeking ourselves back to elegance, in applying our lacquered masks. And at the end of the night, we scraped our masks off, removed our costumes and walked out.

Nicole said, 'My little girl is amazing. Six years old, and she said the other night, "Mummy, do you keep lipstick in your purse?" I don't. But then she said, "So why is it so fresh when you get home in the morning?" Isn't that creepy? So observant. You've all got to remind me: take my bloody lipstick off when I leave!'

We showered at the end of every booking, but with make-up on our faces, it was more difficult to wash them. By the end of shift our faces were stiff with soaked-in cosmetics and the accumulated kisses and sweat of every client. At first I would scrub my face at the end of the shift. Then I just got used to the muck.

The make-up, the dresses, were our tools. They made us feel beautiful, powerful, glorious. But they were a means; in the end the men would strip the clothes off, smear our make-up, mess our hair. It was what was underneath they wanted.

Most men were after a good shag and a taste of glamour, but there were heartening surprises in their choice of lady. Young men adored Lola's maturity; older men valued women who made good, intelligent conversation. Strutting bucks took shy girls and were tender to them. One of the sexiest women I ever saw was Velvet: short, curvaceous and not pretty, she had such a vibrancy, as she floated around with feather boas and sleek stockings, such confidence in herself, that she was irresistible. Blondes, more conventionally beautiful, might be left on the shelf in favour of a

155

scrawny, timid brunette. I loved that—the signs that men were more sophisticated in their attitudes than conventional wisdom suggested.

Part of me considered myself one of the less likely contenders. I was good looking enough, but not ideal. I was only just getting the hang of grooming. I didn't have the most wonderful arse. I cut my legs shaving. My hair was never quite right. And I talked too much.

Everyone noted that I was educated; most of these women, however savvy and sharp, had no tertiary education. It made me self-conscious, but I was proud, too. And so I started to make something of this attribute, rather than camouflaging it. Why not gain attention with something different? It turned out that what was merely 'different' to me was outright weird to some. But not unpopular. And so I became known as much for my eccentric conversation as my sexual attractiveness.

I talked about anything that interested me. I'd learned to rattle on in the cars back in St Kilda: now I could make good sexy chat, or sympathise with a man's job stress, or commiserate on how difficult girlfriends were to find. I could discuss quantum theory and the decline of the Roman empire. I talked about physiology and neurochemistry, about weightlifting, and the perfect packed lunch. I talked, and giggled, and found that I could charm these men with more than just my breasts.

It didn't take long to attract some regulars. Every house has its 'house regs', even if they're loyal to more than one establishment. Some attach themselves to one girl, sometimes for years; others are frequent visitors who will take a different girl each time, but become friends, of a sort, with all. They'd loiter at the front desk, chatting up the receptionist and watching other clients come and go. They were idle men, for whom this place was a kind of club.

The atmosphere could be convivial, or intimidating; at first there was something odd about walking a new client to a booking past a man with whom I'd had sex an hour before, and who snickered knowingly as I collected my condoms from the basket on the desk. But I quickly forgot how peculiar this was.

There were strange men among the Mood Indigo regs. Dirk was a short, stout, leathery man who always wore dirty shorts and desert boots; he'd come in, plonk himself on the couch and wheeze for intros. His face was whiskery and he reeked of alcohol. A session with him was a chore, but he'd book one girl, then another, then another, for an hour each, and he'd do this a few times a week. Where he got his money from, we never knew. He looked and behaved like a bum. But a working girl knows when to look after a good thing. We humoured his coarse manners with coyness, and learned how to deflect his rough kisses.

Another hapless man we saw was Simon, a milkbar owner. It seemed he didn't have anything to do after hours but patronise brothels. Nora had known him for years. He'd sit in the lounge in a lugubrious silence, even after his bookings, just watching us walk past with his long sad greyhound face. He liked to have his anus rubbed; he'd lie, face down, at the start of a booking for the massage; then, slowly, in a tectonic looming, his buttocks would rise until I was face to face with his arsehole. He wouldn't see my sneer of amusement and distaste, the bored yawns as I rubbed and poked. There was no sexiness in him, no joy. It was all about his arse. This was what he did to relax. It was what I did for money.

And Sam, like a house mascot, always appeared early on a Sunday morning, when we were easing towards the end of a hectic shift, and he'd peek at the receptionist's bookings sheet and choose an hour with whichever girl hadn't had a good night. One underdog to another. He was an awkward-looking man, sturdy and ungainly with a plain face and glasses and repetitive conversation; he loved the haven of brothels. A booking with him at the end of a shift was a gift, for the easy money; he very rarely wanted sex of any kind, and insisted instead on giving the lady a long massage. The price we paid was in the soporific effect of his talk and the discomfort of his clumsy idea of a massage. But he could at least be counted on for a pity booking and, with each one of us occasionally needing that, we tried to keep our mockery sotto voce.

Everyone had bad nights. No matter how gorgeous, or popular, or fine you were, there was a perverse cycle of failure. It almost seemed guaranteed that, the more you needed money that night, the worse you'd do: as if the men could sniff the need in you. Maybe they could. All we knew is that the more desperately you tried to get booked, the less likely it was to succeed. The only thing was to be philosophical about it and stop trying; but this was nearly impossible, with the spectacle of failure before the other girls, the humiliation of clients watching when you were refused. Some women needed at least to make their taxi fare home; leaving without a single booking seemed inconceivable, but it happened.

For me, this sense of pressure was incessant; I *had* to make enough for Robbie and me to score. Perhaps a different dress would work; re-do your hair; more make-up. Change your spiel, promise special extras, lower your price on fantasies, look extra deep into a man's eyes in the intro lounge. As the night went on and it would become apparent to all that you were having a bad one, people would make less conversation with you—not, perhaps, from disdain but from pity, and that was almost worse.

It seemed that these moments were the essence of degradation, but I found courage in myself, a resilience. It took strength to persevere with the intros, sitting there with the other girls, and still joke about it, keep the desperation down. Sometimes I was driven to tears, but I held them back; tears would only make me ugly. You learned to go into a room with someone who had just bought your arse for a pittance and vow not to be ashamed, not to let him get to you, to see him off with a bright smile, and walk into the girls' lounge with a blank face.

Then, maybe, a regular might come in and save you; he'd get extra special attention, the temptation of a fantasy ('Have you ever wanted to try Greek? Lots of men like that'), a lingering goodbye at the door. I soon understood that regulars were not only good for company; they were bread and butter.

Other nights you could do no wrong. Perhaps it was the monthly cycle of hormones and pheromones; perhaps it was the strut you got coming off three bookings in a row; sometimes I strode out there and knew I couldn't lose. Everyone wanted me; they queued up and waited. Serendipity would bring in several regs within hours. My hair would get messier and my make-up more smudged as I rushed from one booking to the next, a kind of glory in me. And all the time, totting up the money. Nights like that were rare and blessed.

Some house regulars would ask the receptionist to recommend a girl they might attach themselves to for a while. This was a tricky business; the receptionists weren't meant to play favourites. But they knew which girls were good, and for what. You would be asked to do a particular intro and, if the client liked you, then you would be set. Some men would come in every week, and stay an hour, or several. I must have been doing something right, because whether I realised it or not, I was steered to the company of several regulars who picked me up.

159

There was sometimes a price to pay for this devotion. A very small, fervent man called John discovered me on Nora's recommendation. Once I was in the room he'd step straight from the shower and press himself up against my clothed body. 'I've been thinking about you all day,' he'd murmur, soaking my dress with his skin and his penis. He'd kiss me, clumsily, his moustache wet against my lips. Then he'd drag me to the bed, tear off my dress—I heard the stitches straining—and penetrate me, barely giving me time to scrabble for a condom. Once finished his frantic thrusting, he wouldn't withdraw but, still lying over me, his face a few inches from mine, he'd declare his passionate love for me.

I would demur, recognising that some kind of reality check was required. His eyes, so close, wouldn't quite meet mine. There was a fine line between encouraging the paid fantasy that we were lovers, and abetting a delusion. It took months, but finally my patience broke. 'We're not really in love,' I said to his utterings about being bound by our souls. 'I'm a working girl, John. You're *paying* me.'

A blink. 'You're so afraid to love,' he crooned. 'Don't be so afraid.'

The receptionist told me she'd known him for years. 'He does this all the time. You must be about the twentieth girl he's fallen for. He does this till each one ends up telling him to fuck off.'

'Poor man,' I said, and I meant it, but I refused to see him anymore. A week later I overheard him saying a seductive goodbye to Nicole. And despite all my complaining, I felt a little hurt.

Of course, most of the clients were there to enjoy themselves. They knew the score, they didn't pretend I wasn't being paid. One of my favourite regulars was a short, jaunty man called Stu, who always came in loudly joking with a friend. The two of them would flirt with the receptionist, call out to us in our lounge down the hall

160

and, when I was summoned, greet me with shouts of appreciation. Stu was rich, funny, and charming; he was always promising to take me to posh events to meet celebrities and planning what kind of gown he'd buy me; I'd smile, and tell him he was full of shit. He'd grin, and go back to rhapsodising about my beauty. There was lots of fun to be had with guys like Stu.

When I got home every night, Robbie would be waiting up for me; if Plum couldn't pick me up from work Robbie and I would go out to sit in the freezing pre-dawn air and wait for him to arrive at the boarding house. Across the road a huge park was silent in spectral streetlights. Once Plum had arrived and departed in his dirty Corolla the two of us would fix up, and sit around talking.

It was awkward, adjusting from the cheerfulness of work to the silence of our little bleak room. I would sometimes relate stories from work, but Robbie would either be silent in response, or outraged at how I'd been treated by some client. He obviously didn't like to hear about my experiences with other men. But there wasn't much else to talk about, except gossip about the girls. And that made him feel lonely. While I was at work, he had long, empty nights with no money to go out, no friends. He'd read, or write; walk around the streets; wait for me. Sometimes we were hungry, and we'd walk to an all-night café to buy breakfast, and return home in the thin dawn light.

We didn't often make love. He didn't want to press me, after a night of sex with other men. But when we did, it was still making love. It was almost completely different. My learned tricks fell away; we looked in each other's faces; I forgot I was a prostitute. It was as if I could turn all that away.

But I'd have to sleep through the day, and when I woke up in the afternoons there was only time to score and get ready to go. Robbie complained that I was always too tired to spend time with him. And I began noticing that money would go missing from where I hid it in the room. I asked him where it had gone; he denied knowing it was there. Or claimed that he'd scored twice, didn't I remember? And he had no money of his own.

'Can't you get a job?' I asked, exasperated.

'No one will employ me because of my bad teeth—I'm going to do a trade course—I applied for a job in a factory but I didn't get it—I have to take care of things, you're always at work—It's not easy for me—I love you.'

He did get work from time to time, odd jobs, but sooner or later it would peter out. I let it go. I was making enough money for both of us, most of the time. He ran errands, he scored for us while I was asleep, he had plans to prepare. He was thin and listless and I knew he felt bad that I was doing all the work; I knew he had no confidence. I was finding enough for both of us.

I rang my family every couple of weeks, to say hello. I'd told them I had moved across town, and given them the address and number, but I deflected them from visiting my dingy den. Relations between us had eased, as time went on and I was evidently surviving. Now that I was settled in a proper job, I told my mother.

'I just wanted to let you know, I'm working in a—' I stopped. It was a hard word to say. 'I'm working somewhere safe now. Somewhere inside.'

I heard my mother pause as she took this on. 'You're working there?'

'Every night. It's much better.' *Than the street.* 'There are lovely girls here.' I listened to her soft breathing. 'I don't want you to worry, okay?'

162

'I'm glad,' she said. I could hear her smile. 'That's good news, darling.'

'Lucy, why do you work so much?' Nora said to me. 'You'd do better if you weren't here every night.'

The thought of dropping a shift was tempting but scary. It would be a gamble; what if the clients didn't follow me one night to the next, what if I couldn't make enough to keep Robbie and me from being sick? But I'd been working seven nights a week for so long; I was dazed with the routine of it, and desperate for a moment to myself. So after I'd been there three months I dropped, first to thirteen nights a fortnight, and then, after a while, to six nights a week. It worked: my regulars adjusted and others, who'd taken my steady presence for granted, noticed my absence and seemed more keen. I made the same money by making myself less available. I was moving closer to the organised hauteur of the true professional.

I was, to my surprise, almost happy. It was as if I'd found a kind of life. Almost all of it was spent in artificial light.

It was a small, snug world at Mood Indigo. Within the green walls, sealed off from the outside, we walked in our gowns as easily as if they were streetwear. Raised three inches in our heels, we adjusted to the elevation without noticing.

It was not strange to call someone by a made-up name. It wasn't strange to find condom packets scattered over a table in between takeaway containers and gossip magazines, or a girl absentmindedly chewing a condom like gum. It wasn't strange to have sex with seven or eight men in one night. It wasn't strange to walk back into the lounge clutching your groin and wearing a man's sweat on your face. It wasn't strange, anymore, to walk out into the absolute quiet of 4 a.m. with a cheery 'Bye!' and a pocketful of money.

The women who worked at Mood Indigo were professional prostitutes, and this was a job. It was an extraordinary job; every night we transformed ourselves into princesses and wore out the soles of our shoes in an endless dance between the lounge and the bedrooms. It wasn't, of course, only our soles that grew worn. But we glimmered in the light, proud in our gowns and our flimsy scraps of lace, tall in our heels, and took men by their damp hands to lead them down the hall. Even when we stripped off our clothes and were naked, open to the touch of unfamiliar hands and mouths, we were still princesses. Of a kind.

Then we'd go home, in the last hours of darkness or the stillness of dawn, and sleep all day, as ones enchanted.

Time went by, night after night, month after month. I barely noticed. Every day the familiar: I worked, I worried, I succeeded—or didn't—in making enough money. My manner relaxed; I was liked, I was asked for, I was greeted with smiles from the women when I walked in the door at 7 p.m. The shift, of eight, or nine, or twelve hours, would go by in its blocks of time: an hour, or two, in a room; another hour, or two, of waiting and meeting men and flipping magazine pages. Back into the rooms. At the end of the night I'd be left with stiffened skin and a wad of money, a numb or burning vagina and the din of a night's conversations in my head.

Asleep all day, I missed family celebrations, parties with my friends. Life out there seemed the dream, not this.

People came and went. Women arrived, stayed a few nights, a few weeks, months. Some I got to know; others I glimpsed only at the change of shift when the day girls left to go home to dinner and the night ladies arrived: a bustle at the lockers, people calling out farewells and greetings; the receptionist, harried, doing the paper-work at her desk; women yanking dresses over their heads with their faces turned to the wall.

165

Briony, a sober young woman I barely knew, left and Odile started, a pixie-like sophisticate with a shaved head, a collection of wigs and a gamine smile. Monique vanished and Melanie started. Asia appeared and disappeared, penalised by suspension for mysterious acts of rebellion (talking back to management). Lola sat in state on her nights. Stella kept up her tricks and insinuations. Alexia completed her security training and dropped a shift. Valentina added a shift, trying to save enough for the house she wanted. Nicole's husband started beating her up and stealing money for his gambling habit. There was a fad of girls trying colonic irrigation after one of the receptionists came to work glowing. The magazines in the lounge changed covers; the soap opera we watched at 2 a.m. remained the same.

We called ourselves 'girls'. The receptionists called us 'girls'. But to the clients, the 'gentlemen', we were 'ladies'.

The girls were my social life, my friends, my audience; a strange little community, brimming with intimacy, blocked with secrets. I would walk into the lounge every time to friendly faces and cheery greetings, or suddenly hushed conversations, or the shrill sound of an ongoing gossip. I would take my place, accepted, liked, never quite sure of what to trust.

'So here we are again,' I said cheerily to Odile at the make-up counter.

'For our sins,' muttered Valentina, smearing eyeshadow.

Valentina was a pal; her dry humour was a tonic. I liked her gruff common sense. I watched her apply the emerald eyeshadow to her lids and admired the exquisite length of her golden limbs. She did well, of course, but she had bad nights like everyone else.

Lola implacably rolled cigarettes for hour after hour and held forth on humanity. Nicole offered me spare slices of pizza from the enormous slabs she somehow fitted into her emaciated frame. Her pupils were always huge, and her talk was of her kids and her husband.

Other girls circulated; Sarah became a kind of mate, a tall, rather frightening red-haired girl with eloquent dark brows who also used heroin. We surreptitiously shared the drugs thing; she even came home with me a couple of times to score. She was witty, a little awkward, a little misunderstood, but we all knew that her temper was ferocious and the breadth of her shoulders made me want to charm her.

Then I lent her money and she couldn't pay me back. What I myself had done to my friends in earlier days now enraged me. I shamed her by asking loudly for the money in front of the others. Turning her red face to the mirror she said she'd do what she could. When I came back from my booking the money was tucked under my make-up bag and Sarah had left early. We didn't speak of it again. Shortly afterwards she was 'purged' from the house for allegedly letting a syringe drop out of her bag in front of Bea, the receptionist. I was sorry to see her go. But when I saw her in the street months later I did nothing to hush Robbie's loud sniping as she strode past, her face set. The righteousness of the flawed is frightening.

There were strange characters to whom I grew accustomed. Cynthia was a volatile Italian girl who insisted on a different wig every shift in the belief that it disguised her from a legion of supposed stalkers; she was unreliable in attendance, dressed in sequinned bras, and talked incessantly about her teenage daughter's sex life. Working with Cynthia was tiring.

Shayla was a day girl who occasionally took night shifts. She was loud and blowsy, with a hoarse voice and an appalling Irish accent she put on for the customers; the day-shift equivalent to Stella. She wasn't above lingering for an hour or two into the evening, just long enough to poach some of the early clientele and then leave, her underwear carelessly draped over the back of a chair, the stink of her cheap perfume hanging in the air.

When someone like Carmen, who had helped me on my first night, left, I was sad. But a month later she was just an dim memory. There were always new girls.

One I liked especially, after I'd been there almost a year and poor Asia was long gone, was a black-haired, pink-cheeked girl called Siobhan. She had the same deadpan humour as one of my old friends, and I liked her immediately. We seemed to have a rapport, a similar background. She was beautiful and tough and made the slow week nights go more briskly.

It was easy to become entwined in the sticky threads of complicity. Easy to love a hissed, whispered, gleeful conversation. Alliances were made and fractured. A girl I was pally with for months might inveigle one of my regulars away—that wasn't a crime, but the gloating was.

'Guess Shane got tired of you.'

I shrugged. The last time I'd seen Shane, he'd proclaimed his love. Melanie turned her face to the mirror in triumph. I looked at her with loathing.

Small lies were told; small misinformations circulated. The feeling in the room was of a band of comrades, alternately beset and amused; the laughter was loud, the kindness frequent, the competition tacit and fierce. We were a group of women who found ways to be together, but the ways were not always clear.

Slowly I built up my regulars, my profile. New clients came in to ask for me, recommended by their mates. This seemed odd to me, that a man would tell his mate about a hooker he'd slept with, pass her on. But I knew that prostitutes were a regular, prosaic part of many men's lives. In Melbourne alone there were nearly a hundred licensed brothels, never mind the illegal joints, the strip clubs, the private workers, the street girls, the phone sex lines and the escort agencies. Thousands of women working, and who-knew-how-many times that many men visiting them.

Secret to the workaday world, there was a culture that admitted paid sex as a legitimate pastime. A night out with the mates. On a quiet Monday night they'd come in, when they'd spent all their money and doing the rounds of the brothels was free entertainment. Not to stay, of course; just to meet women, be flattered and wooed, catch a glimpse of flesh, be on their way.

So long as some stayed, we endured it. To go out and offer your sex, your service, your company to a man and be refused—not just once, but again and again, night after night—was something you just had to get used to. You couldn't afford to take it personally, even though it was so entirely personal.

Most men were pragmatic, able to recognise the limitations of our time together, and make the most of what they got. And this made for a happy ease. Sometimes I was late out of a booking because I had been enjoying myself. No matter how often the receptionist or manager chided me, still there were times when I hadn't the heart to interrupt a conversation, or a man gasping towards climax when the buzzer went. Sometimes I saw my clients to the door with genuine laughter and a special last glance.

The men who selected me seemed to be among the better ones; I attracted jovial, sensitive men. Without always having to force a pretence of affection, I could actually find affection. For my regulars, with whom I built more and more of a relationship—

169

keeping up with their news, sharing my own woes, learning their bodies—but also for one-offs—the shy young men, or awkward middle-aged ones. I began to love the tenderness of their skin, the anxieties they confessed, the humility of their needs. I took them to the room as a priest might take a penitent; I laid a calm hand on their shoulders and undressed them gently.

At times I was disconcerted by the aggression of sex: a friendly man's face distorted by the ferocity of pleasure; the greedy ruthlessness of sexual momentum. It could still frighten me, beneath everything. People became strangers, and I could do nothing but cling to arms and ribs and hips as the face above me darkened with blood and I understood that I could only rush up to meet this force, or be battered by it. It was easier to mock the fervour of lust than to admit its fearful power. And I reminded myself that I was the one sought; it was I who was in control. These men, I thought, were diminished by their need.

There were men who cloaked their nervousness in disdain, and men who hid their disdain with charm. I enjoyed the game of guessing what each man would be like, and being confounded so often.

Some were awful at sex—it never stopped amazing me how many men were so inept, so intimidated by women's bodies. They truly had no idea of what to do. Or they were awkward in conversation: bewildered or contemptuous at the idea of talking as well as fucking. But I came to see, more and more clearly, how every man, however unprepossessing, might bear a kind of grace; a sweet body under drab clothes; a sense of humour behind a stolid face; a readiness to admit uncertainty beyond their bravado.

'You're too good to be here,' they still murmured to me. Just as they had in the cars of St Kilda.

170

'So are you,' I'd say, but I'd take their hands and kiss their mouths to make sure they'd keep coming back.

In the rooms I encountered men to laugh with and men to play sexy with; men to confess secrets to; men to giggle and roll around with. Men who made me grit my teeth, or set to dreaming the hour away while they ploughed at me. Men who flushed me full of anger and offence. Men who made me warm with the joy of real human contact, an unexpected kindness, a sincere compliment. They were all different, and yet I came to see that they were all, at base, somewhat the same. Nakedness is nakedness. We all wanted comfort.

My old fascination for the deliciousness of skin and flesh was fully indulged here. I caressed beautiful velvety youths, others plump as seals—every texture and silkiness. Clever fingers touched me more deftly than I'd ever been touched; different sized penises sparked sensations inside me.

My own previous lovers had all been beautiful to me, and with James and Robbie I enjoyed not only passion but the intoxication of love and sex meeting. Here it was just sex, and that in itself was suffused with another kind of intoxication. Sex, fierce, free and unabashed, could be good. Sex, in this world, was my power. I had left the bashful virgin far behind and surged into discovery. What I discovered was that nothing was as I expected. There were men I could barely stand to look at, whose bodies made mine blush with joy. If the connections were right, I might feel something extraordinary.

There was so much bad sex, too. Men who'd grope and pluck at me, who had no rhythm, who scraped at my clitoris with their nails and pinched my nipples, yanked me too abruptly into a new position, who thrust on and on for half an hour heedless of my

171

fatigue and dripped sweat into my gasping mouth. Who grabbed me cruelly, who fucked me like a whore. These were the testing times, when I felt my soul clench; when it was a matter of pride that I didn't protest or throw the man off me. To me it still seemed a professional discipline to resist pain and discomfort. The man had paid for sex; it was up to me to deliver it.

Control: I learned then how much I had. Control, not to squeal when a man grabbed my breast hard enough to make it twinge. Control to keep my legs stretched in the air even when they were trembling. Control to brace against pounding from behind, as my face mashed into the pillow and my arms shuddered and my spine jarred with every thrust. Control, not to gag at a slimy tongue in my mouth, burrowing wetly into my ear, licking at my throat.

Control not to twitch when a fingernail suddenly dug into my anus, when a cock scraped into my vagina against burning skin and I felt my face go pale with pain. Not to laugh when a man grunted, 'You're the best, you're the best, I've never met anyone like you,' and then screwed up his face and howled with orgasm and barely looked me in the eye a minute later. Control to stay polite, to stay charming, to go on feeding compliments, to not spit out my contempt.

Control to be the best working girl I could be.

I really tried to keep my temper. Sometimes I knew that it was just me, and the constant stress of working to pay my habit, the relentless circuit of men, the secret nugget of anger in my heart.

'You can give me my massage now,' said a truculent forty-something man with heavy eyebrows and a pear-shaped body, after he'd finished with a grunt and pulled out of me. 'All over. Feet too.'

I glared at his hairy back. Straddling his buttocks I reached for the talcum powder. The powder clotted in the furze on his back as I shook it out, more and more. From the crease between his buttocks, where it dampened immediately, up his spine and over his shoulderblades. I kept going. And up the back of his neck. All over his dark hair. The powder fell lightly, undetectable. I rubbed his back, the friction of the hair making my fingertips numb, kneaded his callused feet, watched as he showered and dressed in his business suit, put his wedding ring back on. Said goodbye at the door, and smiled as he walked out, oblivious to the back of his head still blotched with white.

It was professional, of course, not to leave any traces on a client, in case they were married. Some girls wore sparkly body creams, or heavy perfumes; I didn't want anyone coming back complaining of glitter flecks in their pubes. I used perfume, but I warned my clients to have a good shower at the end of the booking; if they ignored my advice, that was their problem. The talcum powder man was an aberration.

Some men deserved to be treated kindly, and that was a point, too. Another man came in and confessed self-consciously as he undressed that he had most of his sex in brothels. 'I'm kind of big,' he said.

'How big?' I was smiling.

'Well. My last girlfriend cried when I fucked her.' He dropped his underpants to his ankles.

His penis was as thick as my forearm, and he wasn't even hard yet. I lay there stroking his thigh and listening to his woes. His girlfriends kept leaving him. He was reduced to going to prostitutes, and then he'd found that courteously warning the girls in the intro meant that he was usually declined. I'd heard of other men like this—Valentina returning to the lounge with watering eyes, pointing at a coffee mug: 'It was *that thick!*'—but it wasn't common.

'I can only try,' I said.

'I know. I don't want to hurt you,' he said, and kissed me slowly and drew me up onto him.

It hurt. It was big. I imagined it was like having a baby in reverse. I breathed, and concentrated; I sent breath billowing down through me to my vaginal muscles, trying not to think of pelvic dislocation. Under me, the guy's face was red with arousal and the effort not to thrust. I beamed at him as sweat broke out on my face. 'Slowly does it,' I said. I gingerly moved up and down; only a few slow, tight pumps, and he came.

'Will you treat me special?' a young man in the intro lounge asked for the fifth time.

'You know I will. I'll treat you like a prince,' I said for the third.

He was fastidious in his pride, smirking. 'I don't want to be just another client, you know,' he said. In fact he was my sixth job of the night.

In the room he jabbed his penis into me as hard as he could, but I barely felt it. He was writhing on top of me, groaning and sweating; I gasped and clenched against him, simulating some kind of crisis. I didn't have the energy to fake a full orgasm, but I wanted him to come. 'Oh yeah, baby, baby,' he hissed into my ear, wet breath on my skin. When he'd finished he took his time showering and dressing. I waited by the door, already dressed, the room fixed, my arms full of towels, ready to go. The buzzer went a second time. I could hear the thunk of footsteps passing out in the hall. It was a busy night.

'Mate, I love this song!' he said, still naked, grinding to the Ricky Martin track on the stereo. 'All the girls tell me I'm like Ricky!' He wiggled at me. 'Hey—'

174

'*Yes?*' I hefted the towels ostentatiously, put my hand on the door handle.

'My cock. Tell me honestly. I want the honest truth. Is it—you know, is it—would you say it's big? Is it big? —Or—?' He held it in his hand and grinned at me.

'Honestly?' I said. 'It's kind of small.' He stopped dancing and pulled his clothes on.

Amazingly, he came back to see me again. I wondered if he'd even remembered me. But the next time he made a point of screwing me for a good forty minutes straight.

'This one is so unbelievably ugly,' said Chloe, coming back into the girls' lounge from an intro. There were raised eyebrows. 'I don't mind ugly, but he looks like a fucking toad.'

'That's too bad, Chloe,' said Nora, walking in. 'He's booked you for an hour.'

We were allowed to refuse a booking, but only with good reason. If a girl knew a client in real life, or had heard reports of him being trouble, or if he refused to be checked for diseases, she could decline. Appearance wasn't a good enough reason; and, in any case, it was a question of money. When I had a truly appalling specimen, I tried to think past the exterior, and he had to be pretty astoundingly ugly for me to notice. Hairy backs could be furry and comforting. A plain face could hide a kind heart and clever tongue. A pimply face might need affection. I kissed bald spots, acne-flecked cheeks, ignored dirty fingernails and blotchy patches of moles. It was all flesh.

I had to remember that irritating men weren't, for the most part, malicious. They were just fools, or anxious about having sex with a woman so experienced. Insecure about their bodies, trapped by an idea of what a brothel-going man should be like. I knew all too well what stupid and fearful behaviour felt like from the inside; I knew what frailty might make a person do. I wanted to gentle these men, as I might have like to be gentled myself.

Nevertheless, my little nugget of rage slowly accreted new layers. I felt it harden, shiny in its varnish, a lode of energy for me to rub when I needed it. I was almost always cheerful, polite, agreeable; even when I was sick, sweating, exhausted with hanging out for drugs or simply worn out.

'You're always so happy,' a man said to me.

I looked at him. It was six o'clock on a Sunday morning and I hadn't had a taste for fifteen hours. The shift had started at seven and I'd done nine bookings. My body was feeble, my skin clammy, my eyes burning dry. Allowing someone to touch me was a test of nerves already shrieking. I'd be going home to heroin soon, home to my dank boarding-house cell, to my difficult boyfriend, to a day of sleeping and then rising again to return here. 'Am I?'

'That's why I come to you,' he said, shyly. 'You make everything seem all right.'

I did smile at that, though it almost hurt.

MY FEARS WERE EMOTIONAL, not physical. The only thing I really feared was losing the last of my friends' and family's love, being finally given up on. That was a piercing horror, the thought that there was always still more to lose. And, for now, I had come to a strange peace with my family. I saw them only once a month or so, but I knew they were there, still thinking of me, and that we were perhaps past the worst. Nothing could match the pain of those old days of deception and desperation.

Working itself was not frightening; not to match that. Perhaps it was the drugs; perhaps the secret conviction of my own inviolability, a kind of magic shield around me; but even on the street I hadn't felt anything sharp enough to be called fear. Only the terrible drag of reluctance, horror at the bleak streets and the enormous task ahead of me every night, and a cold, cold terror at what might become of me if I couldn't keep going. It wasn't as if there hadn't been plenty to be afraid of, but I had walked through those black streets tight-wrapped in my determination.

Now that I was in a safe house, fear seemed even further from me. I was nervous, at times, or apprehensive: going in to intro for a raucous group of abusive young men, or being booked by a coarse man reputed to be trouble. But that was dread, not fear. Again and again I simply did what I was told, or had to do, and managed the situation, and came out surprised and stronger. When frightening things had happened to me, I simply seemed to shut down and wait for it all to pass away.

I knew sometimes girls got really hurt; Heidi came out of a booking white-faced one night, after a client had abruptly rammed himself into her anus. She bled for two hours and then went home. Another girl reported having her hair ripped out by a man whose fervour turned into fury.

There was an incident about a month after I started working at Mood Indigo. One morning when I and most of the other women had already left, a man attacked a girl in a room; when she ran out shrieking for the receptionist, he and his friend began to drag the receptionist by the hair up to a room. The only other girl in the building had to race out into the street in a dressing-gown to call the police while her client cowered in his room. I wondered what I'd do if someone assaulted me. There were panic buttons in each room, but they were over by the door, and in any case we had no security guard, only the receptionist. I assumed I would simply handle any situation if it came up.

I learned the importance of asserting myself one quiet Tuesday night.

Two men came in. They were dark and taciturn. There were no

other clients in the house. We intro'd, and the big one chose me. His friend waited in the lounge.

The man's cock was large, and I was studiedly coy. 'You'll have to go gentle with me. That's a lot to handle.'

'You can take it,' he said, and turned around just as I was going to start the massage. He flipped me on my front, squirmed on top of me and jammed himself in.

It hurt, but I tried to angle my pelvis upwards to control the depth of penetration. I was accustomed to men playing a little rough and careless. He put a hand on the small of my back and shoved me back down, then yanked my hips up into place. He fucked me for ten minutes, gradually getting more and more forceful, his thrusts sending percussive blows of shock and pain up through my stomach muscles. On my front, on my back. Then he yanked me up into doggy position again. There was nothing I could do in this position to avoid the full effect of every thrust. Furtively, I edged my fingers in a grip around his cock at my entrance, to make a buffer; the man swatted my hand away. He could hear the breath grunting out of me, feel the tension in my body; he pushed in faster, more ruthlessly.

'I want to fuck your arse,' he said.

'I don't think so.' Already I was feeling the thin edge of panic. This was more than I wanted to handle. *Be clever*, I thought. *Control the situation*. 'In fact it's starting to hurt. How about if I get on top for a while?'

'I want to fuck you. And I want to fuck your arse.'

Paralysis came over me. I didn't reply. He kept pounding, and I kept crouching there, concentrating on relaxing my muscles, waiting, hoping it would be over soon. Moment after moment of me not saying anything, not doing anything, just waiting. He'd

179

booked for an hour; it had been fifteen minutes. Already my body was protesting; the delicate skin inside me abraded. I thought, *I have to stop this*, but I couldn't make myself say it. I just bore down, and waited.

He asked me again for anal sex. *I'm already hurting anyway*, I thought in my daze. *Maybe I can take more. At least I'll get money.*

'It's—it's a hundred and fifty bucks,' I said, raising the usual price. 'And if I can't take it, you don't get your money back, okay? You're really fucking big.'

He stopped, got off me, fetched his wallet, all the time watching me with a smile. A credit card. I took it, and left the room to put the card through, grateful to get out of there. Nora was at the desk.

'Listen, this guy's really rough,' I said. 'I might have to stop the booking. He's a bastard. So if I stop it, don't give him his money back. It'll be his fault. I'm just going to try to hang on.'

Back in the room. The man was lying there, massive, still breathing heavily. I told him he had to go very gentle because arses are delicate, and lubed up generously. I hoped he'd let me sit on top of him, so I could control the penetration.

He had me back in doggy in a second. His cock pushed in.

It was only just inside me, but already I knew I couldn't take it. The pain was incredible; not just in my arse itself, but searing up through all my guts. Goosebumps broke out all over my skin. When I released my breath I was panting shallowly.

'*Stop*,' I said, but he kept going. Further in, then out, then in again. I could feel deep, heavy pain in my abdomen. He went faster and deeper. I pushed my face into the pillow. Back into a haze of paralysis and a confused notion of pride to be retained. Tears in my eyes. I only lasted another long minute; then I wrenched myself out of his grip and faced him.

'You're hurting me! I told you I might not be able to do it.'

180

He grinned at me.

'That's it. I'm stopping the booking. You can get dressed and leave.' I grabbed my dress and shoes and strode out to shower in another room. My anus and vagina were burning, I was bleeding a little; I stayed under the hot water a while, mumbling my rage to myself. The man's gloating was unbearable. I had a vision of myself, alone in the room, crushed under him, tiny beneath his weight.

When I got out he and his mate had left. Nora looked at me, shamefaced.

'I gave them all the money back. They—'

I couldn't believe it. That fucker had just injured and humiliated me and taken all his money and I was left here with nothing. There was no way I could do Greek again for days, so I'd lose more money. And he'd just walked out.

'They were really scary, Lucy. His little friend—he just sat there the whole time you were in the room. Smiling at me in this awful horrible way. I thought they might have had a knife.'

There was nothing I could do. I should have stopped the booking earlier; I shouldn't have taken the money for a service I couldn't do. But the anger sealed another layer around the nugget inside me, and I decided I'd never let myself get hurt like that again.

A couple of weeks later I was booked by a loud, fat man. His face was bristly with whiskers, his fingers thick and aggressive. As I bent over his bulk to suck his little penis, again and again I felt a rough thumb scrape over my anus and poke into me hard. The first time, I said, 'Don't do that, sweetheart!'

The second time, 'I really don't like that. Please don't. I mean it.'

The third time I bit his cock.

The fourth time I straightened and bent low over his face as it peered up at me. 'If you do that again,' I dug my nails viciously into

181

the fat of his testicles, 'I will hurt you.' I squeezed. 'I am completely serious,' I said. '*I'll hurt you.*'

His features were all distorted by lying on his back. He blinked.

'Right? Okay, back we go.'

The rest of the booking was silent. I saw him out with a smile.

For all the faint tensions between us, the girls were a wonderful source of comfort during an arduous night. In our lounge the men were *them*. *They* were always wanting more than they deserved. *They* were idiots, or holy fools, or dopes, or simply gross. *They* were the target of our barbs, our amusement.

It was easier to tell horror stories than convey a pleasant experience. What could you say about a good one? He was nice, he was sweet, he had lovely soft velvety balls. He brought me lines of cocaine, he felt good inside me, his hands were delicious, he had a really proper shower before the sex. He made me laugh. He made me feel beautiful. He made my night.

The good ones were my secret.

We would sit around the lounge on quiet shifts, telling stories all night. Everyone had a worse tale: the one who drunkenly pissed all over the bed; the one whose hair implants were like the bristles on a toilet brush; the one who fell asleep and farted. The one who said, when asked to have a shower, 'But you're joking, right, love?' The one who spent twenty minutes in the shower and then complained when there was only five minutes left for sex.

The one who had to have crusts picked off his cock, it was so filthy under his designer underwear.

Terrible stories, about other brothels and evil managers who slept with the girls and passed around diseases; about gangsters who were rumoured to own brothels; about bitch receptionists who blew clients behind the counter. Ghost stories about cold rooms in which a girl had overdosed and which always smelt of her perfume and echoed with the sound of her heels.

Funny stories, about big men with tiny dildoes disappearing inside their arses ('I tried to hang on, but it just slipped out of my fingers!'), about men with penises as big as the tip of a little finger ('I poked and pried but he was just all foreskin, there was no dick!'). Haemorrhoids, bad breath, blackheads. Wheedling men droning on about fantasies they wouldn't pay for, rich men skipping out on promised payments. The old man who took out his false teeth with a grin and promised to give oral sex like no one else. Another tiny old man who lugged in a sports bag and took out a boxer's headgear and gloves and told tall Sarah that before she died his wife and he had liked a bit of boxing. ('I stood there, hesitating, you know, because I didn't want to hurt him. Then he whacked me in the jaw! And I just *swung* at him, and got him right in the side of the head—he came right there! I didn't even touch him!')

We shared tales of intimacy and mockery. A room full of women all competing, all sharing common experience. We could say 'my cunt' to each other with perfect nonchalance. The stink of sex on another woman was not offensive; to see each other naked was not shocking. To hear another woman describe her experience with one of your regulars, or the man you'd just had sex with, held little emotional tug. We were like mechanics, discussing cars. And to know you were not alone, to understand that the worst thing that happened to you was not the worst, that you were part of a giant community—however secret—of women labouring and discovering and laughing, was to recall the struggles and endurance and humour of women through all times.

The stories were a kind of folklore reeled out, told in the dark

183

quiet hours, with our hands busy painting nails and rolling cigarettes. Some tales didn't really belong to the teller, but had been borrowed and embroidered, spun around from brothel to brothel until even I could no longer always remember if it was I who'd seen the pot plant thrown across the lobby by a naked man, or if I'd only had it described to me so often it seemed real.

Some women genuinely hated their clients. I thought that if that were the case, they should get out of the business. Even on the street, working purely for the money, I had rarely actually hated my mugs. But rage was perhaps sweeter than bitterness.

I wanted to moderate my anger. I didn't want to go that way. Still, we all learned to pick 'types'. The geeks, the blokes, the kinky ones, the homeboys, the working men. For the first time in my life I heard overt racism bandied around. 'Another currymuncher,' someone would say, coming back from an intro. 'God, it's one of those stinky Indians.'

'Actually,' I'd say primly, 'I think he's a Sikh, from Sri Lanka. It's part of his religion to wash several times a day.'

'Huh. Whatever.'

I enjoyed the variety. An Egyptian Copt told me about his faith. A West African man talked about his time as a resistance fighter. A Singaporean youth explained that he was here only because the university in Singapore had fifty times too many applicants. A Chinese student refused to tell me anything about politics at home. It was like a crash course in foreign relations.

If there was any one group I dreaded, it was the Irish. I am from an Irish-Scottish background. It wasn't their Irishness that I hated, but the fact that every single man with that accent came in rolling drunk. We tried to put most of the drawling Irishmen onto Shayla who we thought, with her feigned Irish accent, deserved the consequences.

184

'I couldn't understand a feckin' word that girl was saying,' confessed one man, fumbling at my underwear. Then he fucked me, and fell asleep within seconds. He was huge, bovine and comatose. I struggled to heave him off me, but it was no good. I lay there for twenty minutes under him, until the sound of the buzzer droning on finally made him raise his groggy head. His mate was in another room with Siobhan; it took three of us to drag him across the floor into the shower and wake him up. The Irish were nice, but trouble, and big enough to be a worry.

Most men put aside any religious convictions they had the moment they walked in the door of a brothel, but some retained a doctrine. I heard one girl relate that a Muslim client had made her perform a brief and mysterious 'marriage' ceremony at the start of an hour booking, then ritually 'divorced' her at the end of it. Another reported that an Orthodox Jew had booked her, only to spend the booking railing against her for being a prostitute—'I just *looked* at him, you know?'—and leave in a rage. Christian clients occasionally fingered the cross around their necks and muttered about redemption as they lay sprawled on a plush bed with a naked woman tidying the dirty tissues. I didn't know enough about most of these religions to guess if they permitted the visiting of prostitutes, but I suspected not. In any case, it was none of my business to gauge the severity of the sin. I was not, I felt, the one committing it.

The other least favoured group of customers—and it seemed strange to me, when there were genuinely loathsome gangs of sullen youths, or drunken businessmen, or dirty-nailed tradesmen—were those with disabilities. Occasionally someone would wheel in through the door in a chair. The receptionist would come and ask us specially if we were prepared to intro. I always did, because I needed the money and I wasn't fussed if someone had wonky legs.

185

It could be more demanding, because usually the man needed help dressing and undressing and showering, and it took extra time. And a man with a disability is not guaranteed to be any more pleasant than one without; I was sworn at for putting socks on backwards, for accidentally pinching someone's leg. A young man with cerebral palsy drooled on my face. I had a client with terrible burns which were coarse under my fingers when I massaged him, but the sensation was no weirder than someone else's hairy shoulders. It was an arrogant vanity on my part, to conceive of myself as a carer or some tender angel, but I did like feeling that I'd given some human warmth to people whose chances of sexual affection were slim. What they thought, I didn't know.

It was getting easier, altogether, to indulge in the conceit that I was a merciful bestower of human kindness on the wretched. It was partly vanity. But the more I worked and saw kind souls bereft of affection, miserable men who'd mumble 'I'm just no good with girls', and saw their appreciation, their gratitude for being treated sweetly by someone who stroked their face and remembered their woes, the more I saw all of us prostitutes as a kind of social service. Nurse, therapist, counsellor, big sister, temporary friend. It felt good to make people happy.

I HAD BEEN AT MOOD Indigo for eight months. The more I saw of the meek, the bored, the frustrated, the more I glimpsed how our society worked. Shut inside the brothel all night and asleep all day, I forgot that the world was full of ordinary, happy couples too. I only saw the men, alone.

There was a client called Antonio. Black hair, green eyes, a sweet boyish face slightly pockmarked; he booked me every few weeks and we built up a friendly banter. He would make love to me with his eyes open, gazing at me adoringly. One night he pulled a slender ring off his finger and said, 'I want you to have this.'

'I can't take it,' I said, surprised, pleased. It was a little gold ring with some tiny emeralds, a girl's ring.

'It was my ex-fiancée's,' he said. 'Please. Take it.'

I wore it, amongst my others; too big for me, it slid around my knuckle and there was a time when I thought I might pawn it, but I didn't. Then I came in earlier in the afternoon one day, and Antonio was there, waiting for another girl. Stricken and red-faced, he told me to keep the ring, but he never booked me again.

At the back of my mind was the emerging thought that I was following in the tradition of the great courtesans of history: the sacred prostitutes of Corinth, the intellectual hetaeras of Athens; the *grande-dame* mistresses of the Belle Epoque. Women who were prized for conversation, talent, style and substance as well as sexual gifts. However little I resembled an established woman of fame and fortune, the ideal comforted me. I could talk, I could be a companion; I wasn't just a whore. I studied my sexual arts, practising different techniques and personae. I wanted to be praised for my character as well as my body.

And on the first day of the new year I met Douglas, and sensed an immediate rapport. He was a big, warm, silver-haired fellow, with a cherubic smile and a witty turn of phrase; we discovered that we both loved history and literature, and our booking was spent talking, spinning from one topic to another. He was companionably married, but he liked to spend time with prostitutes. It was his stress relief.

'And then there's the whole thing with Paris in the twenties.' We were engrossed in a discussion of literary heroes. It seemed not at all odd to be talking in the middle of a brothel, in the spa, with the dimmed sound of people passing in the corridor outside. The stereo was playing Eminem. 'Henry Miller,' he went on, 'traipsing around Paris, getting all his friends to cook dinner for him.'

'Anaïs, riding her bicycle to fuck her psychiatrist in the morning. And then to make Henry lunch! Writing her diary next to her husband in bed.' I grinned. 'She was a naughty girl.' I remembered dressing like Anaïs years earlier. At least now I had the lingerie to match the fantasy.

'You look a bit like her.'

Douglas held me against his large pale belly and we snuggled in. I made an effort to fulfil my professional obligations, but he didn't seem to notice my caresses, and I happily ceased. He extended the booking for another hour of chat and I knew I'd gained a fan.

The second time I saw him I asked if we could turn off the porn movie playing on the television so I could watch a documentary about Alexander the Great; and Douglas let me, while he paid a lot of money to watch it with me. This was a test, and an impudent one; but he merely watched, amused, as I enjoyed a moment reminiscent of my old life. And he came back, every week or so. We would hug, and have perfunctory sex, and I'd lie against him and we'd talk. He had worked all over the world in humanitarian aid; he was forgiving of human weakness; when he appeared I always felt glad. His embrace was huge and warm.

Some men lay down obediently, predictably, for the routine of massage-oral-sex, as prosaically as if they were at the physiotherapist. *On top to kiss. Suck him. Here he comes to fuck me. Change position. There, and we're done.* Others preferred to model the experience as if it were a real seduction; as I entered the room to start the booking after their shower, they'd slide up behind me, wrap me in an embrace, kiss me slowly. 'Can I undress you?' they'd murmur, and I'd be coquettish, languid in their arms. It was sometimes ludicrous, sometimes erotic, this step out of reality into passion, however contrived it was. It could make the experience feel all new, or it was a tiresome burden, to pretend 'genuine' pleasure, having to act one layer beyond actual ostentatious faking, as if they were really, *really* making me happy. A booking when a man would say, *Now tell me*

189

what you really like was a tiring one. But sometimes we both ended the booking happy.

It was always a tricky question whether, or how much, to enact pleasure. There was a twinge of conscientiousness in me; if I let bad lovers believe they were good, then how would they ever learn? They'd just go off and tweak and pinch and scrape other women. I didn't believe that most men wanted to be bad lovers. There was also the matter of perfecting the fake orgasm. I heard the yowling of other girls in their rooms, caterwauling that would convince only a truly ignorant man. I imagined trying it on with a client and having him gaze at me aghast or incredulous. My nerve failed; I simply didn't think I could do that. And I liked the idea of being honest with my men. There was, however, male vanity to be assuaged and the fantasy of amazing sex to be maintained.

The last point to weigh was that a little judicious writhing could be effective in hastening a climax. Grace notes. I learned to simulate exactly the tinier signs of arousal: a mouth carelessly open, a pelvis twitching up as if unconsciously; fingers curling, eyelids tightening, brow flickering, a head twisted rapturously to one side. Nothing too ostentatious; let them believe I was a quiet one, that I was the more sincere. I learned to do this so well that I wasn't even aware of it. It seemed that the less respect I had for a man, the more comfortably I'd resign myself to faking.

There was a site on the internet where people could post news and reviews of brothels and working ladies. I didn't have access to a computer. But one day Nora told me she'd seen my name, and handed me a printout. *Lucy gave me an excellent service,* the anonymous reviewer said. *She didn't have an orgasm, but she very kindly explained to me that she'd had a lovely time and she'd rather be honest with me, and I appreciated that. I recommend her highly.* That made my night.

A young man—rough, rolling drunk; straight, he said, from the bush up north—staggered in late one night.

'I want you to teach me how to please a lay-dee,' he proclaimed, stripping off, then reeled towards the shower and hit the glass pane with a painful bang. His manner made me smile; he was like a wide-eyed innocent, and I felt like a learned old pro. Once he'd showered, I started to massage his back, while he wriggled uncomfortably. He had looked a little shocked at the abrupt nakedness when I'd briskly whipped my dress over my head.

'Girls are different from boys, we're much more complicated,' I began. 'It's really important not to scratch at a girl. A clitoris is very sensitive—'

He jerked up, appalled. 'A *what?*'

'A clitoris.' I was amused. Sliding over, I opened my legs to show him.

'Fuck.' He looked aghast. 'You're fucking joking.'

Before I could stop him he'd yanked on his clothes, slung his boots over his shoulder and pelted out the door.

I looked at my watch. A ten-minute booking. It didn't matter to me; I still got paid for the half hour.

'Did you know the female clitoris can extend nine centimetres inside the body?' I told a young stockbroker. 'That's bigger than some penises!'

He looked at me blankly.

'Don't you think that's interesting?'

'I guess.' He kept sucking my breast. I sighed and held his head.

There was chemistry between some people; I was a great kisser with some men, clumsy with others. I met young men with little experience who made love like angels, lyrical sex, deft and fluid. A kind, thoughtful, humorous person was more likely to touch with

191

sensitivity, to enter with tenderness; their mouth might be soft on my skin, their fingers sweet. They were real people, not so concerned with cutting an impressive figure, or admiring their own 'conquest'. Very often, the less good looking a man, the better the lover. With handsome men there was often the sense that they relied on their looks to charm. Not always, and there were the happy occasions when I'd go to bed with a man who was both beautiful and exciting. But it was the gentle, fat men, the scarred men, the ones who were quiet or wry or simply ordinary who gently, quietly, handled my flesh and took their pleasure from mine, and gave it back too.

Of course, I wasn't there for sexual pleasure. I was there to service the men; to open my legs; to be good company. It would be disingenuous to pretend, however, that having sex several times a night I didn't notice if it was good.

'You look happy,' Valentina said when I came back into the lounge after an encounter with a peach-skinned, blond French boy.

'There are times,' I said, sinking on a chair as my legs trembled, 'when I can't believe I get paid for this.'

'And there are the times when if you weren't making this kind of money you'd run screaming,' she said, and turned the page of her magazine.

By then I supposed I'd had sex with hundreds of men. Or thousands. I couldn't begin to conceive of how many, or that it was a fact. Never again would I be able to enumerate my lovers, as I'd once done. There was a kind of pride in that, as well.

It wasn't what I had expected, but I was learning new pleasures for myself. Sometimes a client would enter me and I was rinsed with the joy of it; especially when the heroin was running out of my system and my nerves were sensitised, it was as if a veil of water was running through me and the sensations inside me were full of rippling and buckling delight. Small compensation for the sweating and the fever I had to hide, but it was something new.

Many women didn't like to orgasm with clients, even if they could. It was a private thing, they felt. I agreed with them, and for a long time I resisted any chance to pursue climax; but then, as the opportunities appeared and pleasure seemed more possible, I welcomed the rush of it, the pay-off. The release was also physically helpful, after having sex for hours. But I remained selective; it was still private.

In my bookings I learned and tried positions: back-to-front on top of a man, squatting, wheelbarrowed, scissored, standing and touching my toes…Freed from my natural sexual reticence by the mask of Lucy, pushed by my professional responsibilities, I could play the raunchy babe, the reckless sex-kitten, the sultry temptress. I could thrash around on top of a man and pump hard. I nearly fell off the bed in shock the first time my wearied gyrations on top of a tired man made me come from a vaginal orgasm. And the time a man who dedicated himself to giving oral sex tongued me intently for an hour, I came shrieking, from the tension and the surprise and the sheer relief of finally breaking through a mental barrier of embarrassment. If it was his pleasure to give me pleasure, I needn't feel guilty or selfish; I was discovering that my body held secrets.

The 'fantasies' were interesting, too. Marcel was a lean black man who'd turn up at the very end of a Friday shift, when it was already light outside, after a night's clubbing. He was a slave to a large woman in the bondage scene; he'd come in with his dog collar still fixed around his elegant throat and peel off his leather pants to reveal no underwear, but a shiny silver cock-ring around the base of his slender, erect penis and shaved balls. His knowing smile seduced me; he'd murmur domination talk, pushing me back on the bed with a hint of force, ask me to talk dirty; bite my throat just lightly enough to avoid marks. He'd bring in a gleaming silver dildo and press it into me while I squirmed, as if swooning; tie my hands with a silk scarf to the bed-head and take me from behind, crooning obscenities. It was a game, it was fun. And I was gratified that of all the glamorous women available on that night, he chose me. Perhaps he recognised something in me I had never seen.

But talking dirty usually confounded me. I simply didn't have the imagination for it; all the phrases I could come up with were trite. Marcel prompted me with genuinely sexy thoughts. *You're a lot naughtier than you look, you're a little fox, see how lovely you are with your pink cunt; come on, bite me back,* was one thing. With other men, hissing *I want you to fuck me hard, yeah I like it really hard, I'm a slut, you're so hard* felt wrong, and I resisted.

Dress-up requests amused me, but they rarely worked well. After spending ten minutes digging out the nurse's uniform, rummaging for stay-up stockings and pinning my hair into a severe bun, I'd enter the room to find the client looking sheepish. 'Let me take your temperature, you poor thing,' I'd coo, spreading his legs, but the men hardly knew how to enter into the spirit of the thing. We charged even more to 'act the part' as well as wear the costume, but invariably the client would ask me to just take the damn thing off and get on with the action.

A man asked me if I could do a domination act, no bondage, only talking. I admitted I'd never tried it, but I was prepared to have a go. He'd never done it before either. He booked for an hour, but after twenty minutes of *Lie down, that's it, crawl to me. Slower. Lick my ankle, lick my thigh, but don't you dare touch my pussy* I was desperate for inspiration. He looked as if he felt equally foolish scrambling around on the carpet. We went on for another quarter of an hour and then admitted defeat and just fucked. I was attracted to the idea of being a dominatrix—they charged a great deal, didn't have sex, and it was a fascinating job psychologically—but I could see there was more to it than I could provide.

Dildos were one of the easiest fantasies, and often I didn't even charge extra for them. The little purple anal vibrator that Asia gave me was used until its battery connection failed; some men already knew the joys of prostate stimulation, but most were introduced to it by us girls, desperate to jostle the tired routine of a 'vanilla' booking. A knuckle against the perineum to hasten orgasm; a well-timed, condom-covered fingertip reaching around a backside to slip in. It was a delight to watch men experience the extra frisson for the first time.

I'd never seen porn movies before I started working, but I rapidly understood the idea and tired of them. I had a client called Mark who always insisted on watching one while we fucked. He'd have sex with me, but with his eyes glued to the screen. The pornos owned by the brothel were accompanied by droning synth tracks and featured a lot of headbands and bad tans and relentless grunting. There was something vaguely arousing about penetration shots and the sheer cumulative effect of watching people screwing for hour after hour, but I found them mostly misogynistic and trite and numbingly repetitive.

There was enough sex going on in the rooms.

'Will you do a bi with me?' asked Heidi. She knew I didn't usually do bisexual; I was happy enough in a twin, sharing the client with another girl, but I had always held out on even faking love with another woman. My reason was romantic; I had occasionally been attracted to women, and yet I'd never been to bed with one. I wasn't prepared to lose my 'girl virginity' as a vulgar spectacle. But I liked

Heidi; she always looked out for me. There was a little attraction between us, delicate, furtive, unspoken.

'We can fake it,' she reassured me. It was usual for women to slide a hand between their lips and the other woman's labia, and lustily lick the back of their own fingers, hiding it all with their long hair. Heidi was gay, but I guessed licking a colleague's vagina could be as disinterested as a client's penis was to a heterosexual girl. I just looked at her and smiled.

The man wasn't going to be easily fooled. He wriggled around to peer at us. 'Go on, you love her, you love the smell of pussy,' he was whispering hoarsely. Heidi winked over the man's meaty shoulder and I grinned. There I was, confronted up close with a vulva for the first time in my life. Everything seemed unreal, and yet so right. I glanced up; Heidi was still smiling at me, sending me calm.

Month by month, my vanity grew. I could help people; I could give them more tenderness than anyone; I had a mission. I cosseted my men, with soft kisses to their brows and an affectionate hand in theirs as I walked them out. They told me I was beautiful, special, the sexiest thing they'd ever seen. It was a heady experience to be so adored. Rank after rank of men coming in to compliment me, worship me, to pay for my time, my presence. How glorious I felt.

Some of the other women seemed to understand the glory. The ones who didn't talk about their clients; the ones with a sober dignity, whom I saw walking their men to the door with an arm around their waists, a quiet smiling word, a lingering kiss that wasn't like the dramatic clinch some less-trusted customers received. There was a mien of dedication about them, and I felt myself getting closer and closer to that stature.

Then I realised I had become one of them. It was rare for me to have a night without at least a couple of regulars. My body firmed up under night after night of physical work—holding myself up on my arms for hours of sex or 69-ing, pumping hips, working off calories—and with the new sleekness came more confidence to show off. I scrimped money out of what I needed for drugs and bought some dresses, or was given cast-offs from other girls: transparent shifts, tight lycra slips, a bold pink dress of chiffon. It was a new pleasure to wear fabric so tight, to strut around marvelling at my own elegant curves and planes. New lingerie, to push up my breasts; tiny lace g-strings to tease. As my confidence grew, my clothes grew bolder. Angie wore a see-through dress with no bra, to show off her breast-job, and one night I bought a dress like it. Underneath I had only a bra and g-string; I sauntered into the intros feeling radiant with daring. The men's gazes lingered; but after a couple of nights of poor bookings I realised that less was more. If I gave them a glimpse of everything before they'd even booked me, there was no mystery for them to pursue. Still, the night that I wore that dress I felt like I'd come a long way.

Mostly I wore black, or red; short and tight, and perhaps slightly transparent, but not so brazen. It felt wonderful, and slowly I equipped myself with finery. There was a woman named Dolores who came in occasionally with armfuls of dresses, cosmetics and trinkets to sell. I became a creature of glittery eyes, brilliant red lips and smooth velvet over which men would run their hands.

In the mirrors of the bedrooms I saw myself. Golden-skinned in the soft lighting, lithe and bucking against a faceless man. My own cleft, bent over, looking like some porn shot. My arms reaching up to twine around a man whose dark head bent to my breast.

My own wicked smile over his shoulder.

HOME WASN'T SO HAPPY. In the boarding house with Robbie, things were fraying. I was despondent at the routine of scoring, of scrimping money and chasing around for drugs, the dreariness of waking to the fading afternoon and the sound of schoolgirls walking home past my curtained window.

I'd caught myself, hitting up when Robbie was out, standing in the open door of our room. Already stoned but greedy for more, something to mark a sharp moment in the greasy slide of the day. Knowing that I'd already had enough, still faintly aware that this was a poisonous chemical that killed, that this might be the moment before I died and I'd never know. The drug would rinse through me, stronger and more blissful than I'd ever felt it; my last thought would be surprise and then terror and then the melt. I looked around the drab cream walls of the room, the peeling carpet, the harsh dense light from the lamp suspended above; I heard the people passing in the street outside the opaque window; I thought, quite soberly, *If I have it here, then when I fall I'll be visible from the hall. Someone passing might see me. Someone might save me.* And I'd wrap the old tie around my arm, and find the scarred place on my arm, and plunge the metal in.

Robbie was my companion and a loyal one; he was thin and worn, going nowhere, but he was my friend and my loving boy. Sometimes we lay in the park across the road from the boarding house and I'd hold his hand and we'd smile at each other, startled to find ourselves still a couple after everything. It had been more than a year.

His face was drawn with boredom and depression, his notebooks full of plans and dreams I had no intention of financing, and no heart to criticise. But he could still make me laugh.

Now I took a night off every week, as the season changed and the weather improved again, we could go out. I still slept all day, of course; but in the evening we'd score, and walk into town. Sometimes we'd see a movie or have a cheap meal somewhere. Robbie already spent many of his nights alone wandering town, but for me it was wonderful to see the streets full of people, the world going on. I had the sense of being part of it briefly. The shops were shut, of course. For years now I had walked past shops closed for the night.

It was always too late; too late in the day to do anything but rise and go to work; too late at night for more than reading in bed and sleep. Too late to find my old friends; too late to catch the shops open. Too late to make love, too late to score and make it to work on time; too late for doing anything but drift forwards.

I didn't always make enough money to score. If I had a bad night with few customers, it was a disaster. Waiting for Plum to arrive, wheedling and apologising and promising money tomorrow, when I hoped I'd have it but I wasn't really sure. Sometimes Plum said yes. Sometimes no.

No drugs. Clammy with withdrawal after my fruitless night at the brothel, I would keep pulling the thin sheet of sleep back over me as the hours went past. Dim daylight scorched through my eyelids. Even opening them was more than I could bear. The weird chemicals of withdrawal made my head spin; I had synaesthetic reveries, so tactile I could taste them, smell them over the rankness of my own skin. I'd whimper in confused fright, and hear Robbie next to me, grunting back, or turning roughly to settle again.

Who was I, how had this happened, how could it ever be right, how could I ever open my eyes again? Terror a thin mucus at the back of my throat.

Finally, I'd feel Robbie clamber out of bed; he'd dress, and disappear while I dozed again in my muck. Then he'd be back, hours later, murmuring *Hold out your arm*, and he'd sink the needle into me while I still lay there, my face crumpling with relief. The drug would spangle into me, miraculous; we'd smile at each other. Sweet blood sticky and stoned, running down the white flesh of my arm. Robbie had gone to the dole office and begged money out of them. Or he'd borrowed it from a mean thug down the hall, pawned something for a few dollars, or got credit from the dealer. The catastrophe averted once more. I would have to make twice as much the next night, but at least I would be able to go to work.

We used twice a day at least—once before I went to work and once afterwards, before we slept. It seemed a waste to sleep through the easy first hours following a taste, but if we didn't, we'd doze off in the engulfing drowsiness of withdrawal, and then wake weak and in need. We split 'halves', at over a hundred dollars each time. This

200

was enough to keep us going. But it meant that, with cigarettes and food, I needed to make good money every night. Heroin always soaked up everything. If we had the cash, we could use five or six hundred dollars' worth of drugs in a day. Every fortnight Robbie would get his dole payment, and that was one of my nights off. What was meant to last two weeks was gone in an hour. It was up to me to keep us going.

I thought from time to time that I should look after my own needs before I shared my meagre score with Robbie, but that seemed churlish. And I needed him. For companionship—he was the only person in the world who knew who I was now—for tenderness, and for an anchor. He could score, and that was important. But I resented the burden put on me to keep us going.

One night I came home, brittle and worn. He had made a mess in the room, dirty clothes everywhere; he'd smoked the last cigarette and there was ash all over the bedsheets.

'How was your night with all your rich boyfriends?' he asked, barely looking at me, staring at his book.

'I got fucked up the arse tonight,' I spat. 'Three times. Three times, and each time I got paid less for it. I gave the last one for free, just to get the booking.' I wanted him to hear. Tears were hot in my eyes. I looked at him in loathing.

'What do you want me to say?'

'Just—nothing. Just—' Oh God, I was so tired.

He rubbed my back, and then went out to meet Plum. 'I love you,' he said quietly as he uncapped a syringe.

'I just want this to stop.' I climbed into bed and turned to the wall.

We didn't have many belongings to pawn when we needed money. In my room at the boarding house there were only a few piles of clothes and assorted trinkets we'd collected. I toyed with the idea of selling the piano still at my parents', and dreamed of the sum it might fetch. But I could never quite resign myself to giving up the promise of playing it again. I had some cds, however, and my old bass guitar and amp; these two went in and out of the pawnshop for a pittance. Every time my bass was hauled over that counter and put in a back room I gazed after it mournfully. And one day we didn't have the money when it was due, and when we went back it was too late. I didn't lose many possessions from my habit, but I lost that, and it was like a grief.

With time off I had the chance to see my family again. Every second week I'd leave Robbie to himself yet again and go across town for dinner. It was beyond strange to walk back into my parents' house, the familiar smell and light and objects that now seemed so far away. And yet, for those hours, it all felt almost close. Now that I was working in a safe house, inside, stable, it was like a normal job; I had a place to live, with an address; I had a boyfriend, however unpopular, to keep an eye out for me. My parents were still going to their weekly support group for families of addicts and they looked at me with no less pain but more acceptance. They'd stopped wanting to interfere; they'd learned how dearly that cost. My sister, too, was quicker to hug me, less likely to hang back full of the mulish horror I'd seen in her before. We'd have dinner together and watch television, just as we always had. All around us the rooms full of books, the shelves of music. My room, stacked high with my belongings, at the end of the hall, the door closed. Sometimes I'd take a few things away with me: clothes, books, tapes. Mostly I just left it. The stale scent of that dusty room made me uneasy. It wasn't a smell that belonged in this warm house, with these loving people.

My mother would drive me back to the boarding house. We'd talk.

'Would you consider methadone?' she asked, nearly every time.

I'd shrug. 'It's not that great, I've heard,' I said. 'And it ruins your teeth.'

'Better bad teeth than dead,' she said, and that had to be admitted. But I pushed the possibility of death out of the space between my mother and me. I didn't want her to think of that.

It wasn't the drug, it was managing a habit that was the hard work. If the dealers didn't inflate the price with every step down the chain—if it didn't cost so much—if I had enough money—if there were enough money left over for a life—if the gear weren't cut with nasty powders that scraped my veins—if there were some way to make it *work*—

There were celebrities and professionals who had enormous habits and yet carried barely a crease on their skin to show it. They could afford their supply; they had good, clean stuff. That's what I wanted, I thought—not to have to give up the drug, which was so much a part of me, but to have it without the grinding slavery and sacrifice.

The numbness of my soul I dismissed.

It was too late to think of a simple detox. By now a detox would involve puking and diarrhoea for days, would involve massive disorientation and pain, perhaps hospital. I couldn't conceive of the torture my mind would go through. My parents had mooted the controversial Israeli program, in which an addict was sedated and pumped full of replacement sodium solutions, supposedly to awaken restored after a week in a Tel Aviv centre; but that seemed outlandish, not to mention expensive. I considered returning to rehab, but I simply couldn't face the idea of the detox.

So just before Christmas I decided, after four years of using, to try a methadone program. Robbie had been on the 'done sometime before he'd met me, and grizzled about it still. You were tied to a chemist visit every day, they fucked you around, if you missed a dose there was trouble, it was hell to get off, it was invented by the Nazis to control their soldiers and what did you expect, it was a sadistic government plot to register addicts and keep them controlled and on lists. I thought this was all quite probably true, but it couldn't be worse than having to score, and I was ready to muster some energy for helping myself. If it didn't work, then at least I could tell my mother I'd tried.

Robbie had no choice. If I wasn't going to buy his drugs, he had to follow me.

We registered at a clinic near St Kilda, in fact only a few doors down from my old dealer Jake's flat. There was a lot of paperwork, and a long wait in a room full of whining junkies with smelly clothes. I looked at them in distaste.

The doctor was calm and jaded, with a tweed pocket full of pill bottles and a messy desk. 'How long have you been using? How much? How often?'

I thought of doctors' examinations in my student days. *Have you ever had unprotected sex? Have you ever used intravenous drugs? Ever had anal sex? Ever had an abortion? Ever been tested for HIV or hepatitis C?* I'd put a long line of ticks against the 'No' column. 'I'm awfully boring,' I'd said cheerfully.

Now it was *Yes, yes, yes, yes, yes.* A different kind of smile.

Afterwards, we popped in to see Jake. But no one answered my knock, and I couldn't see the GI Joe on the windowsill when I looked up from the street. For a moment I feared Jake or Vicki had died. Then I remembered someone had said they'd got clean, gone up north. It was a long time since I'd visited St Kilda. Across the road was the flat I'd had with James, its balcony still shaded by the big plane tree. I didn't point it out to Robbie.

We found a chemist just around the corner from our boarding house. We had to be there every day before it closed at seven, to drink a small cup full of red cordial and bitter methadone solution. The dose was high to start with; over the following months it would be reduced steadily, by tinier and tinier amounts as the dosage got towards zero.

The methadone, a synthetic opiate, would hold us and alleviate the symptoms of withdrawal. The idea was that we wouldn't need real smack anymore; but of course our greed was no less. Whether or not our bodies actually craved the drug was almost irrelevant, once we had the luxury of thinking that way. The idea of a day— even half a day—without the solace of a needle was inconceivable. And we were terrified of the methadone letting us down. It didn't seem plausible that a couple of sips of sickly cordial could replace the chemical that crackled from a needle in a vein. So we started methadone, but kept using. Just a little less.

Now, with the promise of getting clean, or at least cleaner, I decided that I wanted a house again. I lay in my ash-stained bed in a waking afternoon daze and fantasised about a living room, about coming home from a shift and being able to make toast and watch television. My books close to me again: rows of books, on a real bookshelf, like a normal person. I wanted to ease a space away from Robbie too, and the money he was inexorably leaching from me. I wanted something of my own.

Now we were on methadone we didn't spend quite so much on heroin, and the difference showed. A little cash, stashed away, hidden from Robbie and the dealers and the other girls, money from fantasies, money from extras; my own money, it felt like. I scraped it together until I had five hundred dollars. I figured that if I had a high rent to meet, I'd economise and use less heroin. And then I looked at the ads in the paper.

Several weeks in a row, after a big Friday night shift and before a busy Saturday night, I got out of bed after only two or three hours' sleep and went to inspect houses to rent. It would have been hard enough, without a car, without a phone at home, dashing between houses that were each open only for twenty minutes. I was dazed with fatigue, my make-up still on, blinking in the light and trying to hide my pinned pupils from agents and owners. I trundled around to various dank cottages and luxurious apartments. I figured that I could share with someone. I warned Robbie that it wouldn't be him.

'It's not that I want to split up with you, but I need someone who can share the rent,' I said. 'I mean it.'

I was resolved to be stern, to ignore his pleas, my guilt at leaving him to his own devices. I felt love for him, but many other things as well.

'Sure,' he said, and yet he did nothing about finding a place to go.

I found mine. It was a renovated Victorian terrace in the next suburb, with hardwood floors, french windows off the bedroom, a little garden, an ironwork verandah, a spa bath, two bedrooms and a new kitchen. And white roses in the front garden. It was perfect, the most beautiful house I'd ever lived in; full of light and peace and room for books and lovely things. I got a reference as an 'entertainment co-ordinator' from Bea, paid my bond in cash, and moved in.

We'd been a year at the boarding house. I left our dingy room with a lingering backwards look. Robbie was hefting his bags of stuff, coming to stay for a little while. I was moving on again.

206

MY HOUSE WAS FURNISHED with my own belongings. I rented a van and moved my stuff out of my parents'; for the first time in my life I had my own house. I borrowed a table, I made a couch out of cushions, I brought along bookcases and put all my books on them. I rarely actually pulled them out to read.

The bedroom was decorated with vintage dresses from my university dress-ups days, and with perfume bottles and candles I bought from Dolores at work. It wasn't like my old rooms in share-houses; this was like the house of a grown woman. I loved spending money on it.

When Dolores came in now I was the first to browse, to set aside cushions, exotic drapes of gauzy embroidered material, elegant dresses, sharp streetwear, girly paste jewellery. With every purchase I felt I was restoring myself in the world.

It didn't take long for my landlady to discover my deception. The first month's rent, though achievable, was late, and when she turned up at my door and I let her in, she looked at me shrewdly. Her little boy, playing in the kitchen, opened the bottom drawer in which we kept our clean syringes; she kicked it shut quickly. I couldn't tell if she'd seen the contents.

'You're not an entertainment organiser,' she stated. I was sitting in my dressing-gown, without my contact lenses in, blinking and dishevelled; at a disadvantage, I let her press me.

'No.'

'I rang to check up on the business,' she said. She glared at me. 'Well.' There was a pause. 'So long as you can make the rent.'

The idea of having someone come to share the house never worked. I realised that I'd have to explain my hours; it would be hard to watch television with a stranger sleeping in the next room. I had no idea how someone would react to the news that I was a prostitute. And, of course, I was a drug addict. And my boyfriend was taking up the space.

He was melancholy, and full of dreams and plans that required more organisation than he was capable of at that time. It was too easy for him to keep extending his stay, his reliance on me and my income; and too easy for me to allow this to go on. I was alone in the world outside the brothel. Robbie was the boy I loved, and he was warm against me in the night; he scored when I needed to sleep; sometimes he brought me gifts—a scarf he'd found in the street, a t-shirt he'd bought, a small tube of chocolates. His sweetness was undiminished by his lack of finances, and the fact that he used my own money for these treats. I understood how much he wanted to be generous in turn.

We fought often; when I came home exhausted from a night's work to find the house uncleaned, him sitting sullenly on the couch, when he reproved me for not having enough time for him.

'I'm *working*,' I said. 'Working for us. I spend half my money on you! And you're meant to be moving out.'

'I just want you,' he said.

I began to calculate the money I spent on him, the hours I worked, the awful transaction that was taking place between us. He took money to score when I was at work, and when I challenged him, my face hot with outrage, he said only, 'It's because I'm miserable.' It was also because he was hopelessly addicted to heroin.

He had odd moments of paranoia, when he accused me of being in love with my clients, of blackening his name with gossip, when he lied to my face over small things and the more I pressed him to tell me the truth, the more vicious the insults he threw at me. I would end up staring at him, this mad stranger; underneath I could still see the man I loved, but he made it difficult to remember that.

More and more I was afraid of what might happen if I separated from him. I couldn't imagine leaving him altogether, he was so frail, so close to despair and defeat. And how alone I would be without him. He was there to talk to when I got home. In the pale dawn light I'd kiss the skin between his shoulder blades and wrap myself around him, and be wrapped in turn.

I still had some friends: Max, who had a steady girlfriend now with whom I got on well, David, and others, like Matilda, who had never told me I wasn't welcome, but whom I had no time to contact. Now I got my own phone. There was little time, between work and sleep, to ring anyone, and I was hesitant to approach old mates, but at least I didn't feel so isolated. I got an email address too, at an internet café. Occasionally I'd make it over to St Kilda, en route to the doctor's for a new methadone prescription, and I'd have a coffee with Max; he talked to me just as he always had, about books and cinema and the problems of love. I never saw any of the films, or read the books, but when he hugged me goodbye at the end of each visit, I clung back.

He knew what I was doing for money. 'I just hope you're okay, lass,' he said. 'Watch yourself.'

'I do,' I said. His neck was warm against my face. 'I do.' Then the tram arrived, and it was time to go home to get ready for work.

I'd started seeing Douglas, my client, outside of work. Not for bookings, but for lunch. He'd asked me after a few months if I wanted to come to a meal and, to my own surprise, I'd said yes. I went off in the bright sunshine one day to lunch at the Windsor Hotel, and we continued our chats about war and history and life's lessons. The two of us sitting at a stiff-linened table, him in his tweed jacket and cufflinks, and me in my tight girlish shirt. The waiter eyed us. We talked about the British in Afghanistan, and the descendants of Alexander the Great in India, about Oscar Wilde and Rabelais and *Fanny Hill*. He joked and made me laugh as I worked my way through the hierarchy of cutlery, trying not to look as though I didn't lunch in fine hotels all the time.

Douglas was warm and unjudgmental and seemed to see something in me beyond the articulate working girl. He knew I used; he knew I had a difficult boyfriend and a demanding job, and that it had been a long time since I'd been out to have fun. And so, every now and then, he organised something for us to do. A picnic, a movie. It was difficult to get out of bed early and go into the world with little sleep, but the outings were wonderful. The simplicity of sitting in a sunny park with good company, of driving out of

210

Melbourne into the hills, of talking with someone who seemed to value me in the way my old friends had. The sunlight made me blink, the colours made me happy.

I rang him once, and asked him to come see me at the brothel. It was the only time I had to spare, and I was desperate for comfort—it had been a difficult week, with Robbie crazed and jealous, the clients wheedling, the money short. I'd been seeing myself from the outside, struggling under the bodies of man after man; wondering what had happened to the dreaming girl in the library, with her Greek books and princess turrets. I had told Douglas my childhood dream of an island where I could sit under the geraniums in dense silence and the humming of crickets; my trite fantasy of worn marble and shelves of golden books. The hunger for it tore at me now.

He arrived, and I pressed myself into the warm wool of his jumper. 'I'm sorry,' I said. 'To make you come in here just to talk.'

He patted my head. In the room we lay together quietly. My belly was taut with unhappiness and the effort to not shatter.

'What's going on?' He stroked my forehead.

'It's my—' I stopped. 'I don't know where I've gone—where I've *gone.*' The world was cracking around me. I was so small. A flood of shame spilled from my eyes. 'I've lost myself—I'll never get out. Where's my island? Where's my island gone?'

He held me. It was dark and safe against his chest.

'I'll never find it.'

'You will.'

Nearly a year and a half since I'd begun at Mood Indigo, things at work were changing. Nora gave up running the place, although it seemed she'd still be around; Bea stepped up. With her bouffant hair and clucky manner, she was like a darling auntie, always on our side, always looking out for us. We looked forward to a new style.

Bea made an announcement one day. 'Staff meetings, they'll be held once a month and if you have any suggestions, let us know.'

'What about having one of us attend the meetings?' I asked. The other girls nodded.

'You, Lucy!'

Bea agreed, and so I became the girls' representative. It wasn't the kind of responsibility I'd ever looked for; I was more one to make quiet suggestions and let others do the shouting. I was, however, astute and articulate. I'd paid a lot of attention to the way the business worked; the issues of regulated prostitution interested me with their paradoxes and intricacies. At times I contemplated becoming a madam myself one day. I had a few ideas of how to create a truly high-quality brothel.

One of the things that made me uneasy in the profession was the lack of rights of working women. As far as we knew we were covered by no union apart from a loose, government-subsidised collective that advocated for prostitutes. Because everyone was anonymous, and paranoid about being 'outed', there was barely any possibility of mobilising for rights. Management could fire a lady on a moment's notice with no consequences. And we all knew there were dozens more women out there to take her place. We were all independent contractors, with no representation or organisation. This move of Bea's, at least, would give us some voice at Indigo.

I took my duty seriously, with a hot sense of justice that was new to me: I went to a staff meeting, gathered around a bed in one of the rooms with the receptionists and Bea, and wrote up my notes. Then I stuck them on the mirror for all the girls to see. This was a licensed brothel, with duties of care.

Our requests were small. We wanted a fire exit; we suggested that the coffee levy was in fact illegal; we wanted better security. 'That's something I'm working on,' said Bea.

Her changes were mild: the book where our periods were recorded—in case of faking—was updated; new bedsheets were bought; a security man was briefly hired before it was discovered that he'd been in jail for rape. Lola listened intently to all the conversations in the girls' lounge and was seen whispering to Bea; the atmosphere altered somewhat. Bea was much busier and brisker now; her tiny lips pursed quite readily.

Then she announced that she'd organised something big. A spokeswoman for an agency came to talk to us, an agency that managed working girls' affairs, providing a contact phone number, carefully phrased references for landlords and employers outside the industry, and a taxation system. We could—in fact, would—give them control of the books and our pay. Tax, the coffee levy, and a handling fee would be deducted, and a receipt given for the cash we then received.

There was discontent in the girls' lounge. Valentina was outraged. 'It's a scam,' she stated. 'The fees are illegal and I don't want my real name on any documents.'

Everyone muttered. 'And did you hear? The receptionists get a cut. And Bea gets a bigger cut.'

We were all astonished. Bea had more responsibilities now, but she knew us well, knew the difficulties of working, seemed concerned to give us the best environment she could. Surely there was a mistake; maybe the management hadn't considered the ramifications. Bea had always treated me as a favourite. I'd even confessed to her one miserable night that I needed to leave my shift briefly to score, and she had patted my knee gently, and never mentioned it again. She kissed me hello when I arrived and shared gossip about the other girls. Now she was working against us.

The agency was a definite; things were going to change no matter what we wanted. And the Goods and Services Tax was about to be introduced—even prostitutes gave a taxable service. Regulation would rule us. I had enough money troubles at that moment: my plan to use my house-budget to control my heroin use hadn't worked; my rent was late. My landlady was literally beating on my door and I needed to get to a dentist for expensive fillings. I absolutely couldn't afford this rip-off. But all we could do was protest, and I did so passionately.

The next Saturday was a bad night. Plum had been cutting our deals and we had had to buy twice as much just to stave off sickness; it had taken all my cash and a plea for credit. The taste I'd had was barely holding me. Stressed by the need for a big night's earnings, of course I couldn't get a booking to save myself. It was busy; all the other girls were in and out of the rooms while I sat at the table, going out again and again to meet the men, the only girl available, practically marked with 'loser' on my brow. If I couldn't make enough cash by Monday I might get evicted; I had to ring the landlady and put her off, and I dreaded making another begging call.

There was a new receptionist, Sophie, on that night, starting off and drowning under the deluge of clients. I heard her spiels and didn't like them; she wasn't trying hard enough to get me booked. I smoked alone at the table feeling more and more tense and desperate; changed my outfit, to red satin pants and a red halter-top.

Siobhan walked in.

'Are you fucking stealing my look?'

I glanced up; she was already dressed almost identically. I hadn't meant to copy her, but perhaps unconsciously I'd hoped to borrow some of her luck. She was my pal. Now she was glaring at me.

'You fucking bitch,' she said, and left the room for her next booking. I was nearly in tears; the night went on and on; all I wanted was to throw it all in and go home. One man after another looked me over and said no. Sophie took ages to do my books at dawn, though I'd only had two small bookings.

At the counter a house reg tried to snoop a look at my booking sheet as Sophie fiddled with it. I scowled at him. Sophie pushed it across for me to sign. 'So I've taken out the GST deduction, and the amount you owe for dinner.' I signed the form silently, walked off through the crowd of girls, went home to eke out one taste between me and Robbie and wait for the sickness to arrive. At least we had the methadone to see us through.

The next night I arrived for work to find Bea standing at the front counter without a smile. Nora, at the desk, threw me a warning grimace.

'Pack up your locker, Lucy, and come and talk to me in room five,' Bea said.

I felt myself go pale all over; jerk into dream-logic. Yes, I was at work, yes I was talking to Bea, and she was telling me to clear my locker. Something was wrong. It must be a misunderstanding. As I yanked dresses out of my locker and shoved them into a plastic rubbish bag my shock shivered into tears. The other girls watched. Then Siobhan and Heidi came over to help.

'I need eight hundred dollars, I have no idea what's—what's *happening*, what the fuck is *going on*? Did someone say something— what's Bea doing, how am I going to pay the rent—'

They shushed me and commiserated. 'It must be a mistake, you haven't done anything. You're one of the best girls here,' they said.

215

Lola rolled cigarettes at the table.

Bea was waiting straight-backed in the room. 'Sophie tells me that last night you refused to pay your GST or dinner money.'

I just stared.

'And when you got your money you walked away calling her a slut.'

The world jerked again; I opened my mouth. 'That's not true, I paid everything, and the other girls were there, they can tell you— I'd *never* call *anyone* a slut—'

'No arguments, Lucy. I'm very disappointed—*No arguments!* And I can't have you abusing my receptionists. You're suspended for a month. Call me after that and I'll see if there's room for you to come back.' Her face was a stranger's: tight and impassive.

I went on protesting, but she walked out. Nora gave me a look; I couldn't tell what she thought. And in a daze I walked through the front door, dragging my bag of clothes. I was too humiliated and shocked even to say goodbye.

I got home, less than an hour after I'd left. Robbie saw the expression on my face and leaped up to hug me. I started to cry. 'That *fucking bitch*—'

Robbie rocked me. 'What?' He kissed my hair.

'We're completely fucked,' I said.

There was no chance for reprieve; at one stroke I'd lost my job, my clients—what would they think had happened?—my friends—I'd never see Valentina again, or Nicole, or Melanie, and what would Bea tell them?— my income, my place. I had drugs to buy for the night and rent to pay. We already owed Plum, and two other dealers; they were holding my phone for credit. I had twenty dollars to my name.

LATER THAT NIGHT I GOT out the phone book. There were a couple of brothels close to where I lived; one I'd heard bad rumours about, the other I knew nothing about. I rang that one.

'You can come in for an interview right now, if you want,' said the woman on the phone. It was ten o'clock. I put on some tight pants, a nice shirt, some make-up to cover the signs of crying.

The house, called Il Fiore, was yet another renovated Victorian terrace, standing in an industrial area of warehouses and grassy lots. When I was buzzed in I caught glimpses of huge gilt-framed mirrors and overstuffed leather sofas in the lounge. The receptionist's counter was black marble.

I was still a little dazed from crying, but the woman who interviewed me was matter-of-fact and I answered her questions confidently enough. Yes, I'd worked before. My name was Lucy. I would work five nights a week if I could, yes, I did anal, yes, I had my own clothes; yes, I had a tattoo.

'It's just, some gentlemen don't like them, so we keep a list,' she said, peering at the rosebud on my shoulder. 'Of course, some of them don't know what they friggin' want,' she added. Her name was Bernadette and she looked like an aged film star. She wore a thick gold necklace. There was a lot of gold in this place.

'Start tomorrow?' she said, 'Then maybe you can meet Helen, the owner.' I agreed, and left. It was a hard night and day, with no earnings, but we made it. I rang the infuriated landlady and promised money soon. At least I wasn't without prospects.

The next night I took in a bag full of make-up and dresses and went to begin the new job. I'd thought I might still go back to Indigo in a month's time—at least for a couple of nights, to say goodbye— and tell my clients where to find me. But the idea of facing Bea again choked me with anger; I had no way of knowing what else she'd said about me. This place, I could tell, was actually a cut above Indigo, and I was glad of that; fuck them, I was moving on.

Bernadette showed me around. This building was two storeys: lounges and a couple of bedrooms below; a proper kitchen next to the girls' room, which had cable television and expensive couches; a tiny laundry and then, upstairs, the other four bedrooms. Each had enormous gilt mirrors, canopies draped at the head of each bed, fake-antique dressers and clothes-stands for gentlemen's jackets, and enormous spas and showers. The towels were new, the bedclothes rich, the carpet soft. Elegant lighting made the place glow in its champagne paint.

'This is Natasha,' said Bernadette, pointing at a very pretty blonde girl in a pink cocktail frock. 'Desiree'—a stunning black girl with long thin dreadlocks. 'Coral'—a tanned woman with short

218

blonde hair and a pale blue velvet gown; 'and Milla.' Milla waved a long elegant arm. The women all smiled coolly at me and went back to their magazines.

'It's a quiet one, Lucy,' said Bernadette, collapsing into her seat by the door to the foyer. 'Though to be honest, I'm glad of a break—last night they were coming in in *torrents*! Weren't they, Natasha? And oh, the heads on some of them!' She grimaced.

'It was 'orrible,' agreed Natasha. She had a pretty Russian accent.

'I don't care, so long as that bozo doesn't come back—the one that grabbed my *ass*—' said Desiree. She was American. This place was a bit more international than Indigo.

I sat there, smiling gormlessly, as a new person will. In the background the stereo played faintly.

These girls seemed pleasant, poised and well-groomed; they perched politely on the upholstery; in their expensive gowns, they seemed almost upholstered themselves. The television was on a cable channel: a Hollywood movie. Bernadette fetched a load of towels from the dryer that rumbled in the kitchen, and started folding them. 'Come on girls, don't just sit there. You know Helen said you had to help with the towels.'

I was shown how to fold each one precisely into a neat bundle, stack them with the folded edges all aligned, and stow them in the bedroom dressers. 'They have to look perfect for when the gentlemen are in here,' Bernadette announced when she took me to a bedroom to demonstrate. She twitched at an arrangement of folded towels at the end of the bed, adjusting one angle so the origami flower-shape was symmetrical. 'You spray with room freshener after every booking, there's disinfectant in the cupboard, you don't leave a stray hair in the shower. Helen likes the place to be kept nice.' There was something reverential in her tone.

My first booking, and the man was a familiar face. 'I didn't know you worked here as well,' said Mark, the porn-movie aficionado. 'I do now,' I said, and hoped he'd take the word back to Bea. I had to ask Bernadette to turn on the video so Mark could have his movie; this wasn't the kind of place where porn ran idly all day long. Over the concealed speakers came the ubiquitous Ricky Martin. Mark asked me to turn it off.

It took some doing to make sure the room was left spotless at the end of the booking; I was conscientious. I didn't think I'd get fired for not making my towel arrangement fancy enough, but I wanted to make a good impression. There was something pleasing in making everything just so.

It was strange to start at the bottom again; to sit docilely in the lounge while girls made jokes about clients I didn't know, about other girls I hadn't met, while my silence went unnoticed. As at Indigo, most of these girls had regulars, while I took my chance at the other visitors and racked up a few bookings. At the start of each I was given a tiny docket to record my booking; Bernadette handed me some condoms and noticed that my tumbler of orange juice for the client wasn't on a saucer.

'A saucer? For a glass?'

'Helen likes it like that.'

As usual, the buzzer went five minutes before the end of the booking; when I was a couple of minutes late, Bernadette chastised me.

'There's no clock in the room,' I said. 'I'm used to a clock.'

'You've got a watch, haven't you?'

'But it's more discreet to just look over at a clock, men don't like it when you look at your watch—'

220

'Just remember, it's Helen who makes the rules here.'

I felt very new again.

The men that night seemed nice, normal, even though there were the familiar Monday-night gaggles of youths sprawled incongruously in their nylon tracksuits on the splendour of the imitation Chesterfield. Bernadette gave them short shrift. 'Are you interested in seeing a lady? We have some lovely ladies on tonight. There's no one you liked? Well, we'll be seeing you,' she sang as she closed the door behind them. We could hear her through the door and watch her on the closed-circuit screen above the television.

'Mary, Mother of God,' she said, coming back in. 'Did you ever see such a bunch of sad-sacks? Give me strength.'

At the end of the night, she said, 'Now Helen will be in tomorrow when I start the shift, and I'll tell her you've done very well. We have a very particular philosophy here, as I'm sure you've seen—only quality ladies, and a very good clientele.' She pronounced 'ladies' with studied decorum. 'She's strict, but a wonderful owner,' Bernadette continued. 'You've done well, Lucy, and I'll see you tomorrow.'

I walked home; it was only ten minutes away, and the streets in this bleak warehouse zone were quiet at four in the morning. Robbie was waiting up.

'It's good. I think I'll stay,' I said. 'Ring Plum.'

'Now, Bernadette's probably told you I run a tight ship, but we're always glad of a new lady. Where were you working before?' Helen looked at me intently.

She was a small, middle-aged woman with a careful fine blonde coiffure. She shook my hand when I came into work the next night; she smiled tightly, and looked me straight in the eye. Her clothes

221

were expensively tailored in pale yellow; she had a little jewelled bracelet on one wrist. Her accent was pure country girl.

'Mood—' I began.

'Oh.' Helen fiddled with her bracelet. 'Well, you've been told the rules, and met some of the girls—'

'The place is gorgeous.'

She looked at me more warmly. 'I'm very proud of it. Now, any problems you have, Lucy, you just let me or Bernadette know. We want you to feel at home.'

In the ladies' lounge there were some new faces. A woman with a cute button face and a mass of curly yellow hair was tugging her generous breasts into a very tight halterneck dress. There seemed to be a lot of blondes here.

'I'm Jessie!' she said, and extracted a hand to wave at me.

'Nina,' said a dignified brunette on the couch, not waving.

Bernadette blasted though the door. 'Okay girls, now Lucy you'd better scoot upstairs to the powder room and get yourself fixed up. Don't be too long, chook. Is anyone going to order dinner? Towels dry?'

Already the place seemed familiar.

One of my first regulars at Il Fiore was Mohammed. He was charming and handsome: with velvety skin the colour of very milky coffee and thick pepper-and-salt hair, he resembled the young Omar Sharif.

'It's important to give a girl time to become aroused,' he said, stroking me gently. His plump mouth kissed my belly again and again; his fingers teased me. I laced my fingers lazily through his hair. As he pleasured me we talked—of his ex-wife, of his life in Australia, of what women liked in bed. His white-teethed smile was easy and his attitude relaxed. 'If I don't come, I don't come,' he said, curling around me. 'I visit here for the experience.' His body was soft as suede.

Wally was shy and almost silent. All he wanted was cuddles; which, when he'd inevitably arrive at 5 a.m. on a weekend night, was a blessedly humble request for a tired girl. He'd lie, full-length on top of me, with his sweet, bashful face pressed into the side of my neck, his weight warm and close upon me; an hour of quiet. That was all. 'Lucy?' he asked once, and I realised I'd fallen asleep.

Paul was furry and naughty and threw himself upon me like a beast; I squealed with giggles and threw my arms around him. He was an example of the client who just wanted a good shag and a laugh; with him I enjoyed ferocious thumping sex, a barrel chest warm with fuzz; sometimes a line of cocaine on the dresser when I walked in. I liked him so much—the ease of it, the friendly acknowledgment of who and what I was—that it was a shock when one night he asked me to see him outside of work. Helen, even more than the receptionists at Indigo, impressed upon us the unfor-givability of seeing clients outside of work. 'It always ends in tears,' she said; but of course she was worried about losing her cut.

'I really can't, Paul,' I said.

And he never saw me again.

I'd thought the regs at Mood Indigo were companionable; here, somehow—perhaps it was due to my own growing sense of security and relaxation—it was easier to appreciate them as individuals. There was still the variety, and still the annoying ones to tire me; but at Il Fiore I felt more settled. The rooms were so plush and Helen worked hard to make the place respectable and impressive. We all took our duties seriously.

Helen put ads in the newspaper, and she singled out particular women to promote week by week. After a few months I appeared several times: *Lucy, vivacious slim brunette. Bust DD.* These ads brought the clients in.

'She's not a double-D,' one man remarked on seeing me in the flesh.

'She certainly is,' snapped Bernadette, and when he was persuaded to a room I showed him my bra label. 'We don't do false advertising,' I said, and was *vivacious* all over him.

The receptionists were monitored as much as we were. Helen had closed-circuit cameras trained not only on the front door but on the reception desk and in the gentlemen's lounge. Later, she had them put in upstairs, so she could observe how often we ducked out to go to the toilet, or took a cigarette break in the powder room while loitering over our make-up. The cameras also fed to a monitor in Helen's home. She wasn't above ringing up at 3 a.m. to chastise the receptionist for allowing a girl to run ten minutes late out of a booking. Some nights Bernadette was very terse with us.

Bernadette worked most of my nights, and we soon made an alliance. She had a wonderful dry wit. Her frequent appeals to heaven always made us all giggle, including her.

'For the love of Baby Jesus,' she'd say. 'Just when I think my jaw's on the floor from the hopeless types tonight, this young idiot just asked me if *I* was working. You can imagine! I just looked straight at him and said, *young man, what would your mother think?*'

I adored Bernadette; her toughness and her affection made a shift more bearable. But other times I wanted to kill her. She played favourites; and sometimes that was me, and sometimes it wasn't. She'd pick on everything, then. 'Lucy, that dress really doesn't suit you. Lucy, you were five minutes late out. Lucy, I was just saying to

Shelley here, how some really good girls never talk about their clients. What's that stink? Is that what you're eating, Lucy?'

Aside from Bernadette, the other night receptionist was Maude, a mild middle-aged Irish woman who was mumsy and trustworthy; she folded the towels meditatively, and patted us on the shoulder as she passed by. Her soft accent soothed us.

I was impressed that Helen, in addition to running the place and doing all the bookwork, still worked behind the counter. She knew what was happening, who was coming in, how the girls worked. She'd sit in the lounge with us at quiet moments just like the other receptionists and chat freely. But we'd be rather more circumspect in our conversation when Helen was on—she had odd moments of over-sensitivity, when she'd walk in the door as a conversation came to a natural hush, and demand that we tell her what we'd been saying. 'Don't hide it from me, I know you girls,' she'd say, glaring, while we protested that we'd only been discussing the television guide. She could be very intimidating, in her tiny stature and her iron stare; we knew that she could have us out on our ear in a trice.

Natasha the Russian girl and Helen had an argument one night, after I'd been there a few months. We could hear voices shouting in a far room; then Natasha swept through with a bright smile and started packing up her locker with leisurely insolence. Helen slammed in and just stood there, watching, with her arms crossed; Bernadette sat nervously on the couch, grimacing. When Natasha was done, Helen said, 'I'll call you a taxi.' Natasha walked out with a careless wave and a pretty 'Goodbye, everyone'. I remembered my own departure from Indigo.

'She was trouble, that one,' Helen said. 'I don't like trouble. Consider yourselves all warned.' She stomped out in her high heels.

225

Conservative ideas about what was feminine prevailed here; if I mused aloud on a feminist interpretation of prostitution I received an alarmed glare. Things were always to be kept 'nice'. Unlike most of the other girls, I was still curious about the running of a brothel and often asked questions. Sometimes Helen silenced me with a defensive hauteur. Obliviously, I went on asking or making suggestions for doing things differently.

'But if we have to pay a coffee fee, surely that should be waived if a girl doesn't drink coffee—'

'I said, leave it, Lucy.'

'I don't know if you're aware, but it's actually not legal to—'

'*Lucy.*'

Conscientious, I would stay behind with the receptionist while she did the books, so she didn't have to leave the premises alone; I spent extra minutes at the end of shift checking the rubbish bins were empty and the sink wiped. It wasn't so much a love of housekeeping as a feeling, retained from my bookshop days, that an employee was also part of a team; that we were all colleagues and the house was as much my pride as Helen's. I didn't hear the smugness in my own voice as I complained about the other women's slackness.

It was easy to camouflage gossip as chat. I was surprised at myself—especially after the claustrophobia of Mood Indigo's hate sessions about Stella and others—to be still so easily seduced into indiscretions about others. It didn't feel good, when I went home; but at the time, part of a group, trusted and initiated, and with something to offer, it was intoxicating. At least here there was no Stella. It was a happier crew.

Siobhan appeared one night. When I saw her sitting on the couch, I was apprehensive. We hadn't parted well after the fiasco of my last night at Indigo. She smiled at me, but kept herself a little distant. I sat with Coral and Jessie, talking about nailpolish.

'So, tell me about Siobhan,' said Bernadette as we shared a quick smoke in the powder room upstairs.

'Oh, she's lovely,' I said. 'I'm really glad she's here. But,' I daubed more powder on my nose, 'I think she used to use. She's great, a really good person to have, but—'

'Ah.'

And Siobhan wasn't there the next night.

What was going on in my head? As with the loan to Sarah, my self-protectiveness about drugs had become the most repellent hypocrisy. Under the guise of allegiance to the business, I maligned an old friend. Disposed of a rival. Reaffirmed my own security. Created another thing to anguish about as I fell asleep. But at that time, it all felt more like a kind of decency.

WE HAD A CALENDAR IN the kitchen. It marked the full moon cycle: something I'd become aware of having a potent effect. Periodically we'd have a weird night, full of drifters and skittish men we'd never seen before; even trustworthy regulars were suddenly rowdy, drunk, obnoxious.

'What's going on?' someone would ask. 'I mean, *what the hell?*'

'Check the calendar.'

The mood would rise into a kind of besieged hilarity. Bernadette was especially good value on those nights. Desiree and I egged her on. 'What's this one like then?' we asked, perking our hair and bosoms before we went out to intro.

'You just wouldn't credit it, he's got a toupée like a dead cat on his head and, I'll tell you girls, the stinkiest feet I've smelt in a long time. No wonder he has to pay for it. God have mercy.'

We unperked our boobs a little.

Jessie and I got to share one character on a particularly challenging full-moon Friday night. Stuart was small, old, with a halo of unruly white curls and a spirit full of pep.

'Now, you're a lovely,' he cooed over me in the lounge. He sprawled back offensively on the couch and stroked his own thigh, eyeing my breasts. 'Tell me, do you like a nice stiff cock up you?'

'Gosh, I love it,' I said.

'I think I'll have a go at you,' he said, 'but I like that gorgeous blonde one too.' He gestured. He leered. I strode back to Bernadette in our lounge. She rolled her eyes and went to take his money.

'He's all mine, I think,' I said to the other girls. 'What did I do to deserve this?' They sat back on the couch in relief.

'You charmer, Lucy,' said Coral. She was filing her nails. Jessie came bustling out from the kitchen with a bowl of noodles. Dinner had just arrived. We always ate late.

'And you!' I said. Her face fell.

'But I'm *starving!*'

'Just think how good those noodles will be after you've sucked his dick for an hour,' Coral said. Whether she was really relieved not to be booked was hard to tell. For all the rustle of men coming in through the door, as they usually did on a Friday, this night was thin on stayers. Any booking would be good, so long as it wasn't an actual lunatic.

Stuart was a lunatic. When Jessie and I got to the room he was naked, turning slowly in circles and the room was tangy with air freshener. There was water all over the carpet outside the shower and talcum powder thickly clotted on the side of the bed. We strained humouring smiles at him.

'Hi, beautiful!'

He turned. We looked. Fitted tightly around his skinny cock were three gleaming silver cock-rings. One was okay; it merely helped a man stay erect. I'd never seen a man use more than one.

'Ah you're here!' he said. 'Come to daddy!'

When Jessie, graciously going first, lowered herself onto him, she grimaced. 'That's some interesting equipment you have there, darling,' she said. Stuart grinned up at her.

'You like a big hard dick, don't you, gorgeous?'

'Of course I do! It's just that—' and she looked to me for support with her clear blue eyes, '—this is a bit *unusual*.'

I found out what she meant when it was my turn. The rings were spaced up the length of his feeble old penis; in between them the flesh bulged. It looked incredibly painful for him, but what I cared about was the discomfort it caused me. Each ring popped into me past the ring of muscle and made a hard nudging shape inside; when I pulled upwards, the rings clocked out again. Each time left me bruised. Jessie gobbled at Stuart's nipples with the relief of one who had done her duty.

But it took forever, it seemed, for him to come—because of the rings. They held back his orgasm and gave him the control to keep inflicting his accessories on us. Jessie and I took turns, one fucking, the other coaxing him with kisses and tickling fingers behind his balls and increasingly hard twists to his nipples. Finally he relented and slipped the rings off so he could blow. Jessie and I were both looking a bit harassed.

'He was just the nastiest old man,' said Jessie when we were back in the lounge. 'Three rings!' The other girls sucked in their breath.

'Some men have just never ever been sexy in their lives,' Bernadette put in. She herself was no maiden, but she had a gilded, well-preserved allure that made young men blush.

'What's the weirdest guy you've ever had, Coral?' someone asked.

'I had this one the other night—do you remember that really shy, drunk young guy in the big coat?'

I recalled him. Bloodshot eyes, corporate haircut, miserable pleading expression hunched inside a big expensive coat.

'He wanted a vibrator, so I got mine out and put it in him. Then he asks if I can smack him a bit. So I give him a bit of a slap on the arse, you know, with one hand while the other's busy jamming the thing up him. He says, *Harder*, so I smack him harder.' She mimes. 'Then he screams out *No!* So I stop.' We were agog. 'He goes, *No, keep going*. So I'm whacking at him and he goes *No!* again.' She paused. 'And then he goes, *No, mummy, no, no!*'

Our laughter was cruel.

A lean, intense man booked me one night. We went into room six, downstairs; one of the larger rooms, it was painted pale gold and had a gentle atmosphere and a big bed. I always liked being in that room. The man, who said his name was Chris, made little conversation as I pulled back the coverlet and spread towels over the sheet.

When we lay down together, he writhed on top of me almost immediately.

'Don't you want a massage—' I started to say, but he knotted his fingers into my hair and yanked my head sideways. He grappled his legs on top of mine. He was lying on me full length, pinning me down.

'Shut up,' he said, and jammed his tongue into my mouth. It wasn't a kiss, it was a gag.

231

I couldn't move at all; my head was pulled right to one side and his fingers had me clamped almost to the scalp. I lay very still. He didn't move his tongue; he didn't remove his mouth. I felt a surge of adrenalin right down through my body.

Then he began to growl. A low, menacing, relentless growling in his throat; I could feel the vibrations of it in my own skull. Against the tension of my reactions, I let my body go pliant.

Don't resist, I thought. *Don't struggle; don't show him your fear. The panic button is on the other side of the room. Wait. Wait.*

I tried to calm my beating heart. I didn't want him to feel it against his own chest, where it pressed upon me. I opened my eyes; he was staring into my face; I closed them again. We had another twenty minutes to go, I estimated. I could just hear the faint sound of Maude's voice at the reception desk. I thought, *I could scream*—if I could get my mouth ungagged—*but he'll be on me while she gets here.* Then I remembered I'd put the latch on. We had latches on the inside of the doors, to prevent drunken clients bumbling into the wrong room.

Time slowed. The growling came and went; occasionally Chris would wriggle on me and push me down harder. I had no idea what he wanted. His weight on me was getting hard to bear: he wasn't large, but he was crushing me. I wriggled a little, as if into his 'embrace'.

Chris jerked his mouth back. 'Don't,' he hissed. I grabbed my opportunity.

'It's just, we don't have much time left and I thought, wouldn't you like me to suck you? You've got to come, and I don't want you to miss out.' My voice was a whisper, because he was lying on my rib cage. My scalp stung where his hand fisted the hair so fiercely.

He looked at me. 'I don't care about that.'

'Didn't you hear the buzzer? That means we only have five more minutes. Come on, baby, let me fuck you.'

'I don't care,' he said, but he abruptly rolled off me. I sat up, feeling all my bones spring back into place. How calm I was; my only thought was to keep control. He flopped onto his back; he wasn't even hard. I got out a condom, put it on his limp penis, sucked at the air-filled latex for a minute or two. I glanced up once: he was staring at the ceiling. Then the buzzer really did go.

'Oh, see? What a shame. And I've got another booking now.'

Chris got up and turned on the shower. 'You're right. Maybe I'll come back later and book you again.'

'That would be gorgeous,' I said, turning away. 'Just a tick, sweetie. I'll let the receptionist know we're coming out.'

I yanked on a dressing-gown from the back of the door and raced out. 'Maude, don't let this guy book me again. And get him out as quietly as you can.'

Back into the room, and Chris smiled at me. His face was wolfish under the mass of curly hair. 'Yeah, I think I'll be back later.'

I gathered the dirty towels. And when he was ready to go I saw him to the door of the room and then quickly strode off into the safety of the lounge. Maude came in a moment later.

I told her what had happened. As I explained I began to shake. 'He *growled*—'

'I told him you were booked up all night,' she said. 'What if he comes back another night? I can write a description of him in the message book, but to be honest, another receptionist—'

I took half an hour off, to have a coffee and a smoke and collect myself. Maude came up to the powder room.

'He came back, and wanted to know when you'd be free for a quick booking. He *was* weird, Lucy. He had the strangest look on his

233

face. I told him he'd upset you, and he shouldn't come back.'

I wished she hadn't told him I'd been scared. Now he'd got what he wanted.

I thought I was fine, afterwards; but later that night I found myself gripping a man's cock harder and harder. 'Ow!' he said. 'Go easy!' I apologised. I hadn't even realised I was hurting him, but when I did, I understood how good it felt.

Sometimes solidarity was our strength. One weekday night our only visitors were group after group of young men sitting with spread knees and insolent glances who inevitably looked and left. Yet another gaggle came in.

'Come on girls, we'll go out together,' said Shelley. She was older than most of us, tanned to leather and intolerant of bullshit. When I wasn't Bernadette's favourite, it was Shelley who received the confidences; I could never quite tell what she herself thought of me. I didn't care much for her blonde hair/tanned skin/pale pink lipstick look, but I liked her humour.

Through the door of the ladies' lounge we could hear the young blokes egging each other on. We took turns in front of the big mirror and readied ourselves. 'Let's go,' said Shelley, and strode out.

'Hi, I'm Shelley,' she sang as we all trooped into the room. There were five young men in tracksuits, flicking through the soft-porn magazines Helen supplied. They blinked up at us. Usually we'd meet a group like this one at a time—all five men sitting around the standing lady, throwing questions simultaneously, so we would have to keep turning our head, keeping up, keeping polite while they eyed our figures and muttered comments to each other. Now, with us all in a line, towering over them in our heels, we looked like a battalion of amazons in velvet.

'I'm Lucy—Jessie—Milla—Coral—Charlene—Jasmine,' we

said in turn, happily. 'We each do the full service. Any questions?'

Our hips cocked out in disdain. The boys blushed and looked at the carpet. It was very quiet after all their rowdiness a moment before. 'No,' said one, with the roundest face. 'You're all very tall,' he observed. There was always one nicer boy in a gang like this. I smiled at him.

'We take our shoes off,' I offered. He looked at me, puzzled, then grinned.

How powerful we felt, standing there arrayed in our glory.

'Okay, nice to meet you,' said Jessie, and we all sashayed back into our room. We burst into giggles.

'That was fantastic,' said Milla. 'I want to do it like that every time.'

Bernadette came in. 'I don't believe it. One of them's going to stay. I told his mates they have to wait outside. He's yours, Shelley.'

Shelley grinned. 'Treat 'em mean…' she said, flicked her hair into place and went out to get him.

All but the very most exclusive brothels would take any girl, however plain she was without cosmetics. What was important was presentation and grooming. We were all gleaming with make-up, hair products and expensive fabrics. It took a lot of maintenance. In between bookings we were constantly refreshing our make-up, brushing our hair, moisturising our skin, painting our nails. We sat on the couch, in our range of pastels and primary colours, like a bunch of debutantes. Only the conversation gave us away.

I wasn't the only brunette, but the house was stacked with gorgeous blondes. Most of us were white. Occasionally an Asian girl would start work, but, as Helen remarked, they just didn't get booked. There were plenty of Asian-run brothels in town; we supposed that clients who especially liked Asian women went there. No matter how gorgeous or professional, the women who tried with us did badly. Desiree was the only black woman on night shift; briefly there was a sumptuous Indian girl who stormed the place with her thin limbs and astounding boob job, sweeping up everyone's regulars in a daze of worship, only to overstep herself with Helen and vanish again. Desiree appealed with her American style and magnificent physique, and her bawdy humour.

You would often hear Desiree's loud voice, even through the kitchen wall. 'I swear, he was fucking me so hard, she was complaining one night, 'I thought my boobs were going to just *fall off—*'

'Desiree!' said Helen, manifesting through the door from the reception area.

'Sorry, Helen,' said Desiree. She appeared holding a bowl of steamed vegetables.

Helen gave her a severe look.

'That fucking cow,' Desiree said to me in the privacy of the powder room, 'has no fucking clue.'

'There's a lot she doesn't know,' I agreed. 'We're on the coalface, we know what's going on, what the men like, how we all talk. But she's a smart lady, Helen.'

'Smart enough to make a shit-load of money,' said Desiree.

When, to my surprise and delight, Valentina turned up at Il Fiore one night I told her the same thing.

'What's it like here?' she whispered. I'd just come into the ladies' lounge and realised, with a little start of pleasure, who the new girl was. The other girls were sitting away from her; I made sure they saw my hug.

'Good. Strict. Much fucking better than old Indigo,' I said. 'But watch out for Helen. She doesn't miss a trick.' I didn't think Valentina would have any problems; she was one of the most professional prostitutes I'd ever met. Valentina looked around the room, at the expensively upholstered furniture, the cable television, the brass light fittings. 'Nice,' she said. I beamed proudly. For once I'd led the change, instead of following. Valentina would see my success here, the ways I'd matured in my work and my clientele. She saw how I jumped into conversations with the other ladies, how comfortable I was.

'It's really bad over there now,' Valentina said to me. 'That agency thing—and Bea—' she shook her elegant head.

A couple of weeks later Helen came up to me as I was getting ready.

'That Valentina, you know her from—' Helen rarely said the name. 'What do you think of her? I don't care for her attitude.'

Valentina was finding some of Helen's rules abrasive to her sense of professional integrity. She took her career seriously, as her own; as she pointed out, we were independent contractors who were merely hosted by a brothel. The brothel rented the rooms to the client; that's what their half of the fee went to. We were, in a sense, service providers who simply used the house as a specialised hotel. Valentina was adamant in asserting her right to do things her own way; nothing big, but she'd clearly affronted Helen, the control queen.

'Valentina's great, she's a really good working lady,' I said. 'Why?'

Helen looked at me. 'Never you mind, Lucy.'

A few days later Valentina didn't come to her Tuesday night shift. 'Personality difference,' said Bernadette. I was sad; I'd enjoyed having her around again. But there was nothing I could do. I had no phone number for her; I didn't even know her real name. For all that we shared years of work and friendship, once we walked out the front door we were all strangers.

I sometimes felt closer to my regular clients. I had some lovely ones on my roster, some of them quite well heeled—an international security guard, a professional gambler, a tiresome stockbroker who was always hassling me to follow his latest tip, and a stonemason with rough hands and Armani jackets. Often men who visited Melbourne for business would pop in every month or so; one of my favourites was Samuel.

Helen took me aside one night. 'I've got a gentleman for you to meet, Lucy,' she whispered. 'He used to see Natasha—though I don't know what he saw in her. Anyway, he's lovely, and if he likes you you'll have a good time. He's in the lounge.'

Samuel was a spry middle-aged man with dark hair and a ruddy smile. 'Nice to meet you,' he said. I sat next to him. Without a general intro, there was time for some chat. He asked me what I liked in a booking; I answered truthfully, to make sure my client had a good time and didn't give me a hard one.

'Is that all?'

'I like touching men,' I said. 'And talking. You let me start talking, you'll never shut me up.'

He smiled. 'I'll take an hour with you, Lucy, and we'll see how we go. I'm looking forward to it.' He stayed three, and became one of my greatest joys. Always gentle, he had a sexual manner that roused me to pleasure; with him I would touch myself, and come. Afterwards, with his lovely gentle hands, he'd give me a proper massage—no clumsy kneading at my vertebrae, but deft strokes that restored me, while we talked drowsily. From time to time a package would come in the post for me: chocolates, a set of expensive lingerie—of the right size—an enormous bunch of perfect white roses.

'I saw your tattoo,' he said the next time. 'I wanted something to be just special for you. You're the sweetest girl,' he said. 'You do me good.'

He did me good, too.

In the closeness of a brothel bedroom emotions were different, faces drew close without trepidation. There were men with whom I thought I might fall in love; men who gave me effortless sexual pleasure; who looked at me with such a gaze as to allow me the luxury of confession. I told many of my clients parts of my life, wanting to impress upon them that a working girl was more than a body and an act. I gave my story away—not the drugs, not the hardship—but the incidentals; and I told some—artlessly or pointedly—that I had a boyfriend, and that I had a loving mother and father. The longer I saw a man, if I genuinely liked him, the more foolish it seemed to keep up pretences. I saw no point in constructing a wholly false background, as some girls did. I was Lucy, but Lucy was not me; she had my stories, but she bragged when I would not have bragged, she felt satisfactions that I would not have. Lucy was braver than I, more open, behind her mask.

My art was to reveal myself, but only as much as I wished.

And I had reached a philosophy about working. Not for me the pretence that this job wasn't really my life; that it meant nothing to me beyond money. This was something that was changing me, empowering me, teaching me. I had never felt so competent, so adored. After several months, I was someone the newer girls looked to; I was asked to counsel the absolute beginners; I held influence. It was intoxicating.

Most of the other women, understandably, pretended to the world that they had other jobs. I didn't bother. Instead, I positively boasted about my work. It seemed as if it conferred a kind of

239

comradeship with the taxi drivers, the early-morning waiters, the convenience-store staff whom I encountered. We were all servicing the night. And there was the affirmation of refusing shame.

'I'm a sex worker,' I'd say, and there'd be a pause. I'd keep my smile steady. My gaze on the face.

'Right. Cool.'

The more I braved out the shock of this admission, the less it came to feel like anything shocking.

I rarely considered anymore the oddness of giving sex for money. It was a job like any other physical task; it involved my hands, just as a sandwich-maker's did; it involved my mind, as a teacher's did. It took physical strength, as a labourer's did. Performing with my vagina was only an extension of manual work. I assessed the number of skills I possessed, engaging my mind and my body, and to me prostitution seemed like a complex, challenging profession that had enhanced me more than it had reduced me.

There were times, as I caressed a simple man's temple, or bent to kiss a voluptuously beautiful body, that I got tears in my eyes. It was as if I were discovering how to fall in love with anyone, for the duration of a booking. It seemed that anyone could be beautiful if I looked for it. *The whore with a heart of gold*, I thought mockingly, but my wryness did not take away the grace.

My look was still changing. In the shops after-five wear was dominated by black dresses, but at Il Fiore the right to wear black was reserved for the first lady to arrive each night, otherwise we'd look like a funeral party. So I bought a luscious crimson velvet gown. Gown was the word: it had a long skirt, to the ankles, with a high slit up the back, a bodice, a wide neckline, and a little plush velvet rose between the breasts. In it I looked like a queen.

I did have some black dresses, glossy as water, which I wore with heavy smudged eyeliner and pale pink lipgloss; half-Lolita, half-succubus, I fancied. I experimented with cosmetics and colours, created ensembles calculated to impress with a mixture of class and arse. In the full-length mirror my skin was pale against the swaying skirts and tiny shoulder-straps. My hair was shiny, my face painted carefully, my toenails were glossy silver. My breasts jutted out in the push-up bras; even I wanted to hold them, they were so appealingly voluptuous. I'd never thought I could be so exquisite.

I loved to step into my high heels at the start of each shift; and I loved taking them off at the end of the night, so I could put on my own clothes. I'd augmented my sleek shirts and pants with a blizzard of delicate fabrics: transparent skirts, ruffled chiffon tops, shimmering scarves and tiny silk flowers for my hair. I wore scarlet lipstick even when I wasn't at work. I felt sexy and sophisticated and a long way from the scruffy streetwalker with day-old make-up and a nose ring.

When I walked in the door of my parents' place for a visit it was in a cloud of perfume. I showed off my new clothes. 'Like this shirt? It's designer.'

My mother felt the fabric. 'It's beautiful.'

'Do you want some dinner?' offered my father. He was putting out plates for the meal.

'It's a bit early in the day for me, thanks Dad,' I said. 'I bought some cushions the other day too. Really pretty ones. And look, this coat!'

My sister was there. She gave me a look. 'Do you know how that sounds?' she said to me later, alone. 'You still owe Mum and Dad money and you're poncing around talking about all the money you've spent on this shit. It's really rude.'

241

'I *need* nice things, though,' I protested. 'It's been so long. It makes me feel better.'

'Well, I understand that. But, you know—' She quirked her lips. 'Just don't forget that you've got responsibilities.'

I scowled. 'I know.'

'Anyway. Do you want to do yoga lessons with me?'

Peace with my family was easier to find now. And there was stability in my work. I felt varnished and fine.

When I arrived at Il Fiore every night I was greeted with scents. Our perfume mixed with the air-freshener, the scented oil that Maude sometimes burned, the powdery smell of cosmetics, and, upstairs in the rooms, the faint ammonia smells of antiseptic and sperm.

At the end of every shift when we cleaned our room and remade the bed, we changed the bin-liner. As I opened its lid each night after a day and evening of dozens of clients, the reeking air billowed out. The thin plastic bin-liner sagged with the weight of semen.

The quiet moment of fixing the room after a busy night was like a meditation. I admired myself in the mirror as I bent over to smooth a pillow-cover, tuck the towel pattern into a tighter shape. I prided myself on my towels by now, on the perfected room I created every night. In the golden mirror I was elegant and suave, and I left behind a room immaculate, as if no one had ever fucked there.

ONE NIGHT AFTER I'D been at Il Fiore several months Bernadette was talking about heroin users. I sat there, amid the other girls, saying nothing. They were all making comments, saying that women like that were sad but not good to work with, talking of times they'd had things stolen. 'You can tell by their eyes,' said Bernadette. 'Their pupils are all small. If you look really closely at someone—' To my horror she got up and came over to me, since I was closest.

She peered into my eyes. 'You can see that their eyes are different.'

I gazed back at her, too appalled to do anything.

'That's how you tell,' Bernadette said, sitting back easily in her corner. I blinked and lowered my eyes. Bernadette went on, describing an experience she'd had with a junkie in the street. She hadn't noticed anything different about me. I was an example of the clean girl.

I had only one small, dark scar on each arm, which I covered with make-up. I'd have to wait in the powder room, where we got ready each night, until I was alone. I always walked with my arms bent. The lighting was low.

There were only two other girls who used. Milla was sweet and young and blessed with an airy manner that made everyone adore her. She was very pretty, and Bernadette especially favoured her. It was an open secret that Milla was battling heroin; she'd lost her father only a year ago, and her drug use was evidently partly in consolation for her grief. Bernadette clucked over her, and Helen allowed her to take long breaks from work and then return. Milla and I eventually intimated to each other that we used; we were almost shy about it. Not once did we suggest scoring together. I felt it would be almost criminal to help her acquire drugs, although of course I knew she would, anyway. And I noted that Milla's usage was not counted a character failing. I thought the time might come when I, too, could be likewise remitted.

Then Jewel appeared. She was an intelligent, funny-looking girl, with a sharp wit and a disarming candour. We became friends through a kind of sorority long before she confessed to me that she used. I hadn't been able to tell; she used amphetamines too, to enlarge her pupils and get her through the night. A couple of times she came home with me to score. When we talked privately at work, it was with the canny realism of women who were keeping under the radar. A quick glance to see if the other was sweating and looking ill, the occasional loan of twenty dollars. Jewel and I kept our using out of the house, but I was glad, somehow, not to be alone.

In fact, the drugs were becoming a more separate part of my life; though they eased my work by numbing my body somewhat, and soothed my emotional reactions, they didn't really seem to belong in the gilded chambers of the brothel. That place, perversely, was almost innocent.

I was using two or three times a day still, in a routine that was as much about habit as it was about dependence. The more time I spent among non-drug-users the less I thought about drugs at work, but once home, the idea was automatic. The dealer was always late; no matter how early I rang, how emphatically I reminded him that I had a job to get to by seven, he dawdled. We had a new dealer now; Plum had retired—perhaps had been retired—and had handed the business over to a sequence of his friends. Tony, Andy, Lee; they were all Vietnamese, friendly, and drove dirty white cars.

When our credit situation was exhausted with one of them, we'd resort to the nearby housing commission flats, where there was always a junkie down in the entrance foyer to ask for a contact or a nervous woman sheltering behind a half-opened door. I didn't like going to the flats; there was a high chance of being mugged by another user, usually on the way out when you'd scored. Robbie was the one who most often went, and he got rolled a couple of times, or said he did. Nevertheless, the flats were a fairly reliable source of heroin. But even going right to the source didn't always get me to work on time.

'Can't you *try*, Lucy?' said Helen for the hundredth time. 'We start at seven, all the other ladies get here on time, I don't under-stand what's so impossible for you.'

'I'll try,' I said, but I already understood that I had a little power here, that she couldn't push me too hard.

There were nights when I was a golden girl. Maude smiled at me as she did my books at dawn. 'That's a good night, Lucy,' she said.

I felt I'd earned every cent. My body was sagging with fatigue and I'd hardly had a chance to eat anything; but I'd had the luxury of long, successive bookings, a double with two genial middle-aged mates who'd cosseted me happily, a man who'd wanted Greek, and a large tip. In my memory, the night was made up of men whose names and faces were already vanishing from my mind. I smiled.

'Never thought an arts graduate would see money like this,' I said.

'Well, you're not an arts graduate right now, are you, honey,' said Maude, gently.

'No,' I said, and took the money.

My relationship with Robbie was getting more impossible. The more coherent I felt in the rest of my life, the more forlorn his appeared to become. He had a place to live with me, and his dreams still, but it was an increasing abrasion between us that I was the one with the money and the house. I caught myself meting out his 'pocket money' in small moments of discipline. I wondered if I was being mean. I didn't really think I was.

He was lying to me so often by then that I felt my own sense of reality grow garbled; he would stare at me and lie, and I'd challenge him, and he'd lie, and his explanations ('You must have forgotten, *you* took that money out of the box'; 'Don't you remember? You *told* me to score twice!') were so vehement that, faltering, I began to wonder if I could state anymore that he was the mad one and I was not.

I was earning money, but it was still all going; paying rent was difficult every month and there were several times when I was threatened with eviction. I had cash but it seemed to go too fast. Robbie scored for me. I was grateful to be spared the toil, but I knew I was paying a high commission. I kept my temper; chose to go on forgiving and believing. The situation was difficult, but tenable. If I really changed things, if I broke up with Robbie altogether, I had no idea what would happen.

In my diary I wrote diatribes of fury that I rarely told him to his face. If there was any use in recounting my outrage to myself, I didn't know. I would close the covers of my journal and raise my head to reassemble my patience once more.

His rages became more spiteful. He refused to move out, or to stop burning cigarette holes in my expensive bedsheets with his nodding cigarette. He would keep saying he respected me, and that was why he stayed on, and he needed me, and Kate, you're the only one I have in the world.

Guilt bit deep; I couldn't practise my credo of compassion at work and turn my back on the one who loved me. But I was getting desperate for a break; warm weather inflamed the differences between Robbie and me. He was uneasy about my friendship with Douglas, who came visiting sometimes to collect me for an outing, and with Max who would ring for a chat; he himself had no friends other than junkies.

'It's easy for you, meeting all those men every night.'

'I've just been working for fourteen hours and you haven't even done the washing up. In four days! What's *wrong* with you?'

Secure at the brothel, I sensed a chance to progress. I could make a profession of this; the professional aspiration made my life manageable.

With summer, the world seemed to open. I was still reading, as I had done through nearly all my exile; one novel after another, and dreaming anew of the day I'd be free to travel and write and create again. It was as if my imagination, so long dulled, was bubbling up

247

again with the warm weather, more fiercely than ever. I was reading of the French Revolution; entranced by the stories of pathos and grandeur and folly, I dreamed of going to Paris. Lying in bed every dawn, with the windows open in my bedroom and the early sunshine leaking in, I read my way back into excitement. My head resounded with the joy of wonder again.

Something was happening. Inside me there was a new fluttering of ambition. An impatience, finally, with the tithes of drug addiction. Now I yearned for a life like I'd had before, so many years ago, with all the imagination and sweetness I had always cherished in myself; but with the safety of what I now considered a fortunate career.

If I could only stop using; but the thought of giving up my precious needles, the one sure thing in every day, was too daunting. The heroin sickened me now, literally; the quality of the gear was slipping, and it was often laced with unknown substances which made our palms and the soles of our feet itch acutely for a minute after the fix, and brought up angry welts on our skin where the blood tracked it through our systems. I realised that heroin only succeeded in making me sleepy and dull, and I wanted clarity now.

But I dared not take that leap, it was always, as ever, too frightening. Every morning and evening I held the needle in my hand, and its bite still gave me satisfaction.

On New Year's Eve I had the night off; Robbie and I spent the evening together, ceremoniously cooking, lighting candles in the little backyard, dressing in our finest clothes. We bought enough gear for a generous taste, and some alcohol too. I wore gold strappy sandles and a sexy lace top, and he held me tenderly at midnight and kissed me. 'Here's to a brand new year,' I said, smiling against his face.

'Here's to spending my life with you,' he replied. He was beautiful that night; we made love in the thick warm darkness, and I hoped it would all be getting better now.

I told my mother some of my concerns about Robbie, and she said, 'Why don't you come and spend a week with us? Just for a break?'

It was a week later, the beginning of January, and things at work were slow after the Christmas rush. Going home, where I'd visited for Christmas Day and revelled in the familiar summery atmosphere and full fridge, was exactly what I needed. I would keep working, but the change would be a kind of holiday.

To be asked meant a lot.

I worried about Robbie, exiled from his family by his history of drug abuse. Christmas had been a bad time for him, and he was miserable and malign. 'I'm just going for a week,' I reassured him. 'You can have some time to think.' I didn't offer to supply him with money for drugs; he could try fending for himself. It would be a good lesson to him: a taste of what would happen if I actually left him for good. I rang the dealer myself and bought enough drugs to last me several days. Usually I didn't dare buy in bulk like this, because in our greed we would simply go straight through it, but I hoped I could monitor myself without Robbie.

'You're so lucky, with your family,' he said forlornly. I squeezed his hand and left.

'Don't go,' I heard him murmur after me.

My mother had made up the spare room for me, and I went to bed the first night ready to sleep late, lie around the garden and appreciate the kindness of my family. I woke up the next morning to see Robbie clambering through the open window from the front verandah.

'*What the fuck are you doing?*' I hissed. 'Get out! My parents will call the cops. What are you doing here?'

'I'm sorry,' he said, and dropped into a crouch on the floor next to my bed. 'I'm going crazy, I haven't had a taste since yesterday—' He kept his eyes on the ground, abashed. I squinted at him furiously; I didn't have my contact lenses in and he was a murky shape on the floor.

'I just want some fucking time on my own,' I said. 'Is that too much to ask? I *warned* you I was going away. It's not my responsibility, Robbie.' I was shaking with the sense of trespass. He was still on the floor, crouched like a creature.

'I'm sorry, Kate, I'm so sorry,' he murmured, and climbed back out the window. I watched him stumble down the path and away.

Not once had he looked at me. I just sat there for a moment, full of grief for his helplessness, and shock that he had violated my parents' home. Then I remembered my bag, on the floor where he'd been crouching. I checked it, already knowing.

He'd taken all the money and all the drugs. A wad of cash and enough heroin to kill him. All the heroin I needed for the next week. He'd taken it all.

By the time I threw on my clothes and ran down the street after him, he'd vanished. I stomped back up to the house and into the room. Shock collapsed into fury.

My mother came running in when I shrieked my rage. 'That *fucking bastard, that fucking little shit!*'

She sat down on the bed, ready for a catastrophe. 'He was just here, he took—' I gestured to the bag. There was no pretending with my mother, she knew what I was talking about. My parents were aware, of course, that I'd be using in the house, and it was understood that, as long as they didn't have to see, they would accept it. They could hardly expect me not to do it. Those days were long past.

'I don't have any more money to score, and the dealer's on the other side of town, I don't know how I'm going to—' I was nearly in tears.

'Okay, well,' she said. 'Maybe this is a sign, a sign that you and he just can't go on anymore. And it's okay, you're here. We'll look after you. You're still on the methadone, right?' I nodded miserably. Every day I went to get my dose—and it was still as high as it had been a year ago when I'd started the program. While I was using there didn't seem any point in dropping it.

'How about—' She looked at me carefully, lovingly, encouragingly. My wonderful, staunch mother. 'How about if I take you to get your dose later, and you just try getting through the day without the drugs?'

I gazed at the blanket beside my knee. The anger was sluicing out of me, replaced by weariness. 'I don't know,' I said. 'I've never—'

'Just one day,' my mother said, and put her hand over mine.

And so I didn't score that day. By mid-afternoon my skin was fever-hot and my bones ached, but it wasn't unbearable; I still had enough residual heroin in my system from the taste the night before to bolster me. I sat around in the garden, and drank tea, and flicked through a book on Paris. Then before dinner my mother drove me across town to the chemist, and half an hour later I felt better.

It was the thirteenth of January. I had been using heroin for almost five years.

THE NEXT DAY I SLEPT LATE; again, I was a little feverish, but I went to the chemist and then to my shift, and although I was uncomfortable, I managed. I didn't think past, *I'm coping.* When I left work I got a taxi back to my parents' place; more than ever, I didn't want to see Robbie in my living room. If he'd overdosed, I thought, I didn't care.

The week at my parents' place ended, and they suggested I stay on. It had been seven days without a fix, only methadone. Each day I'd woken, automatically reaching for the thought of heroin as I had for five years, and then, astonished, recalled that there was none, and I'd lasted another day without it, and I was okay, I was actually okay.

Already the pride at *one more day* bolstered me. I was so full of my achievement that now I dreaded the defeat of that list of days ending with a taste. A moment of satisfaction followed by the banality of failure. Then I'd have to start again, or worse, just go on as before, and these days of success would count for nothing. I knew too well from my old attempts to get clean how bitter that felt; all the anguish swallowed up in the fact that once more I was using. I didn't want that again; I was too far past that; I was somewhere else now, and going ahead.

Eight days without. Then ten. Then fourteen.

Two weeks clean.

It was strange to be back at home with my family. Strange because it had been such a long time, but it was so familiar in its atmosphere and its security, the friendly chat of my father and the scent of his cooking, and my mother bent over her desk working. My father hugged me. 'Love my daughter,' he said.

Something had changed since those old days of fraught struggle and pain. My parents were more at ease; they'd ceased trying to protect me. Now they just loved me. And I was no longer the sullen rebel I'd been when I left.

And yet it was as if, in a way, I never had left. Away from the claustrophobia of my little house and the daily plod down to work, I felt removed from my recent history, and embedded once more in an older life. The grimness of housing commission flats and dull drugs seemed so very far away. It was like a miracle of waking to find myself back in a happier dream.

Going to work didn't seem very different. I'd sometimes wondered if the drugs were what made the work bearable, according to the accepted wisdoms about prostitution and junkies. I'd looked at the other girls and asked myself if their experiences were really so different from mine; clearly, they could work without drugs to blunt them. I'd tried to gauge how much buffering the opiate gave me against the abrasion of constant penetration. My only experience of working 'straight' was when I was detoxing, and that was difficult; but in that state I had been over-sensitised.

Now I found that working without heroin made little difference. Of course, I was still on methadone, a high dose, even if I didn't feel stoned. I went on smiling, caressing, getting fucked, talking with the girls, eating my takeaway, working—perhaps gingerly, as my metabolism adjusted and I walked with a sheen of sweat on my skin. My body responded more strongly to the sex. But, apart from the sudden, periodic recollection that there was no beautiful syringe waiting for me as my reward at the end of the night, heroin left a smaller space inside me than I'd expected.

All those years drowning, and now the addiction was slipping off me as lightly as water.

Three weeks in, and it had been a difficult, tiring, crazy shift. Jewel and I were in the powder room getting undressed, giggling a little with fatigue. 'I need a *drink*,' I said. It seemed like the night to just blow something, to bite in deep. We were ragged with the aftermath of all the night's dramas—floods of clients, crazed receptionist, hectic sex.

'I need a bloody taste,' she said, and I looked at her.

One more time, I thought; just once more, to show myself I don't want it anymore.

'You want to come home to my place?' she asked.

It was full daylight by the time we got a taxi to her dealer's and then to her house. All the way I'd been realising what I was doing, and how it would feel to have broken my record of days clean. I knew I didn't really want it—not the way I'd wanted it other times, coming off a period of abstinence. I wasn't hungry for it; I just felt dull and tired. But I thought I should go through with it. For the last time.

I told Jewel I was getting clean. 'It's so *easy*,' I said, in wonder. She looked at me with the usual scepticism of the long-term user who's heard it all before—the same look I'd have given her. Full of encouragement and not much confidence. Especially as I was watching her mix up.

'Do you still want it?' She held out the syringe. I looked at it.

'Fuck yeah,' I said, and plugged it in.

But it only made me sleepy, blurred and weary. There was no joy in it at all.

And I knew I didn't need this thing anymore. What I needed was myself back. Already I was impatient for the drug to clear out of me and the new life to begin.

Robbie was living alone at my house. I had almost cut communication with him there; I rang a couple of times from my parents' house, and he spat reproaches at me until I hung up. 'I want you out of my house,' I'd said. 'It's time for you to leave. You have a week. I'm sorry.'

'Just because you're so happy—what about me? I've got nowhere to go, Kate!' he said. Whenever he used my name I knew his outrage was half performance.

'Just find somewhere,' I said. 'Things are different now.'

Then he stopped answering the phone. I worried about what he was living on—he had only his welfare payment, and he'd have spent that on drugs. I knew he wasn't ready to get clean; it wasn't his time yet. It was my time, though, and I was full of a steely certainty about what I had to do.

I went over to my house to pick up some stuff about a week

later. It was a blazing hot day. When I opened the front door, the house smelt fuggy and dry. Robbie's things were scattered around; the place was a mess. A dried-out alcohol swab and a dirty spoon lay on the kitchen bench; I passed them with a long glance and looked away. On the table was a note.

I'm sorry, I can't take it anymore. This life wasn't meant for me. I love you.

'Fuck,' I said, and started to cry.

He was nowhere in the house. I had no idea what to do; the note wasn't dated. I thought it might be for real; or was it just one of his tricks? I rang Serena, his ex.

'Oh shit,' she said. 'He was around here the other day. He was really weird, all strung-out, and talking about how he'd held up a service station with a syringe. I think—'

'What the fuck do we do?'

She rang the police and then called me back. There was no record of service stations being held up recently. They'd told her to file a missing person's report. I was cold with horror, and anger too. I called work to let them know I'd be late; I rang the rehab centre, to see if he was there. They couldn't tell me; it was policy. 'Could you tell me if there's any point in leaving him a message?' I asked. 'No,' they said. I rang hospitals. No trace. Was he lying under a bridge, in the bushes of a park, a needle sticking out of his arm, where was he?

There was no sign of him when I came back to the house the next afternoon; nor the next time. I left notes on the bench: *Please call me. I love you. Don't be a fucking idiot.*

I grew used to the idea Robbie was dead. Serena and I met and talked about when to ring his mother, when to go through his belongings, how to arrange a funeral when his body turned up. It seemed like this was something we'd been expecting. I wept for my

256

beautiful boy, vanished and alone, all his dreams and the waste, the thought of his pale skin being rained on at night, his grief, the pity of it. There was nothing I could do.

I went every afternoon to the chemist for my methadone, and as I walked out one afternoon two weeks after the note, I saw Robbie. He stood in the doorway, waiting for me.

'Hello,' he said, and smiled.

I just looked at him. He was thin and unwashed but okay, standing there as if nothing had happened.

'You fucking—*you*—I don't—' I said. He held out a hand as if to embrace me. I slapped it. 'You just keep the fuck away from me.'

I left a note for him at the house. *Leave the key on the bench and stay out.* I put his belongings in a box and dragged them out to the front verandah. *I still love you. But I can't see you anymore. You break my heart, you just crush it.*

That was February. Occasionally I visited my house to find cds missing, or fresh remains of food on the bench. Then I saw Robbie again; he was sleeping on the front verandah, in a bundle of blankets he'd taken from the house. He'd left the key for me as asked, but I assumed he'd made a copy. Once, the bedroom window was smashed in. When I accused him of entering, he denied it; or sullenly refused to say anything. It was strange, being exiled from my own house. I missed it there; I missed the days we'd spent together there; I even missed Robbie, but it felt perilous to be too close to that house. I was comfortable at my parents'. I'd brought over some of my stuff now, and had a proper room set up in my old bedroom; there was a pantry full of food and a computer and the tranquility of suburbia. My own little cottage was swollen with stale heat and the smell of an old life.

'You can stay as long as you want,' said my parents. 'You can come home.'

The lease on my house was up in May; the landlady wanted it back. I didn't mind. Robbie was staking it out, the rent was expensive and I had other plans. I fantasised of Europe. Douglas and I talked, and he said one day, 'You should go. You could just go, you know. Kick around, and have fun for a while.'

I glanced at him.

'Seriously,' he said.

It wasn't that life was so unbearable now, but I felt bound—too bound—by it. When I was an addict, travel seemed a dream of the perfect escape, but so impossible it became forgotten. Now it could be my reward, my chance to re-set myself, to take the next step in following my imagination; my tool to recovery.

My methadone level was still high, but I'd begun to drop the dose, in consultation with my doctor—just a few mils at a time, but steadily. At the rate I was going, I'd be finished with it by about September. The end of my tethering was in sight.

And so I prepared to save money, and to pack up my little house. There was a lot of time still, but I had a whole houseful of stuff: my very own place, with all its furnishings.

I talked to Robbie. The dramas seemed distant now. He was docile, calm, wretchedly thin. He spoke of his despair and loneliness, of the harshness of the world; I put my arm around his bony shoulders. The skin on his face was as delicate as a child's.

'You can stay until the end,' I said. 'But you help me pack, okay?'

So we packed up. I'd come over a few afternoons a week, and return to the house to stay the night after work; of course I let him in to sleep with me. Back to how things had been, but so different.

He was using a little still, but I simply didn't think about joining him, and he kept it out of the house. There was a drought in the heroin supply that summer; it took hours and hours to score, all for an over-priced and thin-quality pinch of powder. Even at those moments when nostalgia for a taste took me, it seemed too much trouble. Where once I would have spent a day traipsing around St Kilda in search of just one cap, now I couldn't be bothered spending a couple of hours on it. When the hunger for the needle really bit at me, we scored some speed.

Robbie and I began making love again. Back in my rehab days, one of the counsellors, an ex-user, had said, 'Just wait till the first time you have sex clean. Better than any drug.' He was right. I still had the opiate methadone in my system, but my nerves were less blunted and my heart felt clear. I made love to Robbie with all the tenderness of pity for what we'd lost, and all the passion of relief. We lay in bed by the candlelight and giggled and talked; a new freshness came over us. A kind of late grace.

Moving out was a time of tension. Everywhere I went there were obligations undone. I was late to work, packing up my books; I was late home to my parents', staying on to do another booking at the end of a shift; I was late to the house to fetch more cardboard boxes and go on piling my stuff into them. Amphetamines, when I used them, made the day longer, but they always left dirt in my veins.

All around me people were suddenly unhappy with me. Helen was out for my blood; she was irritable with everyone. Bernadette picked it up and sniped too. I tried to keep my head down, but it wasn't easy. My mother had a go at me for treating the house like a hotel, breezing in at dawn and only rising to rush out the door. 'I *work*,' I said; but she said, 'And the *housework*?' and I felt neglectful.

I was spending more and more time at my own house, now it was more welcoming; she was anxious that I might fall back into old habits.

By the time I moved out I was shredded with exhaustion. Everything was staggering to an end, but Europe lay ahead.

By September I'd have been a year and a half at Il Fiore. Already it was long enough to consider its rooms my home, its people my community. I knew the moods of the place; I could gauge the climate and the fortunes; I was respected and trusted, I believed. Girls came and went, but there was a solid core of us who remained throughout. The receptionists were like family; Helen had good moods and bad, but maintained her control. The clients washed in and out the door and many of them were familiar faces.

I'd earned myself a nice stable of regulars, and their arrivals jollied me through each shift. I could count on two or three regs per night, usually; there were those who turned up predictably every week, and others who blew in on a whim.

I had a silent, rotund Indian man who could come three times in half an hour. I went through the same routine of coy encouragement every session, and he left with the same smile every time.

John was a builder with a burly physique, a Mills and Boon jaw and the bashfulness of a nineteen-year-old. 'Gee, you look better every time I see you,' he'd say, and I'd cuff him around the cheek. His sweetness undid me; he said he simply couldn't pick up girls.

'But you're *gorgeous*,' I said. 'Are they *mad*?'

He blushed. 'I don't mind. I get to see you.' He was shy in bed, too, holding me as if I'd bruise.

'You can't hurt me,' I said, smiling down at his hesitant face. 'I like to feel you. You can try anything with me. This is *your* time.'

The next occasion I dimmed the lights right down. The room was pitch black—there were no windows, of course. In the dark I took his hand. 'We're going to just feel it,' I whispered, leading him to the bed by touch. I knew the room without having to see. 'Anything you want.' His hands clasped my hips; we moved slowly, with the care of the blind. His body grew taut and his breathing louder. I moved against him. It didn't matter if I screwed up my face or if I thrust against him aggressively, and he surged back with unfamiliar passion.

'Oh, God,' he said and kissed me hard.

When we'd finished I left the lights down while we held each other, and at the end of the booking when I put them up again, it was slowly, with the consciousness of a blessing.

One of the house regulars was Yanni, a young man with an inheritance. He was loaded with money and a group of cousins and friends to party with us. They'd arrive with whoops and jokes and make Bernadette giggle, and then book the largest room, which had a king-size bed and a spa, and plenty of floor-space. Often we'd have three or four men and a few of us all together in there, with towels spread on the floor for extra room, one couple in the spa and two or three on the bed. My knees would knock against those of the next girl as we each straddled a fat belly and pumped and giggled and crooned. A hand crept up, not attached to the man beneath me, to fondle my breasts. The men were drunk and happy to stay for hours on Yanni's credit card. It was a good time, but physically arduous. We had to do all the crouching and thrusting, and Yanni liked nothing better than a 69. An hour or two holding myself up on my trembling arms and keeping my crotch raised above his face while I laved his wet cock was tiring enough, but he liked licking both clitoris and anus, scraping his bristled chin across my tender skin with every stroke. One booking with Yanni made me a lot of money, but it cost me in pain and the effort not to complain. With a customer like that you couldn't be too honest about their shortcomings. Luckily he usually stayed till the end of the shift; I walked away gingerly when he left.

Regs came and went. I'd see one of mine at the desk one night as I strolled by and when I greeted him he'd look behind me, to where Coral or Jessie was walking out beaming. I knew by then that the girl a man liked on a Tuesday wasn't always the same person as on a Saturday. It had happened to me so often I'd lost all the feeling in that part of my pride. Or perhaps I had so much pride I could afford to let a little atrophy.

One regular I knew wouldn't defect was Philip. He was a silent man with a bony, handsome face and a superb body, as clean and pale as a Greek statue. Sheepish down in the lounge, where Bernadette would escort him in to wait for me, in the rooms he would unleash an intense sexuality that genuinely aroused me. It was athletic sex. Pulled into every position possible in half an hour, I became pliable, swooning. The harder his grip, the softer I became. He adored me, and I cherished him. He was the type of regular who found a girl they liked—on Helen's suggestion—and stayed with her until she left. I liked him so much I'd allow the booking to run on while he finished, and Bernadette wouldn't say anything.

Mick was my other favourite. He'd arrive last thing on a Sunday night, usually when I was already in a booking, and I'd come downstairs to find him curled up on the couch, asleep. He worked in clubs and was always drunk, but he held it well. I found his stocky body addictive and I lavished my caresses on it while he lay flat on his back and joked with me. There were times when I thought I was a little bit too fond of Mick.

'Can I please suck your cock?' I'd ask, sliding up his body.

'Hell, yeah,' he'd mumble.

It was the men who recognised who I was who earned my sincere affection. They could ask how my night had been, and not flinch when I told them how many bookings I'd had already; they didn't baulk when I requested money for fantasies. To them I was a lovely girl who was content to work. They got my respect for not pretending otherwise.

One young man reminded me that I was a working girl when I was in danger of forgetting. His name was Gabriel and he was a melancholy boy in his early twenties. He booked for an hour, and then two; he told me that he was depressed. He'd smoked too much pot and become isolated and a little lost. His honesty touched me. I admitted to him that I knew what drug addiction could do. I showed him my arms.

'That's no good, mate,' he said. I kissed him on the cheek. He kissed me back.

He was good looking, with a fine young body and a handsome

olive-skinned face and thick, long black hair; something in him drew me. When he came back less than a week later I was pleased.

'I can talk to you,' he said into my embrace. 'I don't care about the sex.'

I did. I stroked and teased him until he capitulated. My libido was coming back. It was strange, almost shaming, to find myself the one seeking sex and having to cajole it from a client. 'That's so fucking good,' I said, hot-faced. He just looked down at me almost sadly, and went on thrusting. I liked to see him come, the way his face eased, the sense of satisfaction I gained.

He began visiting me several times a week, for an hour or two each time. I was gratified but concerned.

'What about the money, you can't earn this much,' I said.

'Fuck the money, I don't care.' He was miserable that night. I dimmed the lights and stroked his hair. 'I just can't—feel anything, you know? I just want it all to go away.' My heart ached for him. There was something in Gabriel that I knew in myself.

'Listen,' I said. 'This is my email address. You can write to me if things get too hard, if you—you know—'

He took it. 'Okay.'

The next time he brought me chocolate. 'I know you like it,' he said, smiling. Then it was a teddy bear with the saddest face I'd ever seen. Holding it was like holding a baby.

'You should have kept him for yourself,' I teased. 'Don't be so nice to me.'

We were getting very close. If he didn't show up every few nights I was a little forlorn. He emailed me; I replied. I'd told him a lot about me. It felt so good to be open with someone, to share doubt and sadness. I knew something was happening beyond the strictures of work.

265

Then he came in and told me he wouldn't be coming back. 'I'm getting to like you too much,' he said. 'It doesn't seem like a good idea. I won't be using that email address anymore, so please don't write. And, by the way, you should be more careful giving yours out.'

I looked at him and touched his face. 'Are you sure?' I didn't want him to disappear. He was a friend. But I wanted him to be happy, not troubled over a working girl.

'I brought you chocolate,' he said. 'Don't eat it all at once,' and he hugged me, and walked out.

The women I'd known on the street had, mostly, begun in brothels and then fallen from grace. I'd gone the opposite way. I'd worked my way in, and up.

When I passed through St Kilda on my way home, I looked out at the black streets, the occasional pale figure standing under a light, and shivered with pity. For them and for myself. It seemed a cruel exile, out there in the dark. Yet I still had a pride that I'd been there, that I'd had that apprenticeship. It gave me a sense of being equipped, of having perspective. From darkness to the glowing lamps of the brothel, it had been a long slow dawning out of shadow.

From the quiet beginning at Il Fiore I'd risen to being one of their most prized ladies. Even on nights when the drift of clients was slow, I would be booked. I'd stagger into the lounge from one booking, rushing off to the next, bemoaning my fatigue, while a couch-load of less-fortunate women watched me sourly.

Vanity was my fault. Giddy with the adoration of the men, the glow of success and popularity, I thought I could do no wrong. Now that I wasn't using heroin, my mind sharpened; I talked non-stop,

266

glittering and brittle. When Bernadette said, 'I think you eat dictionaries, just to aggravate us with the big words,' I thought it was a compliment. When Coral said, 'For Christ's sake, Lucy, just shut up a minute,' I thought she was joking. When Helen said, 'Lucy, if you're late one more time I'm going to kill you,' I imagined she was bluffing.

Things were going well for me. I was adhering to my methadone program and reducing the dose steadily; there were a few sticky hours every day before my dose, but I managed them and, by the time I'd been to work for an hour, I'd be fine. There was usually a booking waiting for me when I arrived—I'd have to dash to get ready, but I enjoyed the sense of diving into work. My gowns were dirty; there was no time to get them washed.

At home, life with my parents had settled. I scarcely saw them, with the hours I kept, but we had normal conversations when we passed in the kitchen. I drank coffee for breakfast, they were eating dinner. They seemed to have accepted the path I'd taken. 'It's not what we think you'd be best at,' my mother said. 'You have other talents. But if you're happy, then that's okay.' I knew they told their friends what I did; they had resisted shame. That nearly made me cry, my parents' bravery, their faith in me. Sometimes they even dropped me off at work.

'Have a good night,' said my father. He chuckled awkwardly. 'Well, you know what I mean.'

Robbie had found himself lodgings, above a shop in Brunswick Street. The place was dingy but it was right above the major café strip and I sometimes stayed there. It was much nearer work than my place, and saved me a large taxi fare. We were still together; we hung out, we shopped, we spent hours musing over magazines and television and his new obsession, computers. The floor of his little room was always strewn with broken circuit-boards. We went to the chemist together every afternoon, wandered through the shops, and had a coffee in the same café; it became a second living room for us. I still gave him money. It wasn't worth fighting about.

I had booked my ticket to Europe: straight to Rome, where I'd been before. I'd bash around Italy for a month, and then I'd set off to Paris and wherever else I liked. It was nearly ten years since I'd backpacked, and my world had been so narrow for so long. I was a little terrified of breaking out of it. I'd be so alone. Perhaps I would spend the first month crying. Hiding under a bed. How strong had I become? Strong enough to voyage even further from all who still loved me? But I was going. Leaving would solve all my troubles. It was a glowing portal on the horizon ahead of me. I scarcely believed it would ever actually be reached.

Helen looked bewildered when I said I would be leaving in September for a holiday. It did occasionally happen. Shelley had taken two months off, and returned. I said I didn't know how long I'd be.

'But you'll be coming back?' she insisted.

'Sure,' I said. I had nothing against working, but I was intending to go for as long as my money held out.

It seemed the more respectable my life got, the more obligations I had. When I was a junkie on the streets I'd had no bills, no dentist appointments, no visits to the post office. Apart from the terrible burden of using, life had been almost simple. Now my book of lists was full of chores that all necessitated getting up after only a few hours' sleep and trekking into the city. I had to organise travellers' cheques; there was a phone bill to pay, a haircut to get. There was no use in explaining to receptionists that, to me, a ten o'clock appointment was like two in the morning to them. In my skewed schedule lunch-time was midnight. I simply had to stagger out of bed, dress and lurch out to take care of life before I started my twelve-hour shift. More and more I relied on speed to get me through, and the more I took, the more hectically I reeled through the day.

It was fraying my nerves and health. I began to lose weight; people commented on my gaunt face. While I was using heroin, I'd always looked fairly healthy; now I knew there were mutters behind my back. *She's on something.*

There were reserved bookings end-to-end and I started every shift late. The receptionists had to make excuses for me; I chattered on, glib in my confidence that I was a star girl and everyone would wait. It was winter, and the world was closing in with darkness. I thought, *I'll be crawling onto that plane.*

As my methadone dose dropped, I felt the effects more and more. Only weeks before I was to leave, I reached the lowest levels of dosing; I was clammy and exhausted almost all the time. It seemed more than I could manage just to lie in bed and keep breathing; but I had things to do. And the end was in sight. For the first time in more than five years, I'd be free of chemicals. Anything I felt would be my own.

Something hard and purified came up inside me. I was driven by routine and responsibility. I *had* to get to work; I *had* to visit the doctor; I *had* to pay the bills on time. Ahead of me the thought of Europe was like north on a compass, drawing me closer. I lay on beds under grunting men and dreamed of peace.

Even after my very last dose, there was the backlash of the drug as it wrenched one last time at my shredded system. The next month, the month before I left, was the hardest. Every afternoon when I woke I felt I could have slept on for ever; lying there, willing strength into my muscles, I wondered how I could do it. Once up I was better, as long as I kept moving. But I was increasingly disorganised at work, or took nights off altogether. Helen called me into a bedroom at the start of my shift one evening.

'What's going on, Lucy?' She wasn't fierce, but she sat there with her hands folded in her lap and looked at me. 'You're late all the time, even worse than usual! And you look *dreadful*.'

Now was the time. I was sick of dissembling—after all these years, I was too tired to lie. My head pounded and my eyes were sticky with fever-heat. I had never known if she suspected I used drugs; she was a canny lady, but then again, she liked 'types', and I wasn't the using 'type'. 'Helen, I'm having a hard time,' I began. 'I used to—I used to use heroin.'

She stared at me. She had a great poker-face, Helen.

'I've been on methadone for two years now,' I extended history to spare her the thought of me using while I worked for her. 'I've just finished the program, I've done really well—been clean all this time. But it's really hard, the finishing—it makes me tired and vague, it fucks up my head a bit—'

There was a pause. I stared at my knuckles.

Helen smiled, a sympathetic smile, concerned. 'What do you need?' she said. 'I've got some valium, you can have that—I mean, if you're a bit stressed, it's marvellous for that. You do look awful.'

'I was thinking—if I'm late, that's why. If you can just be a bit patient with me...'

'Well. It's not fair on the other girls, to let you be late when they're all ready at seven. But if you feel sick and you have to leave early, you just tell Bernadette or Maude, and they'll make a note in the book.' She stood up. 'I'm glad you're okay now, Lucy.'

270

She gave me a little hug. 'Now, you'd better get ready. I think Gary is coming in for you in ten minutes.'

'Okay.' I went upstairs to put eyeshadow on my hollow eyes and powder to cover the sweat.

Business as usual, with man after man and happy conversations in the ladies' lounge. I raved on and everyone grew used to my hyperactive rush and weirdly jolly moods. I wasn't aware of how lax I was becoming, how carried away with the impression that I was perfectly charming until one young man said, 'Do you think we could just concentrate a moment here?' I hastened to put the condom on, forgotten in my hand as I made a point about the nature of capitalism.

In my high heels I could run up the stairs now. My lace panties grew frayed with the tugging on and off my hips. I knew sometimes I struck the wrong note, that I was too loud, or too brash. It felt good to be brash, to lead a room in jokes and walk into a conversation that opened up to let me in. I loved these women, so brave and so witty. In their company I felt loved.

'I'll be sad when you leave,' Milla said. 'I wish I could go overseas.' She was fresh out of a stint in rehab, and quiet.

'I'll be back,' I said, and nudged her.

Coral grinned at me. 'You'll go to Italy and fall in love with a gorgeous Italian hunk. That's your type, isn't it, Lucy?'

Bernadette put in, 'Lucy likes the weird ones. She was all over that skinny little runt before—did you see him? Eyes like a bloody bug.'

'I have lots of types,' I said. 'God knows, I've seen a few.'

*

271

I wondered how I would feel if I fell in love again. I wondered if I'd need to. At times it seemed that I already had enough of men. I could be besotted with them for an hour, cuddle and ravish them, and then watch them leave, before I welcomed another. I had my fill of adoration; now, when some man offered me a compliment, I turned it aside.

'You're too good to be here,' said an adoring, round-bellied young Greek.

'I don't even know what that means,' I said.

What more did I need? I had flesh, flattery and company. I had intimacy, if I allowed it; I had cock. Men waited hours for me. I thought it would have to be a pretty good offer for me to bestow my body on someone new for free.

And Robbie waited for me; when I got to his place I would slip into bed next to him and put my arms around him and he'd mumble something and pull me in tighter. When we walked down the street he held my hand. He listened to my grumbles and shared his own. Sometimes I was even still in love with him.

The thought of a new man, the right man, almost frightened me. How would I ever meet him, and how could I explain myself? I had been a drug addict, I was a prostitute. These things didn't shame me, but I had no illusions that they wouldn't alarm a man from outside.

'Outside' was how it felt. This world was cosy, cloistered, and it was all I'd known for such a long time; I'd been subterranean. The dazzle of the world, in daylight, would blind me.

THE LAST DAYS CAME RUSHING up fast. There was much to do; I dashed around, meeting Douglas, Max and other friends for farewell coffees, arranging bills to be paid, buying luggage. My bones ached and I sweated, but I was taut with urgency and there was no stopping me now. Robbie walked too slowly for me; I charged along the streets. My energy was draining fast. I knew I'd only just make it onto that plane, and there was a lot to do before then. I felt my smiles grow manic.

At work I promised to come back, probably in a few months. My clients were mournful.

'Who else will I stay with?' they asked. I briskly suggested other girls. I didn't want sentimentality; it cheapened the real sentiment I felt.

And then it was my last weekend at work. I'd given myself a week off before the flight; I'd finish on Sunday night, always my favourite. There was a list of pre-booked regulars—Philip, Mick, and others—ready to spend a last happy hour with me. Flowers arrived on Saturday from Samuel. I was looking forward to my last shift. Bernadette would be on, and some of my favourite girls; we'd have a good time.

Then, on Sunday morning, I turned my head on the pillow and pulled my neck. It hurt, and through the day—an afternoon picnic with Robbie—it grew worse, until I could barely move. I was dismayed: such a stupid little problem. I rang Helen.

'I can't come in. I mean, I can come in, but I can't do sex,' I said. 'I can't move my head.'

'I've just about had it with you.' Her voice was unexpectedly sharp. 'It's always some excuse or another.'

'I was thinking, I could come on Monday, if I'm better—'

'Look. This is ridiculous. You've been pulling tricks on me. All that sucking up to the receptionists, all that nosing around—and now this.'

It was like being fired from Indigo.

'Don't bother coming on Monday. I'll just tell your clients you were sick. I can't believe you, Lucy—' She hung up.

Propped up on pillows, I stayed the night with Robbie, immobilised. Something as banal as a cricked neck had ruined everything. I couldn't believe I wouldn't see my regulars again. What would they think? The girls—I'd wanted to give them cards, and my number. Helen was just having a mood, surely she'd let me work one last shift. Her spite was stripping me of my right to leave graciously, as if I had been only one more casual girl who came and went, whose name no one remembered.

I went in on Tuesday evening, to see if Helen was there. Maude was on the desk. 'Oh, Lucy, honey,' she said. 'What happened on

Sunday? All your regulars were here, Bernadette didn't know where you were, you should have called.'

'I did!'

'There was no message from you. Bernadette was so upset. She wanted to say goodbye.'

My lips pressed tight, I went to my locker, swung the door open: another girl's stuff was inside. Maude came up behind me. 'It's all packed up in a bag for you, love.'

Someone had bundled my dresses and make-up into a rubbish bag and put it in the storage cupboard. Samuel's roses were in there too, wilted. 'Okay,' I said. Maude looked at me. 'We'll miss you,' she said. 'Come back soon.'

There were some new girls in the lounge; I smiled at them awkwardly. Already the place was less familiar to me. But then I heard Jessie come clomping back from a booking. We hugged. 'See you soon, darl!' She rushed off to do her hair before the next client. The house was quiet, glowing, just as it always was.

'Call me a taxi?' I asked Maude.

On the plane to Europe I slept and slept. I was out of energy, and I'd wanted to depart without this bitterness. The disappointment curdled in me. But I was on my way somewhere else.

Robbie had been sad. Our late-blooming tenderness made him hard to leave, but I never once thought of not going. We made love a last time; sweetly we kissed goodbye on the street outside his place.

'I'll be back soon,' I promised. How would he get along on his own? So lonely, so struggling and brave.

'I wonder if you will,' he said, and walked around the corner.

My family was happy for me. They took me to the airport; they gave me long hugs.

275

'My darling girl,' said my mother. My sister grinned from behind her, and then flung her arms around me.

'Look after yourself, you idiot,' in my ear.

'I'm so proud of you, Katie,' said my father. I looked at them, and left them there, arms around each other, and walked through the departure gate.

I found myself settling in Rome. A friend of a friend offered me a room; my nerve failed, after all, to go adventuring alone through the continent. In the upstairs apartment I was safe, looking out on the city.

When I first arrived I cried almost every day for a month. Over nothing; over the state of the world; the news I saw on television; over the loveliness of the autumn sunshine on soft old stone. Great, wrenching sobs that came and went in moments and left me dazed.

Just occasionally I allowed my heart to stroke the sharp edge of the pity for what I'd done to myself, and to others. I'd lie in bed at night, weeping for the hurt I'd caused the ones I loved, back in the black days. And for how low I'd brought myself, this fragile girl. For the things I'd missed, while I was in the dark.

All I did, in the daytime, was walk. On the move until I was too baffled by weariness to feel anything. I wandered, almost every day, through the soft ochre streets, the narrow old spaces, learning the city, studying it. I made myself a scholar again, and sat in the cold sunshine of a city that had withstood destruction and rebirth many times, and let myself be suffused with dreaming. I walked in different weathers and times of day, learning about change and constancy. In quietness, I walked Rome. Sometimes I worked up the courage to venture further.

*

At times I caught the phantom whiff of withdrawal sweat on my body, long after the last chemicals had drained from my metabolism. In my mind would rise spectral cold streets, desperation, sweaty fear. I washed myself in warm showers again and again, but still the smell was in my nostrils.

I had recurring dreams about heroin. I would be walking down a night-time street littered with full syringes, all jacked up, ready to be taken in my hand and plugged in. I'd resist, walking and walking, tempted and appalled. Then I would capitulate, and put a needle through my skin, and already, in my dream, I was aghast. I would wake, suffocated by regret, relieved to have awoken.

In Naples I spent a bleak day, feeling foreign and lost, wandering the streets. I walked further and further out of the areas I knew, heading vaguely for the citadel on a hill above the teeming city. Over me the sky was white and pitiless. The streets grew more ragged, the people fewer and grimier, and then I found myself walking through an underpass, my feet crunching, as in my dream, on broken syringes. There were fit wrappers all around, and an eerie quiet. The walls of the tunnel were dank old stone. At the end, using an ancient wall for a surface, an old man dressed in rags was stirring a syringe-end in a spoon.

I walked up to him. Everything was silent up here. '*Scusami*,' I said. 'Do you know where I can buy some of that?'

He looked at me. Then resumed his stirring.

'Do you know? Some of that—*eroina*?'

He was silent. I hesitated, and then I walked away, and got bitterly drunk in my little room instead. Scratched my skin with a blunt knife in the freezing cold. Anything to replace the bite of the needle and its luxurious savagery.

Gradually, the urge lessened. I knew that if I did drugs once, I would have no way of not doing them again. The thought of the day after stilled me. The greed for obliteration remained, but I learned to quash it. I sat, instead, in my apartment, and drank sweet lemon liqueur, and sang along with Billie Holiday, and nursed myself slowly, slowly into peace.

At the beginning when men sucked their teeth at me in the street, or gave me lascivious stares, I straightened my back. I knew my price exactly. I absorbed the desire of those men, and it gave me strength. I had been a princess, and I still walked as if draped in a velvet gown.

But those men would whistle at any woman. Here, out in the daylight, amidst the smooth-groomed European women, I began to feel awkward and ragged. Without make-up and lighting, my face was pale and thin. My clothes grew too tight as I put on weight. I stumbled on the uneven cobblestones. Loathing myself, I went to a hairdresser and had all my hair cut off short; anything, to try and feel sleek again. I thought maybe I was just a messy child, after all.

The world still startled me, even after half a year away from Melbourne. There were times when it was all too bright. And then I closed my eyes again, and stayed in the apartment, miserable and panic-stricken for days, wondering what I could possibly do with my life.

Then I met a commonsensical, charming young man and fell in love, easily, after all. To fuck in a Naples apartment with someone I barely knew was one thing. That had had the same wicked glee as work. Faced with Raffaele's sweetness, with passion washing through me like rain, all my tricks fell away. In his bedroom I touched him tentatively. I felt as raw and innocent as a child. He gazed into my eyes and I blinked.

278

'I was a *putana*,' I said to him finally. I didn't know the proper word: I used the term for 'whore'. But he understood. In the crook of each of my inner arms was a small, depressed hollow, scooped out of my flesh, where the scar tissue had collapsed. Raffaele looked at me steadily. He placed his hand against my cheek. 'I'm not perfect,' I said, lowering my face. He raised it.

'No one is perfect,' he said. He stroked my scars gently with his rough fingers, and pulled me over him.

In an out-of-the-way church in Rome, twilight staining the space and antique chandeliers hanging dark, I stood alone and lit a candle. *Serendipity*, I prayed. *Thank you for saving me.* I was very far from being religious, but someone had to be thanked. *Thank you to all who have loved me. Thank you for saving me, for this newness.* And every time I visited a church, I lit a candle, and stood to pay respect to my fortune.

Months went past, in this odd dreaming—half lost in fantasies about the ancient past, and half dreaming up a new self with Raffaele. Then my sister came over from Australia, and we went backpacking. She made me giggle, with her joy at my wellness, and her own bravado at travelling, and we stomped through dusty countries as best friends. The first thing she said when I greeted her at the airport was, 'Your pupils are so big. You look different.' Her laugh was pure joy.

I sat beside her on the beach of an Adriatic island, in the ruins of a medieval harbour, under sweet pine trees, with the transparent water cooling our feet as we read and smoked and ate a picnic in the drowsy sun. Back in Rome, Raffaele was waiting for me. It was my thirtieth birthday.

279

My sister took a photo of us, our healthy, tanned faces and dirty hair and bottles of orange juice raised in salute.

'I am so fucking happy,' I said. 'I don't think I could ever be happier.'

She kissed me on the cheek. 'It's about time,' she said. 'My silly sis.'

Melbourne was drizzly and grim with winter when I got back after a year away. My old room at my parents', the scent of it and the songs I'd left behind on the stereo made me sick with memories. I changed it all, and began again.

How strange I felt, and how strange the city! I walked it in my Italian leather coat, with my new haircut, to meet friends, forgetting how the streets lay, forgetting that my friends hadn't seen me for years. 'You look great!' they said, and looked at me carefully. 'You look *great.*'

Robbie rang me. I put off calling him back. There was something repellent about those memories. It was as if I had a new skin that would peel if I brushed it against old things. I let the sunlight soak and firm me.

My piano is still in the same room as when I was a child. The keys are yellowed and the notes are out of tune. It wants to play better than I allow it, with my clumsy fingers. But when I play Schubert, still the gold light falls down the hallway and still my mother comes in to put her hands on my shoulders with pride.

In the living room when I visit, we watch television, my parents and I. There is a story on the news about drug users. We watch footage of young people mixing up on a coffee table. I see the familiar orange-capped syringes, the red-printed swab packets, the

280

powder in the spoons. I watch it, and my parents watch it. We are all suddenly very carefully quiet.

When I go to St Kilda for a coffee, the place is a palimpsest of memories. Time and space collapse; the place is full of ghosts of me. Walking exhausted in the rain down this footpath, being picked up on that corner. Here is where the police stopped me; here is where, a year before that, James and I kissed rapturously in the early days of our romance. Here is where I used to have coffee with my friends; here is where I stashed my fits under a bush. There is a working girl I used to know; we pass each other without sharing a look. The footpath under my feet is unmarked by all my footsteps, after all.

I get the tram into town and we pass along one side of the block I used to walk. I peer out into the night, past my own reflection glazed on the tram window. There are a few figures out there, standing under the lights. I watch the cars pass them, each one driven by a solitary man. I watch them all with a mixture of solidarity and pride and sorrow.

Night-time streets seem grimy to me, glossed with the residue of my weariness, my desperation. I hate walking through wet streets in the dark. The asphalt and the chilled air seem to reek of alcohol swabs and loneliness.

The tram rushes me away. My reflection, in the window, stays steady beside me.

I am buoyant, polished, secure. I'm on my way to meet Max and David; I tell them stories from my old life, as an outlandish adventure. We all laugh, and then quieten, and my smile is happier than either of theirs.

Walking in the city, a scruffy young man veers towards me. He's saying something about 'bigger than…' I expect he's leering at my breasts. Then I realise he's offering to sell me a deal. He must have seen the scars on my bare arms. Is that all?

'Not anymore,' I sing as I pass him, and catch a puzzled expression on his face before I walk on.

EPILOGUE

I OPEN THE SUITCASE AND the first thing I notice is the scent. Stale perfume, musty fabric. It's been years since I saw these dresses. And here they are, slumped in skeins of varied colours and textures, embracing each other. They've been lying in the dark like this, as if in a tomb, faintly holding the shape of my body. I'd forgotten I had so many. I begin to pull them out, one at a time, shaking out their crushed forms to catch the light.

I'm looking for a dress to wear to a party. I once had more beautiful gowns than I could wear; surely there is one for me still.

I hold gauzy black, slithery purple, plush, flowered velvet. Tiny beads clink around halter-necks; my nail catches a fragile lace hem. I lay the dresses out on the bed carefully. Here's a see-through slip of chiffon, and I remember wearing this to greet clients; this piece of nothing and only a g-string and bra. I'm wonderstruck as I finger the transparent fabric. And this, my first working dress, red velvet but a dowdy cut. I wore it so often, the only one I had for a time, that it still reeks faintly. I put it aside.

Another, sunny pink with ruffles; tiny baby-doll frocks of budded lace and thin velvet shoulder-straps; shiny scarlet slacks cut tight; elasticised lace in maroon; a long black dress, slashed to the hip.

I strip, and begin to try the dresses on. I'm not sure what I'm expecting. The first is hard to get on. And the next. When I last wore these I was pared down by drugs and sex, my body lean, hard. Now the material is tight across my breasts, strains over my hips. I take each dress off hurriedly, and try the next. The sheer ones are worse: my bulges skulk under the dappled shade of fabric. I can't imagine wearing these even for a lover. I feel blobby and celibate and rather like a child playing dress-ups. I take them off and throw them in a pile.

I find my favourites: elegant, after-five gowns. I wore these in the last house to seduce. Slick black satin, cut to drape, edged with fine lace. Chartreuse-green sheen, ruffled like a bell's lip at my knees, worn with bright pink lingerie, designer label: a tea-party fantasy with breasts. And my magnificent crimson velvet, heavy in my hands.

The material of the satin is gorgeously chill against my skin. I strap on the shoes in the suitcase, four inches of glossy black heel; my pelvis tips forward, my bosom juts. I stand tall. The chartreuse resurrects my pallor: icy green against marble. Then the next, black silk slips against my thighs and in the mirror I see my smile become mocking, enigmatic. Last, I put on the velvet—long, slit up the back, bodiced across the belly, a tight velvet rose between my breasts. I hold myself erect, proud. I feel gorgeous.

My dresses were my costumes, my armour: my becoming. I put them on each night and stood taller. I put them on and became a woman. And at the end of the night I took them off, after one last vain glance in the mirror, and put on my own clothes with another kind of pride.

It occurs to me that none of these dresses has been washed since I stopped working. The collars are pale with make-up from where I stripped them over my face for every client; the underarms dusty with deodorant. The smell is of stale perfume and a faint tang of sweat beneath the musk of dust. There must be, still, the invisible stains where mouths nuzzled at my nipples, where hasty men pulled me, still dressed, to their naked dampness.

These days I usually wear comfortable trousers and boots. And the freeness of my body, now, under the loose embrace of these fragile scraps, is startling. My ankles tremble in the high heels; my flesh feels untethered, unstable. Or perhaps freed, blithe, careless.

I run fingers up my naked thighs, under the hem of the dress, raise it with a mocking smirk towards the mirror. It feels delicious, this gloating. Then I see the empty room, how ridiculous I am. And I let the hem fall, and strip it all off me.